PLANNED COMMUNITY LIVING

PLANNED COMMUNITY LIVING
HANDBOOK FOR CALIFORNIA HOMEOWNERS ASSOCIATIONS

A PRACTICAL AND COMPREHENSIVE REFERENCE GUIDE FOR HOMEOWNERS ASSOCIATIONS, BOARDS, MEMBERS AND PROPERTY MANAGERS

By John B. Linford, Esq.

Published by Bench Mark Enterprises LLC

Cover design and illustration by Ty Baker

Library of Congress Catalog Number: 96-96606

ISBN 0-9652973-0-6

This book is dedicated to the memory of William G. von Platen, Colonel, United States Air Force, Ret. A man of honor, wisdom, and vision. He served his community association as he served his country, with loyalty to its members, courage to stand for what he believed in, and absolute discernment in governing for the common benefit of all. 1920 - 1993, Bear Valley Springs, California.

This book is meant to educate and should not be used as an alternative or substitute for competent legal advice from experienced attorneys. The author has exerted every effort to ensure that the information presented is accurate and up to date as of the time of publication. However, in light of constantly changing laws, it is possible that new legal principles may affect the validity of some of the information presented in this book.

TABLE OF CONTENTS

CHAPTER PAGE

INTRODUCTION xxv

I. COMMON INTEREST DEVELOPMENTS - GENERAL OVERVIEW 1

GENERAL CHARACTERISTICS .1

ASSOCIATION 2

GOVERNING DOCUMENTS 4

TYPES OF COMMON INTEREST DEVELOPMENTS 5

A. The Planned Development 5

B. The Condominium 6

C. The Community Apartment 7

D. The Stock Cooperative 7

THE RIGHTS AND DUTIES OF THE PROPERTY OWNERS AND THE ASSOCIATION VARY WITH THE TYPE OF CID 7

ASSOCIATION'S FINANCIAL RESOURCES 9

COMMUNITY COOPERATION .9

II. MANAGEMENT, PRESERVATION AND MAINTENANCE 11

OPERATION AND MAINTENANCE RESPONSIBILITIES 11

LAND USE CONTROL 14

III. LAND USE CONTROL AND PROPERTY REGULATION 17

WHAT ARE CC&Rs? 17

A. Covenants 18

B. Personal Covenants 18

C. Real Covenants 18

D. Historical Development Of Real Covenants And Equitable Servitudes 18

E. Equitable Servitudes 19

F. Conditions 20

G. Restrictions 20

H. The Declaration 20

I. Modern Use And Application Of Declaration In The Common Interest Development 21

ENFORCEABILITY AND VALIDITY OF COVENANTS AND RESTRICTIONS: INTERPRETATION AND APPLICATION 22

A. Which CC&Rs May Be Enforced Presumption Of Validity 22

B. Challenger Bears Burden Of Proving Unreasonableness 23

C. Test Of Reasonableness Of Covenant Or Restriction 24

INTERPRETATION OF GOVERNING DOCUMENTS . . .24

A. Responsibility And Judgment Of The Association 24

B. Specific Prohibitions Or Limitations Against Enforcement of Certain Covenants Or Restrictions 25

C. Liberal Interpretation Required To Promote The Operation Of The Common Interest Development 25

D. Statutory Limitations On Enforcement Of Restrictions 26

(1) Mobilehomes 26

(2) Solar Energy Systems 27

(3) Real Estate For Sale Signs 28

(4) The American Flag 29

(5) Restrictions On The Installation Or Use Of Video Or Television Antenna 29

(6) Family Day Care Homes And Homes For The Elderly - Community Care Facilities 30

(7) Occupancy Or Property Use Restrictions Based On Age 35

E. Restrictions Against Selling, Leasing Or Renting Separate Interests 36

F. Statutes of Limitation 37

G. Other Considerations Which May Affect The Enforceability Of Particular Covenants And Restrictions 38

(1) “Vagueness Or Ambiguity” 38

(2) “Equitable Estoppel” 38

(3) “Waiver” 39

(4) “Change In Conditions Or Circumstances” 39

(5) "Unclean Hands" 40

(6) "Laches" 40

H. Covenants And Restrictions Which Differ From Governmental Zoning Ordinances, Regulations And Licensing Requirements 40

ENVIRONMENTAL OR ARCHITECTURAL CONTROL RULES 42

ASSOCIATION RULES, AMENITY AND FACILITY RULES 44

IV. ENFORCING THE DECLARATION OF COVENANTS, CONDITIONS AND RESTRICTIONS AND OTHER GOVERNING DOCUMENTS 47

A. Associations And Property Owners May Both Enforce The Declaration Of CC&Rs 48

B. Methods Of Enforcement 48

C. Internal Disciplinary Measures 48

(1) Conduct Of Disciplinary Proceeding Must Be In Executive Session If Requested By The Member 48

(2) Suspension Of Membership Rights After Hearing Affording Due Process Safeguards 49

(3) Membership Suspension Procedures Must Be " Fair And Reasonable" 49

D. Possible Availability Of Automatic Suspension Without A Section 7341 Hearing 52

E. Recording A "Notice Of Noncompliance" Or "Notice Of Violation" 53

F. Monetary Fines And Penalties 54

(1) Executive Session Board Meeting May Be Required 56

(2) No Statutory Hearing Required 56

(3) Adoption And Distribution Of Uniform Schedule Of Penalties 56

G. Lawsuits And Alternative Dispute Resolution 57

(1) Injunctive Relief 57

(2) Declaratory Relief 57

(3) Association Must Act In Good Faith And Follow Its Own Standards And Procedures 58

H. Alternative Dispute Resolution 59

(1) Types Of Lawsuits Subject To Mandatory ADR Resolution Efforts 59

(2) Initiation Of Alternative Dispute Resolution Procedure 60

(3) Response To Request For Resolution 61

(4) Completion Of Resolution Process 61

(5) Prerequisite To Filing Certain Lawsuits 62

V. COMMON AREAS AND COMMUNITY AMENITIES AND FACILITIES 63

A. Access To, Use And Enjoyment Of Common Areas And Facilities 63

(1) Non-resident Property Owners 63

(2) Persons Not Property Owners 65

(3) Traffic And Parking Regulation 65

B. Maintenance And Repair Of Common Areas And Community Facilities 67

(1) Routine Maintenance 67

(2) Responsibility For Damage To The Common Areas 68

C. Construction Defects 68

(1) Developer Liability 68

(2) Association Liability 69

(3) Legal Recourse Should Be Sought Promptly 69

(4) Statutes Of Limitation 70

(5) Statutes Of Repose 71

(6) "Patent" Deficiencies 71

(7) "Latent" Deficiencies 71

(8) "Substantial Completion" 72

(9) Disclosure Of Litigation To Property Owners 72

(10) Mandatory Alternative Dispute Resolution 73

(11) Certificate Of Merit Required Before Filing Suit Against Architects, Engineers, Surveyors And Contractors 74

(12) Association Has No Duty To Inform Prospective Purchasers Of Separate Interests About Construction Defects 75

VI. ASSOCIATION STRUCTURE AND GOVERNANCE: GOVERNING DOCUMENTS, LAWS AND REGULATIONS 77

A. Corporate Structure And Governance 77

B. Governing Laws And Regulations 78

(1) The " Davis-Stirling Common Interest Development Act" 80

(2) The California Corporations Code 81

(3) Other Applicable Statutes 84

(4) Common Law Or Case Law 85

(5) Department of Real Estate Regulations 85

(6) Use Of Qualified Legal Counsel 87

C. Governing Documents 87

(1) Land Use Regulation Documents 88

(a) The Declaration Of Covenants, Conditions And Restrictions 88

(b) Architectural Or Environmental Control Rules 88

(c) Association Rules 88

(2) Corporate Or Administrative Documents 89

(a) The Articles Of Incorporation Or Articles Of Association 89

(b) Bylaws 90

(c) Board Of Directors Resolutions And Policies 91

(d) Rules Of Parliamentary Procedure 92

D. Relationship Between Governing Documents And Applicable Laws 93

E. Amending The Governing Documents 95

(1) Amendments During Period Of Developer Control 95

(2) Amendment Of Declaration Of Covenants, Conditions And Restrictions 95

(3) Civil Code Requirements Governing Amendment Of The Declaration Of CC&Rs 97

(4) Amendment Of Declarations Which Specify The Required Level Of Approval By Owners 97

(5) Amendment Of Declarations Which Do Not Specify The Required Level Of Approval By Owners 98

(6) Amendments Of The Declaration Of CC&Rs To Delete Provisions Related To Developer's Completion And Marketing Of Development 99

(7) Petition To Reduce Membership Voting Requirements To Amend The Declaration Of CC&Rs .99

(8) Amendment Of Articles Of Incorporation 100

(9) Amendment Of Bylaws 101

(10) Majority Voting Requirements 101

(11) Supermajority Voting Requirements 102

(12) Petition To Reduce Membership Voting Requirements To Amend The Articles Of Incorporation And Bylaws 102

E. Duration Of The Association 103

VII. THE ASSOCIATION MEMBERS 105

A. Members 105

(1) Definitions Of Member and Membership 105

(2) Which Persons Are Entitled To Be Members . . 106

(3) Multiple Memberships .106

(4) Membership Certificates 107

B. Responsibilities 107

C. Powers And Authority 108

D. Specific Rights 108

(1) Election Of Directors 109

(2) Removal Of Directors 110

(a) Removal By Vote Of Members 111

(b) Removal By Lawsuit 112

(3) Amendment Of Governing Documents 114

(4) Approval Of Assessment Increases 114

(5) Attendance At Board Meetings - " Common Interest Development Open Meeting Act" 115

(6) Inspection Of Association Books And Records 116

E. Membership Protections 120

(1) Notice And Delivery Of Information To Members 120

(2) Discipline In Executive (Closed) Session 121

(3) Suspension Of Membership Rights 121

(4) Suspension Of Membership Rights When Member Owns More Than One Separate Interest 123

(5) Members Cannot Be Disciplined For Exercising Their Rights To Seek Judicial Redress: 124

F. Meetings And Voting 125

(1) Time And Conduct Of Regular Meetings 126

(2) First Meeting Of Members 126

(3) Time And Conduct Of Special Meetings 126

(4) Notices Of Meetings Of Members 127

(5) Voting At Meetings Of Members 129

(a) Number Of Votes: Distribution Of Voting Power Between Developer And Other Members 129

(b) General Voting Power Rules 129

(c) Exercising Jointly-Owned Property Votes 130

(d) Cumulative Voting 130

(e) Proxies And Meeting Ballots 131

(f) Membership Action Without A Meeting By Written Ballot 132

(g) Form, Content And Use Of Proxies 133

(h) Inspectors Of Election 137

(i) Members' Eligibility To Vote 138

G. Delegation Of Common Area And Amenity Use Rights By Members To Tenants And Lessees 139

H. Limited Liability Protection For Members - Minimum Insurance Requirements 140

VIII. DIRECTORS, OFFICERS AND MANAGEMENT 143

A. Directors 143

(1) Elected Officials 143

(2) Qualifications 147

(3) Policy Makers 148

(4) Decision Making And The "Business Judgment" Rule 148

(5) Fiduciaries 149

(6) Responsibilities 149

(7) Standard Of Care 152

(8) Committees 153

(9) Rights 156

(a) Notice Of Board Meetings 156

(b) Filling Vacancies 156

(c) Right To Resign 156

(d) Removal From Board 156

(e) "Absolute" Inspection Rights 157

(10) Meetings And Board Action 159

(a) "Common Interest Development Open Meeting Act" 161

(b) Board Action 164

(11) Immunity From Tort Liability For Certain Volunteer Directors And Officers 166

B. Officers 168

(1) Duties 168

(2) Appointed Or Elected by Board 168

C. Management 169

(1) Management Agent's Pre-Contract Disclosure Requirements 170

(2) Management Agent's Maintenance, Accounting And Disposition Of Association Funds 171

(3) No Commingling Of Funds Without Permission 171

(4) Legal Relationship Between Association And Managing Agent 172

(5) Scope Of Managing Agent's Authority 172

D. Indemnification Of Directors, Officers And Agents . . . 175

IX. FINANCIAL STRUCTURE: ASSESSMENTS, FEES AND RESERVE FUNDS 179

A. ASSESSMENTS 179

(1) Nature Of The Assessment 179

(2) Authority For Assessments 179

(3) Commencement Of Assessments 180

(4) Developer's Obligation To Pay Assessments 181

(5) Limited Exemptions May Be Provided Under The Governing Documents 181

(6) Increasing Assessments: Prerequisites To Valid Assessments And Assessment Liens 182

(7) Limitations On Assessments And Increases In Assessments 183

(a) General Limitation 183

(b) Specific Limitations 183

(c) Notice Of Increased Assessment 184

(8) Assessments Are Both A Personal Obligation Of The Owner And A Lien Against The Separate Interest 184

(9) Nature Of Assessment Lien 186

(10) Required Contents Of Notice Of Delinquent Assessment 186

(11) Priority Of Assessment Liens 187

(12) Duration Of Lien 187

(13) Enforcement Of Assessment Obligation In General 187

(14) Nonjudicial Foreclosure 187

(15) Judicial Foreclosure 189

(16) Competing Liens And Encumbrances 194

(17) Effect Of Foreclosure Of Senior Liens 195

(18) Subordination By Declaration 195

(19) Effect Of Property Owner's Bankruptcy On Assessment Obligations 196

(a) Automatic Stay Of Bankruptcy Court 197

(b) Recording Assessment Lien 198

(c) Association's Remedies In Bankruptcy 199

(d) Effect Of Bankruptcy 200

(e) Are Common Interest Development Assessments " Post-petition" Or " Pre-petition" Debts Of The Property Owner ? 201

(f) Specific Bankruptcy Code Provisions Now Address Common Interest Development Assessments 201

B. BUDGETS AND OTHER DOCUMENTS 202

(1) Pro Forma Operating Budget 202

(2) Review Of Financial Statement 203

(3) Assessment Lien Enforcement Policies 203

(4) Summary Of Insurance Policies 203

(5) Summary Of Alternative Dispute Resolution Procedures 204

(6) Notice Of Members' Rights To Obtain Minutes Of Meetings 204

(7) Copies Of Governing Documents Upon Request By A Property Owner 204

C. OPERATING FUNDS AND RESERVES 205

(1) Nature Of Reserves 205

(2) Use Of Reserve Funds .206

(3) Mandatory Reserve Studies 206

(4) Periodic Reviews Of Reserve Accounts 207

(5) Withdrawal Of Funds From Reserve Accounts 207

(6) Borrowing From Reserve Funds 207

(a) Generally 207

(b) To Pay For Litigation 208

(7) Periodic Review Of Operating Funds And Accounts 208

CHAPTER NOTES AND REFERENCES 209

INDEX 293

INTRODUCTION

Imagine a large, beautiful and magnificently manicured English garden surrounded by 18th and 19th century period houses, all of which enjoy and share in common the use and benefit of the garden. Next envision a would-be developer's proposal to raze the garden square, its flowers, trees and shrubs, and replace them with newly constructed residences, altering, if not destroying, the beauty and serenity formerly enjoyed by all of the home owners. If you can visualize all that, you have conceived the basic ingredients which led to one of the earliest legal rules still in encountered today in modern homeowners or community associations.

In 1848, the English Court of Chancery decided what was to become a dramatically influential case in the law of real property. The case, entitled *Tulk v. Moxhay,* involved a parcel of land which included Leicester Square, a "pleasure garden", surrounded by dwelling lots. The defendant purchased the land from a seller who had, prior to the sale of the land to the defendant, acquired the land with a deed which contained a promise or covenant that Leicester Square would be preserved as a pleasure garden for the benefit of the surrounding dwelling lots.

When the defendant ventured to build houses on Leicester Square, the original seller, with whom the deed covenant had been made, filed suit to stop the defendant from proceeding with the intended construction. The Court of Chancery ruled that the covenant requiring Leicester Square be used and maintained as a pleasure garden for the surrounding lots was valid and enforceable against the defendant, even though it might not be enforceable as a "real covenant". The court decided that it would be unfair to allow the original promisor to shed the burden of the land restriction simply by selling the property. In ruling that the covenant was enforceable and that Leicester Square must be maintained and preserved as a garden in accordance with the covenant, the law of "equitable servitudes" was first announced:

> "... for if an equity is attached to the property by the owner, no one purchasing with notice of that equity can stand in a different situation from the party from whom he purchases."

After the 1848 Tulk v. Moxhay decision, the law governing restrictions and limitations on the use, occupancy and enjoyment of land, has undergone tremendous evolution. But, the basic principles remain the same and can be traced back through the history of the law of real property to the year 1848 and the English Court of Chancery. For example, the California

Supreme Court recently commented that the resolution of land use restriction issues frequently "requires us to penetrate a legal thicket entangled by the ancient doctrines of covenants that run with the land and equitable servitudes. The task is not easy. 'The law of easements, real covenants, and equitable servitudes is the most complex and archaic body of American property law remaining in the twentieth century.' ... 'The law in this area is an unspeakable quagmire. The intrepid soul who ventures into this formidable wilderness never emerges unscarred. Some, the smarter ones, quickly turn back to take up something easier like the income taxation of trusts and estates. Others, having lost their way, plunge on and after weeks of effort emerge not far from where they began, clearly the worse for wear. On looking back they see the trail they thought they broke obscured with foul smelling waters and noxious weeds. Few willingly take up the challenge again.' It is, however, necessary to take up the challenge. ... Although the relevant doctrines go back centuries, they are more vital than ever today as California becomes increasingly crowded and people live in closer proximity to one another. Planned communities have developed to regulate the relationships between neighbors so all may enjoy the reasonable use of their property. Mutual restrictions on the use of property that are binding upon, and enforceable by, all units in a development are becoming ever more common and desirable."[1]

The form of notice of declarations of covenants, conditions and restrictions which most commonly binds property owners in planned developments, condominiums, community apartments and stock cooperatives, is the "constructive notice" effected when the declaration is recorded in the public land title records.[2] Property owners, whether or not they have actually promised or covenanted to follow the declaration, are nevertheless obligated to do so because of the "constructive notice" imparted when the declaration is recorded and the legal principles first announced by the Court of Chancery in *Tulk v. Moxhay.*

The modern American law of real covenants and equitable servitudes finds no greater emphasis or more frequent use than in the context of "common interest developments": planned developments, condominiums, community apartments and stock cooperatives. It is this subject and the integrally related subject of homeowners or community associations which form the essence of this book.

This book is intended for use by non-lawyers. It is intended as a comprehensive guide and resource for association directors, property owners, members, and property managers. As a result, the author has attempted to avoid, whenever possible, the use of "legalese" and esoteric language all too frequently encountered in statutes and judicial opinions.

Unfortunately, it is not always possible to avoid the use of such language. Sometimes another word or phrase cannot be substituted accurately in place of a legal term of art without losing significant meaning. In such cases, the use of a legal term of art is immediately followed or preceded by text explaining in plain English the meaning of the more mysterious language. Occasionally, a statute or judicial opinion is of such significant importance that it is quoted in the text.

PLANNED COMMUNITY LIVING

CHAPTER I

COMMON INTEREST DEVELOPMENTS—GENERAL OVERVIEW

GENERAL CHARACTERISTICS

This book is intended to be used as a general guide and reference source for condominium and homeowners associations, boards of directors and the property owners. The ever increasing importance that homeowners associations and land use restrictions play in our lives has recently been highlighted by the California courts:

> "Homeowner associations play an increasingly important role in the daily lives of Californians. It is common knowledge that much of the new housing developed in recent years- including single-family detached dwellings- is subject to CC&Rs enforceable by such associations. Some large homeowner associations have budgets which put them on par with small cities and towns."[1]

As a general reference source, this book is not intended to be a substitute for competent legal counsel and it should never be used as a substitute for such advice. It is intended only to provide associations, boards of directors and property owners with general information regarding issues and questions that frequently arise in the context of community or homeowner association living. The reader is encouraged and strongly urged to seek the advice of competent legal counsel experienced in such matters whenever the need may arise.

A residential "common interest development", referred to in abbreviated form in this book as a "CID", is a subdivision which has certain legally defined characteristics and in which the property owners and other residents live in a shared community environment. Real estate developers frequently subdivide land and create common interest developments to meet several market demands. Land is an increasingly scarce resource. Common interest developments often combine many individually-owned properties, together with desirable recreational facilities, into areas significantly smaller than those required in the traditional single-family, detached residential dwelling community. Many home buyers enjoy using facilities such as swimming pools, tennis courts, golf courses, clubhouses, equestrian centers and other amenities, but do not have the financial capacity to bear the expenses for such facilities individually. Local governments are receptive to the creation of common interest developments because the association and its members, not the government, will bear the financial and management burden for the operation and maintenance of the infrastructure and facilities of the development.

There are four types of CIDs generally recognized by California law: the planned development, the condominium, the community apartment project, and the stock cooperative. Of the four types of CIDs, the most common are the planned development and the condominium.

ASSOCIATION

Each CID is required to be operated, managed and maintained by an association,[2] ordinarily consisting of all of the CID property owners.[3] The primary purposes of the association are to manage, maintain, and preserve the development for the common benefit of all of the property owners. In many cases, the association also serves to provide and foster community and social recreation and activities for the residents of the development. Although the characteristics of each CID and the rights, duties and responsibilities of the associations and the property owners are to a large extent defined by law, each CID is also defined by its own geographic location, its own community and social needs, and its own "governing documents".

Common interest developments are subject to and governed by a variety of laws and regulations. The first comprehensive statute to be enacted in California to govern CIDs is commonly referred to as the "Davis-Stirling Common Interest Development Act" which was enacted in 1985 and which became effective in 1986.[4] The Davis-Stirling Common Interest Development Act provides the basic framework of statutory law applicable to CIDs. However, a great many other statutes, as well as many published court decisions and regulations also apply to the operation and affairs of CIDs. Within the past ten years, the California legislature and courts have been very busy promulgating new, additional laws which directly or indirectly affect CIDs and their property owners.

This book is intended to provide practical and ready assistance to associations and property owners alike with regard to their respective rights and responsibilities arising out of community ownership and living.

This book also provides the reader with a comprehensive discussion of the legal issues most commonly encountered by associations and property owners, supported by analyses of and references to the appropriate legal authorities.

Although the four types of common interest developments differ markedly from each other legally, they do share many important common characteristics. Each is a real estate development, designed for either or both residential and/or nonresidential or commercial purposes. In each type of CID, the property owner holds separate legal title or an exclusive right to possession to lots, parcels, spaces or units on which the owner resides. These separately owned lots, parcels, spaces or units are referred to by the law as "separate interests".

One or more additional lots, parcels, spaces or units are then either typically owned in common with the other owners of the separate interests, or owned by the association which operates and manages the CID. These lots, parcels, spaces or units commonly owned or owned by the association are referred to by the law as "common areas". The common area or areas may also consist simply of mutual or reciprocal easement rights which are legally attached to each of the separate interests.[5] The common areas, whether owned in common by all of the property owners or the association, are intended to be for the benefit, use and enjoyment of all of the property owners.

The owners of separate interests may also have an exclusive right to use a certain specified portion of the common areas, for example, patio or balcony areas. These areas are generally referred to by the law as "exclusive use common areas".

The design, purpose and use of the property can make the allocation of the various areas and the owners' rights and interests more complex. For instance, an owner's separate interest or exclusive use common area may also be subject to easements in favor of the other property owners so they can have access to their separate interests.

When a real estate developer proposes to subdivide land and create a CID, the developer must, in addition to other legal requirements, obtain the approval of the California Department of Real Estate.[6] The Department of Real Estate has enacted a series of detailed regulations requiring that proposed CIDs meet a number of specified standards with respect to the configuration of the development, requiring the developer to meet specified development and financial standards, and prescribing minimum standards for the management, maintenance and operation of the development, the creation of an association to manage the CID, and the mandatory and permissible contents of the association's governing documents.[7]

The Department of Real Estate regulations and requirements are intended to protect home purchasers and ensure that only viable and operable developments and associations are established.

Ordinarily, every property owner is automatically made a member of the property owners association which operates, maintains, and manages the CID. The affairs of the CID are managed by the association, which may be incorporated or unincorporated.[8] The property owners are the association members and they are equivalent to the shareholders in other types of corporations. That is, the members elect the governing board of the association and ultimately control the operation and business affairs of the association. As the developer sells each additional lot, unit, condominium or apartment in the CID, the developer is gradually relinquishing control of the association to the purchasers who become voting members of the association.

The association is charged with the responsibility of repairing, maintaining and replacing common areas and member facilities located on common areas. Both the property owners and the association may enforce the declaration of covenants, conditions and restrictions.[9] However, it is the association that is legally responsible for enforcing the declaration.

GOVERNING DOCUMENTS

In order to ensure the maximum beneficial use and enjoyment of the CID by each property owner, a "declaration of covenants, conditions and restrictions" is prepared by the developer. The developer then records the declaration in the county land title records before the first separate interest is sold to a buyer. The main object of the declaration is to preserve and maintain the esthetic and environmental desirability of the CID and to make clear the respective rights and obligations of the management association and the individual property owners with respect to one another and the CID.

Other important association documents are ordinarily prepared by the developer as well, including articles of incorporation or association, bylaws, architectural or environmental control rules and association rules. Taken together, all of the association's documents are referred to by the law as "governing documents". In addition, prior to the sale or financing of any separate interest in the development, the developer must apply for and obtain from the California Department of Real Estate a public report which describes the development and the features which are to be provided to prospective purchasers. Before the Department of Real Estate will issue a final public report for the CID, it will review the contents of the governing documents and require that the developer include certain mandatory provisions with respect to assessments, reserve funds, the rights of association members and the power and authority of the association to govern the CID. During its review of the project, the Department of Real Estate will also satisfy itself that the governing documents are binding on all purchasers of property within the CID.[10]

During the period of time that the subdivider or developer continues to own or control a sufficient number of separate interests so that the developer controls one-fourth or more of the votes of the association, no amendment of the governing documents which would materially change the rights of the property owners, either directly or as a member of the association, is valid without the prior written consent of the Department of Real Estate.[11]

TYPES OF COMMON INTEREST DEVELOPMENTS

As previously mentioned, there are four types of CIDs generally recognized by California law: the planned development, the condominium, the community apartment project, and the stock cooperative.

Planned Development:

A "planned development" is a CID, other than a community apartment project, condominium project or stock cooperative, which features either or both of the following: (1) the common area is owned either by the association or in common by the owners of the separate interests who possess appurtenant rights (see definition of "appurtenant" on page 8) to the beneficial use and enjoyment of the common area; (2) the association has the power to enforce an obligation of an owner of a separate interest with respect to the beneficial use and enjoyment of the common area by means of an assessment which may become a lien upon the separate interests.[12]

A planned development is similar to a condominium project in that subdivided parcels are individually owned and there is common ownership of, or interests in, common areas or other separately owned parcels. The major legal distinction between the two is that in the case of a planned development the unit owner also receives separate fee title to the land beneath his unit. Another major distinction is that the creation of a statutory condominium project requires the preparation and recordation of a condominium plan, final map or parcel map which contains sufficient detail to locate all of the boundaries of the condominium project as well as all of the boundaries of each condominium unit (see condominium discussion below).

Condominium Project:

The definition of a condominium is somewhat esoteric because the concept of a condominium is itself legally involved and complex.

A "condominium project" is defined as an estate in real property consisting of an undivided interest in common (with other owners) in a portion of a parcel of real property, together with a separate interest in space, the boundaries of which must be described, in a recorded condominium plan, final map or parcel map, with sufficient detail to locate all boundaries of the space. The area within those boundaries may be filled with air, earth, water or any combination thereof, and need not be physically attached to land except by access easements and, if necessary, vertical and/or lateral support.[13]

The "condominium unit," or separate interest, is a separate ownership in a condominium project consisting of a cube of space as defined in the condominium plan, final map or parcel map (with sufficient detail to locate all the boundaries of each "unit"), together with an appurtenant undivided interest in the common areas.

The cube of airspace which is called the "condominium unit" or separate interest in a residential condominium project is surrounded by the structural portions of the building which is common area. Depending on the legal descriptions in the condominium plan, final map or parcel map, the unit or separate interest may include the interior unit, garage(s) and/or storage space(s).

The common area is the entire condominium project except for the areas designated as units or separate interests in separate ownership. Thus, the boundary walls of a unit outside of the unfinished surface areas are common areas. The common areas include all bearing walls, utility lines and conduits, halls, elevators, stairs, walkways, open-space areas, driveways, recreational areas, and the like.[14]

Unless provided otherwise in the condominium plan, final map or parcel map, if walls, floors or ceilings are designated as the boundaries of the unit or separate interest, the interior unfinished surfaces of the perimeter walls, floors, ceilings, windows, doors and outlets located within the unit are part of the separate interest and any other portions of the walls, floors, or ceilings are part of the common areas.[15]

In a condominium then, the unit owner owns the wallpaper, paint, and other finishes within the unit and is responsible for their care maintenance and replacement.[16] The unit owner also owns all interior walls, except for bearing walls and, subject to easements for the common areas, wires and pipes that pass through the unit.

Community Apartment Project:

In a community apartment project, the homeowner owns an interest in the development and an exclusive right to occupy a designated residential unit or apartment. The separate interest in a community apartment project consists of this exclusive right to occupy a designated unit.[17]

Stock Cooperative:

In a stock cooperative, the homeowner owns a share of stock or a membership interest in the corporation formed for the purpose of holding title to the real estate and an exclusive right of occupancy in a specific portion of the real estate. The right of occupancy is transferable only with the share or shares of stock or membership certificate.[18]

THE RIGHTS AND DUTIES OF THE PROPERTY OWNERS AND THE ASSOCIATION VARY WITH THE TYPE OF CID

The legal and practical meaning of the terms "separate interest" and "common area" differ dramatically depending on the type of common interest development involved. In a planned development, the separate interest is a separately owned area, parcel or lot. In a condominium, the separate interest is the exclusive right to occupy an individual unit. In a community apartment project, the separate interest is the exclusive right to occupy an apartment. In a stock cooperative, the separate interest is the exclusive right to occupy a portion of the real property. The common area means the entire common interest development except the separate interests.[19]

The term "exclusive use common area" means a portion of the common areas designated by the declaration for the exclusive use of one or more, but fewer than all, of the owners of the separate interests and which is or will be "appurtenant" or legally attached to the owner's separate interest.[20]

In the context of CIDs, the word "appurtenant" means the owner's undivided interest in the common area and the owner's interest in the exclusive use common area are legally connected with, attached to, or bound with, and cannot be separated from, the owner's separate interest. In other words, a separate interest cannot be sold, transferred, assigned or conveyed without its appurtenant interests.[21]

Unless the declaration of covenants, conditions and restrictions provides otherwise, any shutters, awnings, window boxes, doorsteps, stoops, porches, balconies, patios, exterior doors, door frames, and hardware incidental thereto, screens and windows or other fixtures designed to serve a single separate interest, but located outside the boundaries of the separate interest, are exclusive use common areas allocated exclusively to that separate interest.[22]

Generally, in all CIDs the owner of the separate interest is responsible for the repair, maintenance and replacement of his or her separate interest and, ordinarily, any exclusive use common area appurtenant to his or her separate interest. Conversely, the association is ordinarily responsible for the repair, maintenance and restoration of the common areas.

Unless the declaration, or condominium plan in the case of a condominium, provides otherwise, if walls, floors or ceilings are designated as the boundaries of a separate interest, then the interior surfaces of the perimeter walls, floors, ceilings, windows, doors and outlets located within the separate interest are part of the separate interest. All other portions of the walls, floors and ceilings are part of the common areas.[23]

Section 1364(a) of the California Civil Code provides the following:

> "Unless otherwise provided in the declaration of a common interest development, the association is responsible for repairing, replacing, or maintaining the common areas, other than exclusive use common areas, and the owner of each separate interest is responsible for maintaining that separate interest and any exclusive use common areas appurtenant to that separate interest."

The allocation of responsibilities dependent on common areas, separate interests and exclusive use common areas, determines to a large extent the respective rights and obligations of the property owners and the association.

ASSOCIATION'S FINANCIAL RESOURCES

During the initial formation of the CID, the developer is legally bound to provide certain financial assurances with respect to the completion of the CID and all of the planned improvements and the establishment of reserves and operating funds for the continued operation of the CID by the association.[24] This is necessary in order to ensure the continued viability of the CID and association as the developer continues to sell more separate interests and gradually relinquishes a controlling share of the separate interests.

The association is empowered by law, indeed it is obligated, to levy and collect assessments from the owners of property within the CID to pay for the costs of operation, maintenance, restoration and repair of the CID, and to establish reserves for the replacement of CID facilities when the need arises.[25] A complete and detailed discussion of assessments and reserves is found in Chapter IX.

COMMUNITY COOPERATION

Community association living can be a pleasant experience where property owners may enjoy many amenities and facilities that would not otherwise be available to them, or available only at significantly higher costs. Community association living, however, also carries with it certain responsibilities for both the association and the property owners. Fulfillment of those responsibilities is necessary for successful and harmonious community living, the full use and enjoyment of the development by all owners, and the management, maintenance and preservation of the development as a whole.

Chapter I is intended to provide a broad, general overview of CIDs. The remaining chapters in this book discuss in detail the various legal and operating characteristics of CIDs and the rights, duties and responsibilities of the associations and the property owners.

CHAPTER II

MANAGEMENT, PRESERVATION AND MAINTENANCE

As briefly mentioned in Chapter I, the primary purposes and responsibilities of the CID association are to operate, manage, preserve and maintain the assets of the development. These purposes and responsibilities have many facets and will vary according to the type of CID, the terms of the association's governing documents, the particular facilities and amenities located in the development, and the needs and desires of the property owners.

Among the association's responsibilities, perhaps most important are the duties to operate and maintain the common areas and community facilities and amenities and the enforcement of the land use regulations found in the association's governing documents. These responsibilities, when fulfilled, benefit not only the association's assets, but the individual property owner as well. Although real estate values may be subject to many factors beyond the control of individual owners and the association, prudent and consistent management of the association should tend to stabilize, if not enhance, the value of individually-owned properties within the development.

OPERATION AND MAINTENANCE RESPONSIBILITIES

Subject to certain parameters imposed by law, an association's maintenance and operation responsibilities should be set forth in the association's declaration of covenants, conditions and restrictions, and perhaps supplemented by other association governing documents.

As described in Chapter I, the law sets the fundamental maintenance responsibilities, but permits those responsibilities to be changed or modified according to the terms of the declaration of covenants, conditions and restrictions.[1]

Section 1364(a) of the California Civil Code provides the following general rule with respect to maintenance, repair, and replacement obligations:

> "Unless otherwise provided in the declaration of a common interest development, the association is responsible for repairing, replacing, or maintaining the common areas, other than exclusive use common areas, and the owner of each separate interest is responsible for maintaining that separate interest and any exclusive use common areas appurtenant to that separate interest."

As Section 1364(a) specifies, the respective maintenance responsibilities of the association and the property owner can, and often are, allocated differently according to the terms of each association's particular declaration. For this reason, the association and the property owners must become familiar with the relevant language of the declaration and pay particular attention to those provisions addressing maintenance responsibilities.

The association's legal authority and responsibility to levy and collect assessments is closely tied with the association's operation, maintenance, repair, replacement, and restoration obligations under applicable law and the association's governing documents (see the comprehensive discussion of assessments in Chapter IX). Section 1366(a) of the Civil Code provides that:

> "Except as provided in this section, the association shall levy regular and special assessments sufficient to perform its obligations under the governing documents and this title. ..."

The level of regular and special assessments which will need to be levied and collected by the association should correlate directly with the association's operation, maintenance, management and replacement activities.

With respect to a few particular maintenance problems likely to be encountered with some frequency, the legislature has chosen an allocation of maintenance responsibility along logical lines dependent on the type of CID involved. But again, for the most part the legislature has permitted the rule to be modified by the declaration.

For example, unless the declaration provides a different scheme of maintenance responsibility, the property owner may bear the maintenance responsibilities for certain areas or improvements in the CID which benefit that owner's separate interest, even if the area or improvement is located outside the boundaries of the separate interest. Several types of areas or improvements are specifically defined by statute to constitute exclusive use common areas for which the property owner is responsible for maintenance, repair and replacement. Section 1351(i)(1) of the Civil Code states:

> "Unless the declaration otherwise provides, any shutters, awnings, window boxes, doorsteps, stoops, porches, balconies, patios, exterior doors, door frames, and hardware incident thereto, screens and windows or other fixtures designed to serve a single separate interest, but located outside the boundaries of the separate interest, are exclusive use common areas allocated exclusively to that separate interest."

Another example of the legislative allocation of maintenance responsibilities lies in the repair of termite damage. Unless the declaration provides a different allocation of responsibility, in a condominium project, a community apartment project, and a stock cooperative, the association is responsible for repairing and maintaining common areas damaged by termites. Because of the all-inclusive definition of common area in a condominium this can be a significant potential financial burden for condominium associations. On the other hand, in planned developments, the owners of separate interests are responsible for the repair and maintenance of the separate interests which have been damaged by termites. Section 1364(b) of the Civil Code provides the following:

> "(1) In a community apartment project, condominium project, or stock cooperative ..., unless otherwise provided in the declaration, the association is responsible for the repair and maintenance of the common area occasioned by the presence of wood-destroying pests or organisms.
>
> "(2) In a planned development, as defined in Section 1351, unless a different maintenance scheme is provided in the declaration, each owner of a separate interest is responsible for the repair and maintenance of that separate interest as may be occasioned by the presence of wood-destroying pests or organisms. Upon approval of the majority of all members of the association, the responsibility for such repair and maintenance may be delegated to the association, which shall be entitled to recover the cost thereof as a special assessment."

In spite of any terms of the association's declaration to the contrary, both internal and external telephone wiring designed to serve a single separate interest are deemed to be exclusive use common areas for which the owner of the separate interest is responsible. Section 1351(i)(2) of the Civil Code reads as follows:

> "Notwithstanding the provisions of the declaration, internal and external telephone wiring designed to serve a single separate interest, but located outside the boundaries of the separate interest, are exclusive use common areas allocated exclusively to that separate interest."

The association's maintenance obligations are not limited to the daily operation and maintenance of the CID common areas and facilities. The association must also plan for the future. This means the association must establish and follow procedures for the accumulation of reserve funds for the replacement and major maintenance of common areas and facilities as the need may arise from time to time. This is an extremely important association function which cannot be overlooked. If reserve fund planning is not instituted and followed in a wise and prudent fashion, it is likely the association and property owners will be unable to meet the financial obligations necessarily resulting from the physical depreciation of the CID's common areas and community facilities. For this reason, the legislature enacted Sections1365 and 1365.5 of the Civil Code which require the association's board of directors to prepare, or cause to be prepared, maintain and regularly review reserve fund account statements and reconciliations.

As can be seen from a reading of the above-referenced statutes, the association's and property owner's respective maintenance obligations will be prescribed to a great extent by the terms and provisions of the association's declaration. Both the association and the property owners must familiarize themselves with the terms of the declaration in order to have a clear understanding of their respective obligations. A little time spent studying the declaration and the other association governing documents can go a long way in encouraging community harmony and avoiding misunderstandings and needless litigation.

LAND USE CONTROL

A detailed and comprehensive discussion of land use control and regulation is found in Chapter III.

Although an association may manage, maintain and operate its own assets in a wise and prudent fashion, it must also administer its land use and architectural or environmental control obligations as well in order to adequately protect, preserve and maintain the CID as a whole.[2] Many people purchase property in a CID after visiting the development and forming a belief with respect to the general appearance and condition of the community. Most purchasers rely on their belief that the association exists to maintain and preserve the community in the general appearance and condition with which it is viewed and in accordance with the association's governing documents. Included in this belief is the understanding that the association will enforce the land use and architectural controls provided in the declaration and other governing documents to enhance and preserve the aesthetics and environment of the community, the owners' full use and enjoyment of their separate interests as well as the common areas and community facilities, and the value of the separate interests.

It is because of these reasonable expectations of prospective purchasers and property owners and the need to maintain the design, purpose and plan of the community for the common benefit of all owners, that the law imposes an obligation on the association to enforce its declaration and other governing documents.[3] Likewise, it is for the same reasons that the law imposes an obligation on property owners to comply with all of the reasonable land use and architectural control restrictions which may be included in the association's declaration.[4] In order to achieve and maintain the quality of community living desired by most residents, a significant level of cooperation between the association and all property owners must be encouraged and established. Where a sense of community pride and spirit is shared by all, or at least a majority of the property owners, maintenance and preservation of the development is more expediently achieved and at significantly lower costs.

CHAPTER III

LAND USE CONTROL AND PROPERTY REGULATION

WHAT ARE CC&RS?

The abbreviation that many of us commonly see used and referred to in CIDs, "CC&Rs", is a shorthand way of referring to a declaration of covenants, conditions and restrictions.

Generally speaking, all common interest developments have a declaration of CC&Rs which has been recorded in the public land title records of the county in which the CID is located. The declaration typically contains restrictions limiting the use of the separate interests in the development to specified purposes, defining what construction and architectural standards must be followed in the development and otherwise specifying the respective duties of the association and the property owners.

A clear understanding of the purpose and scope of the declaration and its terms is essential to the proper and orderly operation and management of the association and the development.

In order to adequately grasp the meaning and implications of CC&Rs, the reader should examine and understand several legal definitions and parts of the history of property law. To begin with, "statutory law" or "statutes" consist of that body of law which is prepared and enacted by our legislature. Please see Chapter VI for a detailed discussion of the laws which apply to and govern CIDs.

"Common law" is the phrase most often used to describe the body of law that is created when our courts, ordinarily appellate courts with jurisdiction to review the decisions of our trial courts, render decisions which are published in opinion form and collated into books of case law reporters. Sometimes, the decisions of the courts directly or indirectly tell us how to interpret the statutes enacted by the legislature.

The phrase, "covenants, conditions and restrictions", must be broken down into its three fundamental parts to adequately understand what is meant by each component.

Covenants:

A "covenant", in the context of real property law, is an agreement to do or refrain from doing some certain thing and ordinarily relates to the use of land. A covenant is ordinarily created by words in a deed or another written document which show the agreement. The agreement does not have to be signed by the promisor, that is, the person promising to do or refrain from doing something.

Personal Covenants:

If the covenant is a "personal covenant", it is binding and enforceable only as between the original parties to the agreement and is governed to a large extent by the principles of contract law. As a simplified example, if John Doe "covenants" or promises with his neighbor Jane Roe that he will not keep or permit barking dogs on his property which annoy or disturb Jane, and the covenant is a "personal covenant", Jane may enforce the covenant against John to make John quiet his dogs. But, a buyer of Jane Roe's property probably will not be able to enforce the covenant against John Doe when John's dogs begin barking at 2:30 a.m. Likewise, if John were to sell his property, Jane could not enforce the covenant against the buyer of John's property. After all, the buyer did not promise Jane anything.

Real Covenants:

On the other hand, if the covenant is a "real covenant", it is binding and enforceable not only between the original parties to the agreement, but also as to their successors in interest. The covenant, in a legal sense, attaches to the land itself, not the owner of the land. In the example given above, even after John Doe sells his property, Jane could enforce the covenant against the new owner. In legal language, the property now owned by John's buyer ("successor in interest") continues to be "burdened" by the "real covenant".

Historical Development Of Real Covenants And Equitable Servitudes:

Much of our law governing real covenants is derived from ancient English common law and many of the decisions rendered by English courts in the 17th, 18th and 19th centuries continue to influence modern court decisions.[1] While the reader may find this strange, it does tend to lend stability, uniformity and some predictability to our laws. Two fundamental aspects of real covenants have long been recognized by the law. A real covenant is said to have both a "burden" and "benefit" side. The same real covenant may have a burden which burdens or imposes responsibilities on the owners of the burdened land, and a "benefit" which benefits other land and its owners. In the example given above, Jane's land is benefited by the real covenant, while John's land is burdened by the covenant. In the case of real covenants, the benefits and burdens pass with changes in ownership by implication of law, not under principles of contract law.

Other names ascribed to real covenants are "running covenants" and "covenants that run with the land", words which attempt to describe the chief characteristic of the covenant, that is, that it attaches to the land itself regardless of changes in ownership.

In order to be a "real covenant" or "covenant that runs with the land", several essential ingredients are necessary: (1) the written instrument creating the covenant, for example, a deed or declaration, must disclose the parties' intention that the covenant run with the land, (2) the covenant must "touch or concern the land", in other words it must affect the parties as owners of particular estates in land or relate to the use of land, and (3) the parties' successors in interest must acquire the estate or interest in land of their predecessors, the covenanting parties.

Equitable Servitudes:

Because of the very technical nature of real covenants, sometimes covenants which the original parties intended to be binding on their successors were not. For instance, at one time in history, the law courts[2] decided that if the benefit side of a covenant did not run for any particular reason, then the burden side should not run either. As a result, the equity courts slowly began to evolve a doctrine called "equitable servitudes" to afford protection to parties who thought they had fulfilled all the technical requirements of real covenants, but later found an essential ingredient was missing. Today, even if a covenant does not meet the technical requirements to "run with the land", it may be enforceable as an "equitable servitude" if the person bound by the restriction had notice of its existence.[3] If a covenant is enforceable as an equitable servitude, it will be enforced by the courts against the parties and their successors in interest despite the fact that it does not qualify as a real covenant.

As mentioned above, our law of real covenants and equitable servitudes can be traced to early English common law. In the earliest reported decision on the subject, of which the author is aware,[4] the English Court of Chancery in 1848 held that a covenant in a deed by which the grantee covenanted to use and maintain Leicester Square as a pleasure garden for the enjoyment and benefit of the dwelling lots located around the square was enforceable in equity even if not enforceable at law as a real covenant. The equity court held that the covenant was binding on the grantee's purchaser who had notice of the covenant and that he was, therefore, prohibited from building dwellings on the square as he had intended.[5]

Conditions:

The word "conditions", as used in declaration of covenants, conditions and restrictions, is usually a misnomer and is technically incorrect in this context. A condition, in the context of real property law, refers to an event or occurrence, which triggers a certain result upon its happening. Declarations of covenants, conditions and restrictions rarely contain conditions. As an example, a breach of a true condition that certain land shall only be used for a park, would result in title to the land reverting to the grantor. True conditions are extremely uncommon in declarations of covenants, conditions and restrictions.

Restrictions:

The word, "restrictions", as used in declaration of covenants, conditions and restrictions, generally refers to restrictive covenants, that is, covenants which prohibit or limit certain types of land use or activities on the affected land.

The Declaration:

The "declaration" is that document which contains a variety of different covenants and restrictions affecting certain specified land. Declarations recorded in the public land title records after January 1, 1986 must include a legal description of the CID, a statement that the CID is a community apartment project, stock cooperative, planned development, condominium project, or a combination of such CIDs, the name of the association and the restrictions which are intended to be enforceable equitable servitudes. The declaration may also contain any other information which the party originally signing the declaration or the property owners consider appropriate.[6]

Modern Use And Application Of Declaration In The Common Interest Development:

During modern American legal history, in order to effectuate and implement the desired benefits of land use control, particularly in planned development settings, the courts and legislatures have taken steps to liberalize the enforceability of covenants as equitable servitudes. The law has done so in order to preserve and maintain the environment intended by the original covenanting parties, often land developers and subdividers.

Within the last ten years, in order to keep pace with the ever increasing popularity of CID living and ensure the continued viability of the land use regulations making CID living a possibility, the California legislature enacted Section 1354(a) of the Civil Code which states that:

> "The covenants and restrictions in the declaration shall be enforceable equitable servitudes, unless unreasonable, and shall inure to the benefit of and bind all owners of separate interests in the development. Unless the declaration states otherwise, these servitudes may be enforced by any owner of a separate interest or by the association, or by both."

Whether or not a property owner knows of the existence of the recorded declaration, he or she is bound by its terms and provisions. One of the chief tenets found in most areas of real property law, including common interest development law, is that when a person has notice (knowledge or awareness) of a fact, rule, or standard, whether the notice is actual (personal knowledge) or constructive (knowledge imputed by operation of law whether or not the person has actual knowledge)[7] that person cannot escape the responsibilities, duties and obligations that necessarily flow from that knowledge. When documents such as a declaration of CC&Rs are recorded in the public records, the law deems that the entire world has constructive knowledge of the documents.[8]

The covenants and restrictions in a recorded declaration can be many and varied, addressing a wide array of different topics such as general land use restrictions, for example, limiting use of lots to residential as opposed to commercial or business purposes, animal control restrictions, minimum building and safety standards, aesthetics and preservation of the overall scheme and design of the development.

Sometimes people confuse the aspects of covenants and restrictions found in recorded declarations with other features and characteristics commonly (but not always) found in CID living. For example, many parcels of land throughout California are subject to recorded declarations containing covenants and land use restrictions, but there is no owners association in existence and one was never intended. This does not mean that the declaration is unenforceable. Generally speaking, any land owner whose property is benefited by a covenant or restriction may cause enforcement of that covenant or restriction as against the burdened land. In other words, an owners association is not synonymous with a declaration of covenants, conditions and restrictions.

Likewise, not all subdivisions and subdivided land projects constitute CIDs. If a subdivision is not a CID as defined by statute, then the comprehensive body of statutory law implemented to govern CIDs will generally not apply to that subdivision. The chief characteristics of a CID are that a separate interest coupled with an interest in the common area or membership in the association is or has been conveyed (legal title transferred) and a declaration, condominium plan if any exists, and a final map or parcel map have been recorded.[9] Please see Chapter VI for a detailed discussion of when a CID is created and to what laws a CID is subject.

When a CID has been created and an owners association does exist, it may have many functions, responsibilities and powers, including the power to enforce the declaration of CC&Rs and the power to adopt more detailed rules to implement the broader covenants and restrictions. If it exists, the owners association may be either incorporated or unincorporated. If it is incorporated, the association will have articles of incorporation by which it was created or incorporated, and ordinarily will also have corporate bylaws which govern the corporate aspects of the association and the benefits, responsibilities and conduct of its members and affairs.

As succinctly stated by the California Supreme Court: "How courts enforce recorded use restrictions affects not only those who have made their homes in planned developments, but also the owners associations charged with the fiduciary obligation to enforce those restrictions."[10]

ENFORCEABILITY AND VALIDITY OF COVENANTS AND RESTRICTIONS: INTERPRETATION AND APPLICATION

Which CC&Rs May Be Enforced - Presumption Of Validity:

Associations and property owners need to be familiar with their particular declaration of CC&Rs. However, the declaration cannot be viewed in the abstract alone. A vast and relatively comprehensive body of law has evolved governing the meaning, interpretation, validity and enforceability of covenants and restrictions. In the event an association or a property owner has serious questions with respect to the meaning or validity of particular covenants and restrictions, the advice of legal counsel experienced in such matters should be sought. The meaning and validity of any given covenant or restriction will often be influenced both by the language of the declaration and the specific facts and circumstances involved. This book is intended as a general reference guide only, and no general conclusions can be or are stated with respect to the meaning or enforceability of any particular restrictions or types of restrictions.

Not all covenants and restrictions contained in any given declaration may be enforceable. Remember that Section 1354(a) of the Civil Code states that, "[t]he covenants and restrictions in the declaration shall be enforceable equitable servitudes, unless unreasonable ..." The covenants and restrictions set forth in a recorded declaration of covenants, conditions and restrictions are presumed by the courts to be reasonable, valid and enforceable.[11]

Challenger Bears Burden Of Proving Unreasonableness:

The person challenging the validity of a particular covenant or restriction bears the burden of proof to establish that the restriction is unreasonable with respect to the development as a whole.[12] Prior to the California Supreme Court's decision in *Nahrstedt v. Lakeside Village Condominium Association, Inc.* in late 1994,[13] several lower appellate courts had ruled that the challenger could show the covenant or restriction was unreasonable as applied to the challenger or his property.[14]

In *Nahrstedt v. Lakeside Village Condominium Association, Inc.*, the Supreme Court held that the challenger, in order to show that a covenant or restriction is unreasonable and therefore unenforceable, must prove that it is unreasonable with respect to the development as a whole, not merely with respect to the particular facts and circumstances of the challenger's property:

> "Under the holding we adopt today, the reasonableness or unreasonableness of a condominium use restriction that the Legislature has made subject to section 1354 is to be determined not by reference to facts that are specific to the objecting homeowner, but by reference to the common interest development as a whole. As we have explained, when, as here, a restriction is contained in the declaration of the common interest development and is recorded with the county recorder, the restriction is presumed to be reasonable and will be enforced

> uniformly against all residents of the common interest development unless the restriction is arbitrary, imposes burdens on the use of the lands it affects that substantially outweigh the restriction's benefits to the development's residents, or violates a fundamental public policy."[15]

In a lawsuit brought by the association against a property owner alleged to be in violation of the association's declaration, the property owner bears the burden of proof to show that the particular restriction or covenant is unreasonable. And, the proof must establish that the restriction or covenant is unreasonable with respect to the CID as a whole, not merely with respect to the facts or circumstances peculiar to the objecting property owner.

Test Of Reasonableness Of Covenant Or Restriction:

The general rule which is now followed by the courts in determining whether a particular covenant or restriction is reasonable is whether the covenant or restriction is either (1) "arbitrary", that is, it bears no rational relationship to the protection, preservation, operation or purpose of the affected land, or (2) violates a fundamental public policy, or (3) imposes burdens on the use of the affected property that substantially outweigh the benefits of the restriction.[16]

INTERPRETATION OF GOVERNING DOCUMENTS

Applying the standard of reasonableness to particular covenants or restrictions may often prove troublesome and frustrating for associations and property owners alike. But associations and owners should both at least recognize the standard which is now applied by the courts.

Responsibility And Judgment Of The Association:

Associations have the responsibility of interpreting and enforcing the development's declaration of CC&Rs independently of what any given property owner or group of property owners might think or assert.[17]

However, where there are serious disputes between property owners as to the meaning or application of a particular covenant or restriction, the association need not vigorously advocate any particular interpretation. Instead, it is enough if the association seeks a judicial declaration of the meaning of the covenant or restriction.[18]

Commensurate with the level of responsibility placed on associations for interpreting and applying the declaration of CC&Rs, the law has developed a level of protection insulating the association's decisions from unwarranted attack. Neither the courts nor minority members of the association can substitute their business judgment for that of the association where the association's board of directors has acted in good faith and with a view as to the best interests of the association and all of its members.[19]

Whenever serious questions arise with respect to the meaning, application or enforceability of particular covenants and restrictions, associations and property owners should seek the advice of competent legal counsel experienced in such matters. The meaning, application and enforceability of any given covenant or restriction will often vary according to the language of the declaration and the specific facts and circumstances involved. A little homework and time spent with legal counsel at the outset may save countless hours and expensive legal fees later on, should a dispute or lawsuit evolve from the questioned covenant or restriction.

Specific Prohibitions Or Limitations Against Enforcement Of Certain Covenants Or Restrictions:

Some covenants and restrictions are void and unenforceable as being against public policy or in violation of constitutionally protected rights. Clear examples of such restrictions are those that purport to limit the ownership or occupancy of property based on race or some other protected classification of people, such as religion, sex, ancestry, national origin or disability.[20]

Liberal Interpretation Required To Promote The Operation Of The Common Interest Development:

The California legislature has also adopted a statute instructing courts to interpret covenants and restrictions liberally in order to facilitate the operations of CIDs. Civil Code Section 1370 specifies that:

> "Any deed, declaration or condominium plan for a common interest development shall be liberally construed to facilitate the operation of the common interest development, and its provisions shall be presumed to be independent and severable. Nothing in Article 3 (commencing with Section 715) of Chapter 2 of Title 2 of Part 1 of this division shall operate to invalidate any provisions of the governing documents of a common interest development."

The liberal construction requirement of Section 1370 means that when called upon to interpret a declaration of CC&Rs, the courts should do so in a manner which will implement and be consistent with the operations of the CID, maintaining and preserving the overall design of the community. The Section 1370 language establishing a presumption that the terms and provisions of a declaration are independent and severable means that in the event a court finds that any particular covenant or restriction is invalid or unenforceable, the remaining terms and provisions of the declaration should be treated as independent with continuing validity.

Statutory Limitations On Enforcement Of Restrictions:

Other covenants and restrictions may be invalid and unenforceable, or limited in effect in application, because of statutes which have been enacted to address specific subject areas of concern to the legislature. Some statutes operate prospectively only.[21] That is, they affect or have an impact only on those declarations or covenants or restrictions which are adopted by an association after the effective date of the statute. Other statutes operate prospectively and retrospectively, that is they may affect or have an impact on declarations, covenants or restrictions whether adopted before or after the effective date of the statute.

Mobilehomes - Manufactured Homes:

An example of a statute having a prospective effect on the validity of covenants and restrictions is Section 714.5 of the Civil Code. Those restrictions in declarations adopted after January 1, 1988 attempting to prohibit the sale, lease, rent or use of property on the basis that the structure intended for occupancy is a mobilehome or manufactured home are invalid under Civil Code Section 714.5. Section 714.5 states that:

> "The covenants, conditions, and restrictions or other management documents shall not prohibit the sale, lease, rent, or use of real property on the basis that the structure intended for occupancy on the real property is constructed in an offsite facility or factory, and subsequently moved or transported in sections or modules to the real property. Nothing herein shall preclude the governing instruments from being uniformly applied to all structures subject to the covenants, conditions, and restrictions or other managing documents.

"This section shall apply to covenants, conditions, and restrictions or other management documents adopted on and after the effective date of this section."[22]

By its own express terms, however, Section 714.5 does not invalidate or otherwise affect restrictions adopted prior to January 1, 1988.

Solar Energy Systems:

Although a declaration may contain enforceable restrictions regulating the design and placement of solar energy systems, restrictions that flatly prohibit the installation of such systems are invalidated by statute. Civil Code Section 714 protects and encourages the use of solar energy systems in the following manner:

"(a) Any covenant, restriction, or condition contained in any deed, contract, security instrument, or other instrument affecting the transfer or sale of, or any interest in, real property that effectively prohibits or restricts the installation or use of a solar energy system is void and unenforceable."

"(b) This section shall not apply to provisions which impose reasonable restrictions on solar energy systems. However, it is the policy of the state to promote and encourage the use of solar energy systems and to remove obstacles thereto. Accordingly, reasonable restrictions on a solar energy system are those restrictions that do not significantly increase the cost of the system or significantly decrease its efficiency or specified performance, or that allow for an alternative system of comparable cost, efficiency, and energy conservation benefits. ..."

Section 714 goes on to define the parameters by which a restriction may be deemed reasonable, and prescribes a civil penalty of up to $1,000 which may be imposed, in addition to other legal relief, against any entity that willfully violates the statute. Civil Code Section 714.1 then clarifies the association's right to enforce reasonable restrictions with respect to solar energy systems:

"Notwithstanding Section 714, any association, as defined in Section 1351, may impose reasonable provisions which:
"(a) Restrict the installation of solar energy systems installed in common areas, as defined in Section 1351, to those systems approved by the association.

"(b) Require the owner of a separate interest, as defined in Section 1351, to obtain the approval of the association for the installation of a solar energy system in a separate interest owned by another.

"(c) Provide for the maintenance, repair, or replacement of roofs or other building components.

"(d) Require installers of solar energy systems to indemnify or reimburse the association or its members for loss or damage caused by the installation, maintenance, or use of the solar energy system."

Real Estate For Sale Signs:

Whether they are found in a deed, a declaration, a mortgage, a deed of trust, or any other instrument, restrictions which would prohibit or restrict a property owner or his or her agent from displaying signs advertising the property for sale, lease or exchange are invalid and unenforceable. Believing that people should be free to advertise their property for sale, the legislature enacted Civil Code Section 712 which reads as follows:

"(a) Every provision contained in or otherwise affecting a grant of a fee interest in, or purchase money security instrument upon, real property in this state heretofore or hereafter made, which purports to prohibit or restrict the right of the property owner or his or her agent to display or have displayed on the real property, or on real property owned by others with their consent, or both, signs which are reasonably located, in plain view of the public, are of reasonable dimensions and design, and do not adversely affect public safety, including traffic safety, and which advertise the property for sale, lease, or exchange, or advertise directions to the property, by the property owner or his or her agent is void as an unreasonable restraint upon the power of alienation.

"(b) This section shall operate retrospectively, as well as prospectively, to the full extent that it may constitutionally operate retrospectively.

"(c) A sign that conforms to the ordinance adopted in conformity with Section 713 shall be deemed to be of reasonable dimension and design pursuant to this section."

Thus, associations are not entirely precluded from regulating the property owners' use of real estate for-sale signs to maintain and preserve the aesthetics of the development, but any such restrictions should be drafted and/or applied in conformity with the requirements of Section 712.

The American Flag:

Section 434.5 of the Government Code prohibits covenants or restrictions which, when applied, would deprive a person of the right to display the American flag. In addition, no restrictions regulating the display of the American flag based on aesthetics alone will be enforceable. Section 434.5 provides the following prohibitions:

> "(a) No person, private entity, or government agency shall adopt rules, regulations, or ordinances, or enter into any agreement or covenant, which prevents any person or private entity which would otherwise have the legal right to display a Flag of the United States on private property from exercising that right, unless it is used as, or in conjunction with, an advertising display.
>
> "(b) As used in this section, "legal right" means the freedom of use and enjoyment generally exercised by owners and occupiers of land.
>
> "(c) Nothing in this section shall be construed to prevent a city, county, or city and county from imposing reasonable restrictions as to the time, place, and manner of placement or display of a Flag of the United States when necessary for the preservation of the public's health, safety, or order. However, no restrictions solely to promote aesthetic considerations may be imposed."

Restrictions On The Installation Or Use Of Video Or Television Antenna:

Civil Code Section 1376, which became effective on January 1, 1996, renders void and unenforceable any prohibition against or restriction on the installation or use of a video or television satellite dish antenna that is less than 36 inches in diameter. The statute does permit an association to impose reasonable restrictions on the installation or use of video or television antennas,[23] if the restrictions do not signigicantly increase the costs of the system or significantly decrease its performance.

Residential Use Restrictions As Applied To "Family Day Care Homes":

Association declarations frequently include a restriction providing that "no business or commercial activity shall be conducted or maintained on any lot or unit", or "the use of all lots within the development shall be limited to single-family dwelling purposes", or another variation of language intended to limit the use of property within the development to single-family residential uses.

Beginning in the 1970s and continuing through the 1990s, the California legislature began to enact a series of statutes designed to encourage and foster the development and use of small residential facilities for impaired adults, the elderly and children in existing residential neighborhoods and settings. The statutes are commonly known as the "California Community Care Facilities Act",[24] the "California Residential Care Facilities for the Elderly Act",[25] the "California Adult Day Health Care Act",[26] the "California Child Day Care Act",[27] and the "Family Day Care Homes Act".[28]

The importance of the statutes as they relate to CIDs is the effect the statutes have on covenants and restrictions which prohibit the use of land for purposes other than single-family, residential purposes. The statutes in effect require that certain day care facilities be treated as a residential use of property and a single-family use of property. The use of property for such facilities then complies, by operation of the statutes, with contracts, deeds and covenants which restrict property to residential and/or single-family uses and purposes.

Community Care Facilities:

A "community care facility" is defined by statute to be a facility, place or building which is maintained and operated to provide nonmedical residential care, day treatment, adult day care, or foster family agency services for children or adults, including those who are physically handicapped, mentally impaired, incompetent persons, and abused or neglected children.[29]

Residential Facilities Serving Six Or Fewer Disabled Persons:

Covenants and restrictions limiting the use of land to noncommercial, residential, single-family purposes can no longer be applied to prohibit the land from being used for a "residential facility", serving six or fewer persons.

Health and Safety Code Section 1502(a) includes eight different types of facilities in the broader category of "community care facility" including a "residential facility"[30] defined to mean a family home or group care facility providing 24-hour nonmedical care of persons needing personal services, supervision or assistance in daily living, "adult day care facilities"[31] defined to mean any facility that provides nonmedical care to persons over the age of 18 needing personal services, supervision or assistance in daily living on less than a 24-hour basis, and "small family home"[32] defined to mean any residential facility that provides 24-hour care for six or fewer foster children who have mental disorders or developmental or physical disabilities.

Health and Safety Code Section 1566.5 then provides the following:

> "For the purposes of any contract, deed, or covenant for the transfer of real property executed on or after January 1, 1979, a residential facility which serves six or fewer persons shall be considered a residential use of property and a use of property by a single family, notwithstanding any disclaimers to the contrary."

Residential Care Facilities For The Disabled Elderly Serving Six Or Fewer Persons:

Covenants and restrictions limiting the use of land to noncommercial, residential, single-family purposes can no longer be applied to prohibit the land from being used for a "residential facility for the elderly", serving six or fewer persons.

Health and Safety Code Section 1569.2(l) defines "residential care facility for the elderly" to mean:

> "... a housing arrangement chosen voluntarily by persons 60 years of age or over, or their authorized representative, where varying levels and intensities of care and supervision, protective supervision, or personal care, or health-related services are provided, based upon their varying needs, as determined in order to be admitted and to remain in the facility. Persons under 60 years of age with compatible needs, as determined by the department, may be allowed to be admitted or retained in a residential care facility for the elderly."

Health and Safety Code Section 1569.87 then provides that:

> "For the purposes of any contract, deed, or covenant for the transfer of real property executed on or after January 1, 1979, a residential facility for the elderly which serves six or fewer persons shall be considered a residential use of property and a use of property by a single family, notwithstanding any disclaimers to the contrary."

As quoted above, Section 1566.5 requires that a "residential facility", serving six or fewer persons, be treated as a residential use of property and the use of property by a single family. Likewise, Section 1569.87 requires that a "residential facility for the elderly", serving six or fewer persons, be treated as a residential use of property and the use of property by a single family.

Both Section 1566.5 and Section 1569.87, by their own explicit terms, apply only to covenants executed on or after January 1, 1979. However, in 1994 the California Court of Appeal was called upon to consider the validity of a declaration of CC&Rs recorded in 1974 which included a provision stating that, "no business or commercial activity shall be maintained or conducted upon any of the [lots]". In this case, the property owners remodeled their home to make it suitable for use as a licensed "residential care facility" for six or fewer non-ambulatory elderly adults. The association filed suit seeking an injunction to prohibit operation of the facility as being in violation of the association's declaration of CC&Rs.[33]

The court held that neither Section 1566.5 nor 1569.87 could be given retrospective effect to invalidate covenants recorded prior to January 1, 1979. However, the court also held that the 1993 amendments of Government Code Sections 12955 and 12955.6[34] had the effect of invalidating or repealing those portions of Sections 1566.5 and 1569.87 which limit the statutory effect to covenants executed on or after January 1, 1979.[35]

The final result of this court decision is that all covenants, regardless of when they are adopted, which prohibit or restrict the use of land for purposes other than single-family, residential use cannot validly be interpreted or applied to prohibit or restrict the use of property for a "residential facility" serving six or fewer persons or a "residential facility for the elderly" serving six or fewer persons.[36]

Family Day Care Homes For Children:

Similar to residential care facilities for the disabled and the disabled elderly, the California Legislature has enacted a body of statutory law promoting the establishment of child day care facilities in existing residential neighborhoods. The intent of the legislature with respect to promoting child day care facilities is expressed in Health and Safety Code Section 1597.40(a), part of the "California Child Day Care Act", as follows:

> "It is the intent of the Legislature that family day care homes for children must be situated in normal residential surroundings so as to give children the home environment which is conducive to healthy and safe development. It is the public policy of this state to provide children in a family day care home the same home environment as provided in a traditional home setting."

Health and Safety Code Section 1596.750 defines a "child day care facility" as:

> "... a facility that provides nonmedical care to children under 18 years of age in need of personal services, supervision, or assistance essential for sustaining the activities of daily living or for the protection of the individual on less than a 24-hour basis. Child day care facility includes day care centers, employer-sponsored child care centers, and family day care homes."

A "family day care home" is a home which regularly provides care, protection, and supervision of 12 or fewer children in the care provider's home for less than 24 hours per day while the parents or guardians are away.[37] A "large family day care home" is then defined to mean a home which provides such care to 7 to 12 children, including children under the age of 10 years who reside in the home.[38] A "small family day care home" is defined to be a home which provides such care to six or fewer children, including children under the age of 10 years who reside in the home.[39]

Section 1597.40 of the Health and Safety Code invalidates covenants and restrictions which directly or indirectly prohibit the use or occupancy of land for family day care homes for children. Section 1597.40 became effective in January, 1982 and provides in relevant part that:

> "(b) Every provision in a written instrument entered into relating to real property which purports to forbid or restrict

> the conveyance, encumbrance, leasing, or mortgaging of such real property for use or occupancy as a family day care home for children, is void and every restriction or prohibition in any such written instrument as to the use or occupancy of the property as a family day care home for children is void.
>
> "(c) Every restriction or prohibition entered into, whether by way of covenant, condition upon use or occupancy, or upon transfer of title to real property, which restricts or prohibits directly, or indirectly limits, the acquisition, use, or occupancy of such property for a family day care home for children is void."

Section 1597.40 probably operates retrospectively to invalidate restrictions adopted before January, 1982. There may be some legitimate legal arguments that such statutes, which have the effect of terminating protections provided by restrictive covenants, may constitute an impairment of private contractual and property rights in violation of the United State Constitution, article I, section 10, and the California Constitution, article I, section 16. But such arguments have never been addressed in a published California court decision.[40]

Several other statutes designed to prevent discriminatory practices related to land use may affect the validity or enforceability of particular covenants and restrictions. For example, the California "Fair Employment and Housing Act",[41] the California "Unruh Civil Rights Act",[42] and the federal "Fair Housing Act",[43] all contain provisions which may invalidate or limit the effect of particular covenants and restrictions.

For example, Civil Code Section 53(a) contains a blanket prohibition against the enforcement of covenants and restrictions which discriminate on the basis of specified protected classes or categories of people. Section 53 reads as follows:

> "(a) Every provision in a written instrument relating to real property which purports to forbid or restrict the conveyance, encumbrance, leasing, or mortgaging of that real property to any person of a specified sex, race, color, religion, ancestry, national origin, or disability, is void and every restriction or prohibition as to the use or occupation of real property because of the user's or occupier's sex, race, color, religion, ancestry, national origin, or disability is void."

Whether or not an association's declaration or other governing documents contain covenants or restrictions rendered void under Civil Code Section 53, the California "Unruh Civil Rights Act" prohibits all "business establishments" from discriminating against persons in the providing of privileges, services, facilities, and accommodations on the basis of sex, race, color, religion, ancestry, national origin, or disability.[44] The California Supreme Court has held that an association which engages in typical business transactions such as hiring property managers, procuring insurance, maintaining common areas and collecting assessments, is a "business establishment" within the meaning of the "Unruh Civil Rights Act" and therefore subject to its prohibitions of discriminatory policies and practices.[45]

Occupancy Or Property Use Restrictions Based On Age:

The California legislature has determined that there is an inadequate supply of housing available to meet the special living environments and services which may be necessary or appropriate for senior citizens. In order to encourage the growth of such housing, the legislature enacted Civil Code Sections 51.2 - 51.4 to permit certain residential developments to set age restrictions preserving the development for senior citizens. Civil Code Section 51.2 states in relevant part that:

> "(a) Section 51 [Unruh Civil Rights Act] shall be construed to prohibit a business establishment from discriminating in the sale or rental of housing based on age. Where accommodations are designed to meet the physical and social needs of senior citizens, a business establishment may establish and preserve that housing for senior citizens, pursuant to Section 51.3, except housing as to which Section 51.3 is preempted by the prohibition in the federal Fair Housing Amendments Act of 1988 ... against discrimination on the basis of familial status. ..."

Under Civil Code Section 51.2, an association's declaration may include restrictions based on age which are consistent with the standards and ages specified in Section 51.3 of the Civil Code. Generally speaking, the statute defines a "senior citizen" to be a person 62 years of age or older, or a person 55 years of age or older and living in a "senior citizen housing development"(as defined in the statute). The statute then defines "qualified permanent resident" as a person 45 years of age or older and meeting certain other criteria.

Civil Code Section 51.3 then specifies that the covenants, conditions and restrictions may limit occupancy, residency, or use on the basis of age, but not more stringently than to require that one person residing in each dwelling unit be a "senior citizen" and that each other person residing in the same dwelling be a "qualified permanent resident".[46]

Declarations which contain lower age restrictions than those specified in Section 51.3 are nevertheless enforceable to the extent allowed by the statute if the restrictions were in existence on or before January 1, 1984. Civil Code Section 51.3(h) reads:

> "The covenants, conditions and restrictions or other documents or written policies applicable to any condominium, stock cooperative, limited-equity housing cooperative, planned development, or multiple-family residential property that contained age restrictions on January 1, 1984, shall be enforceable only to the extent permitted by this section, notwithstanding lower age restrictions contained in those documents or policies."

Restrictions Against Selling, Leasing Or Renting Separate Interests:

Covenants and restrictions limiting or conditioning a property owner's right to sell, transfer, lease or rent his or her separate interest are valid so long as they do not constitute "unreasonable restraints against alienation" and are reasonably applied by the association.[47]

An association's declaration may contain enforceable restrictions requiring the association's approval of a property owner's contemplated sale, transfer, leasing or renting of a separate interest.[48] However, the association's right to withhold consent or approval of such sale or lease is not absolute. If the association has justifiable reasons for limitations on the leasing or renting of separate interests which are reasonably related to the purposes for which the association exists, for example, preserving a stable community of owner-occupied residences, the limitations will probably be enforceable.[49]

In exercising its authority to approve or disapprove transfers or assignments, an association must act reasonably and exercise its power in a fair and nondiscriminatory manner. The association may withhold its approval only for reasons which are rationally related to the protection, preservation and proper operation of the property and the purposes for which the association exists as stated in its governing documents.[50]

An owner's membership in a CID association is not transferable, except upon the sale or other conveyance of all of the member's title in the separate interest. Civil Code Section 1358 provides that when an owner's "entire estate" is transferred by conveyance, judicial sale or other voluntary or involuntary transfer, the transfer also conveys the owner's membership interest in the association.[51]

When a member rents or leases his or her separate interest, the member has not transferred his or her "entire estate" within the meaning of Civil Code Section 1358. Instead, the member continues to own and hold a "reversionary interest", which will entitle the owner to full possession and enjoyment of the property once the lease or rental agreement has expired or has been otherwise terminated.

The governing documents of many associations do permit the owner of a separate interest to delegate his or her common area and amenity use rights to a tenant or lessee of the owner's separate interest. The question is sometimes raised whether, after such delegation, both the owner and his or her tenant may use the common areas and facilities of the development.

However, nonresident property owners who lease or rent their property may be lawfully excluded from using the association's common area facilities and amenities, at least where the property owner has delegated his or her use rights to the lessee or tenant and the recorded declaration or rules adopted by the association pursuant to and consistent with the declaration authorize such use prohibitions.[52]

On the other hand, it is clear that a CID association may not discriminate among its members by prohibiting nonresident members from using and enjoying the common areas, including recreational facilities within the development, solely because the members are not resident members.[53]

Statutes of Limitation:

Statutes of limitation are laws which preclude or bar the successful prosecution of a lawsuit after a specified period of time has elapsed, even though a legitimate claim may otherwise exist. The period of time within which a lawsuit must be filed varies according to the nature of the alleged wrong and the nature of the legal theory involved. The function of statutes of limitation is to promote justice by preventing surprises through the revival of claims that have been allowed to slumber until evidence has been lost, memories have faded, and witnesses have disappeared. The policy supporting statutes of limitation is that even if a person has a just claim against another, it is not unjust to require that the claimant put the other person on notice to defend the claim within the period of limitation, and the right to be free of stale claims in time comes to prevail over the right to prosecute them.[54]

Generally speaking, the statute of limitations applicable to written land use covenants, including those contained in declarations of CC&Rs, is the four-year statute applicable to legal actions arising from written instruments.[55]

The four-year period of limitations commences to run when a demand for performance of the covenant or restriction is made and a party fails or refuses to comply with the demand for performance.[56] In other words, where a covenant or restriction contained in a written declaration of CC&Rs creates an obligation for a person to perform some act or refrain from doing something and a demand is made that the covenant be performed or complied with, the party seeking enforcement of the covenant must file a lawsuit, if ever, to enforce the covenant within four years after the demand for performance is made.[57]

Other Considerations Which May Affect The Enforceability Of Particular Covenants And Restrictions:

A variety of other factors discussed in the following paragraphs may affect the enforceability of particular covenants and restrictions. Most of the considerations discussed below, however, turn on the particular facts and circumstances which may or may not be present in any particular case. Associations and property owners should consult with competent legal counsel experienced in real property law and common interest development law should questions regarding the enforceability of a particular restriction arise.

Sometimes a covenant or restriction may be too vague or ambiguous for the courts to enforce. Where a covenant or restriction is ambiguous, that is, it is susceptible to having two or more meanings because of indefiniteness in the language, it will ordinarily be interpreted most strongly against the party seeking to enforce the restriction.[58] On the other hand, while the language of a restriction may appear vague or ambiguous on its face, the courts may enforce it despite the ambiguity if its meaning can be objectively ascertained by reference to common understanding or experience.[59]

The law has long recognized an equitable doctrine commonly called "estoppel" which is often invoked when one party seeks to enforce a promise, covenant or restriction against another. The doctrine of estoppel can be raised as a defense to enforcement of a land use covenant or restriction when one party makes a misleading statement or engages in misleading behavior or conduct and the other party, believing the statement, behavior or conduct, relies on it. For instance, it is possible the doctrine of estoppel could be invoked to preclude enforcement of a restriction if the association or a person acting with its authority states, or otherwise overtly leads property owners to believe that the restriction will not be enforced.

In order for the doctrine of estoppel to operate, generally the presence of four elements is required: (1) the party to be estopped had knowledge of the true facts involved in the particular circumstance, (2) that party intended that its statements, behavior or conduct would be acted upon, or that party acted in such a way that the other party was entitled to believe that the conduct was intended to be acted upon; (3) the "innocent" party was ignorant of the true facts; and (4) the "innocent" party relied upon the other party's statements, conduct, or acts to his or her detriment.[60]

Sometimes the courts may rule that the enforcement of a particular restriction has been "waived" through inaction and complacence over a period of time. The legal theory underlying the doctrine of "waiver" is that the party now seeking enforcement has failed to seek enforcement against similar violations by other persons and has, through such inaction, induced the other party to believe that the particular covenant or restriction is no longer subject to enforcement.[61]

Merely because enforcement of one covenant or restriction may not have occurred, however, does not necessarily mean that enforcement of other covenants and restrictions have been waived.[62]

Likewise, even if violations of a particular restriction have been tolerated and waived in a particular portion of a development, enforcement of the same restriction may not have waived in other parts of the development.[63]

Where a change in surrounding property conditions or other circumstances frustrates or defeats the purpose of a particular covenant or restriction rendering it of little continuing value or benefit, the courts may not enforce it where enforcement would lead to unfair or inequitable results. This is often referred to as the doctrine or defense of "changed circumstances".[64]

The extent or degree of change necessary to establish the defense of changed circumstances is a question of fact which can only be determined on a case-by-case basis. Not all changes in circumstances or character or property use are sufficient to render a restriction unenforceable. If the original purpose or benefit of the restriction can still be satisfied or achieved, the restriction will generally be enforced.[65]

If a court determines that there has been a change in surrounding circumstances, the court can conclude either that the restriction is unenforceable, or that the restriction should be interpreted differently in order to accommodate the changed circumstances.[66]

When a party who seeks an injunction to prohibit the violation of a restriction has also violated the restriction, the party opposing enforcement may be entitled to maintain the doctrine of "unclean hands" as a defense to enforcement.[67]

If enforcement of a covenant or restriction has not been timely sought or has been delayed unreasonably, and the party now seeking enforcement has either acquiesced in the violation of the restriction or somehow prejudiced the other party by the delay, as for example, by allowing construction to continue in violation of a lot line setback restriction, enforcement of the restriction may be barred by the equitable doctrine of "laches".[68]

If monetary damages are sought against a person or entity for violation of a land use restriction, the applicable statute of limitations is probably four years under California Code of Civil Procedure Section 337, which applies to an action premised on a written contract or liability on a written instrument.[69]

Even if a declaration of CC&Rs is not viewed by the courts as a written contract for purposes of applying the appropriate statute of limitations, California Code of Civil Procedure Section 343 provides a four-year limitations period for actions not otherwise specifically covered in the Code of Civil Procedure.

Covenants And Restrictions Which Differ From Governmental Zoning Ordinances, Regulations And Licensing Requirements:

Private land use restrictions, which are otherwise reasonable and enforceable, may prohibit or limit land uses, conditions, activities and conduct which are otherwise permitted under applicable zoning ordinances.

A restriction that is reasonably related to a legitimate purpose of an association and which prohibits conduct or activity that interferes or is reasonably likely to interfere with the rights of other persons in the peaceful and quiet enjoyment of their property will be considered to be reasonable and enforceable by the courts.[70]

It is now an established rule that a private land use restriction may prohibit an activity or condition that is lawful and otherwise permitted by zoning ordinances.[71]

For example, in *Wilkman v. Banks,* recorded CC&Rs prohibited the construction of hospitals and sanitariums on any parcel within the subject tract of land. Despite the restrictions, the owners attempted to build and maintain a sanitarium on their lot after the city government enacted ordinances permitting such land use. In affirming the trial court's injunction prohibiting the violation of the restrictions and covenants, the appellate court stated:

> "Appellants cry with alarm against the enforcement of an agreement [the restrictive covenants] they and their predecessors had made to preserve the home-like character of their community and make the novel plea that is unreasonable and unjust for a court to enforce the compact. We know of no authority to warrant the ruthless renouncement of a contract [the restrictive covenants] made to preserve and protect the rights of the contracting parties. *The fact that the City of Los Angeles has rezoned [the tract] to allow the construction of hospitals and sanitariums therein is not authority to violate the restrictive covenants.* An act of sovereignty with respect to lands already restricted by a general plan against specified uses confers no authority to violate the existing restrictive covenants as to use. One is a legislative enactment for the general good, authorized by the police power [the ordinance] and confers a merely permissive right; the other is a contract of individuals made for their own enjoyment [restrictive covenants], is protected by the federal constitution, ... and in no sense interferes with the zoning ordinance."

Similarly, the fact that the Federal Communications Commission has issued a declaratory ruling which preempts state and local governmental regulation of amateur radio operators does not preempt or render invalid private restrictive covenants regulating the placement and height of radio antennae.[72]

The foregoing principles may have far reaching effects in the association's continued efforts to maintain and preserve the CID for which it is responsible. For instance, in the author's opinion, although an association's covenants and restrictions may not preclude the use of land for small family day care homes under Section 1566.5 of the Health and Safety Code (see discussion above), the facility or structure used for the small family day care home must still comply with the association's architectural and land use covenants and restrictions.

ENVIRONMENTAL OR ARCHITECTURAL CONTROL RULES

Associations, especially larger associations, will typically have a governing document separate from the declaration of CC&Rs which provides greater detail and more specificity with respect to acceptable building and construction location and design, minimum building and architectural standards, permissible alterations, landscaping requirements and the process by which the association's approval of such activities must be sought. This document is often referred to as the association's "architectural control rules" or "environmental control rules", or "environmental control committee rules".

Ordinarily, when the original developer of the CID prepares the declaration of CC&Rs, it is designed and prepared to be somewhat broad and flexible so that it will endure the test of time and changing circumstances without having to be amended. This broadness and flexibility inherently creates some terms which are quite general in nature. The purpose of the "architectural control rules" or "environmental control rules" is to provide more detailed specifications for use in the day-to-day operations of the CID and the decisions which the association will have to make with respect to land use and construction issues.

Generally speaking, such rules are a great aid to the association and the property owners because they provide detailed guidance with respect to what designs, locations, materials and construction techniques are and are not acceptable under the declaration of CC&Rs. However, such rules must be consistent and not in conflict with the broader terms and conditions stated in the declaration of CC&Rs.[73]

Associations typically have an environmental control or architectural control committee, appointed by the board of directors, whose task it is to review and approve construction and alterations proposed by property owners, interpret and apply the rules to existing buildings and structures and assist property owners and contractors with questions they may have regarding the rules or the declaration of CC&Rs. When initially created, a

CID's environmental control or architectural committee must consist of no less than three and no more than five members.[74]

An association's authority to adopt and enforce architectural or environmental control rules and other association rules must be derived from its fundamental governing documents, the declaration of CC&Rs, articles of incorporation or association and bylaws, and applicable laws and regulations. If an association's rules exceed the scope of authority granted, the rules and decisions of the association are likely to be held invalid by the courts.[75]

As discussed in Chapter IV, the provisions of a recorded declaration of CC&Rs are presumed to be valid and enforceable and are treated with a substantial level of deference by the courts.[76] The same degree of deference is not necessarily accorded to architectural control, environmental control or other association rules. Such rules will often be given greater scrutiny by the courts to ensure that the rules have been adopted in good faith to further the purposes of the development and are consistent with the association's underlying governing documents.

As recently stated by the California Supreme Court,[77] the potential for abuse justifies closer scrutiny of association decisions which implement the underlying governing documents:

> "Restrictions on property use are not the only characteristic of common interest ownership. Ordinarily, such ownership also entails mandatory membership in an owners association, which through an elected board of directors is empowered to enforce any use restrictions contained in the project's declaration or master deed and to enact new rules governing the use and occupancy of property within the project. ... Because of its considerable power in managing and regulating a common interest development, the governing board of an owners association must guard against the potential for the abuse of that power. ... Therefore, anyone who buys a unit in a common interest development with knowledge of its owners association's discretionary power accepts 'the risk that the power may be used in a way that benefits the commonality but harms the individual.' Generally, courts will uphold decisions made by the governing board of an owners association so long as they represent good faith efforts to further the purposes of the common interest development, are consistent with the development's governing documents, and comply with public policy."

Although architectural restrictions need not be precise, they must contain reasonable standards for architectural review.[78] In reviewing and approving or disapproving proposed construction, improvement and alteration plans submitted by a property owner, the association must follow its own rules and procedures[79] and act reasonably and in good faith.[80]

In exercising its power of approval or disapproval, the criteria applied by the courts for testing the reasonableness of the action are (1) whether the reason for withholding approval is rationally related to the protection, preservation or proper operation of the development and the purposes of the association as contained in its governing documents and (2) whether the discretionary power was exercised in a fair and nondiscriminatory manner.[81]

Where the association's declaration includes language stating that the association or architectural control committee may take the attractiveness or exterior or physical appearance of an improvement into account in reviewing the improvement as proposed by an owner, the association and the committee are entitled to apply both subjective and objective criteria in evaluating the merits and acceptability of the proposed improvement.[82]

ASSOCIATION RULES, AMENITY AND FACILITY RULES

Associations frequently have other rules and regulations, in addition to the architectural or environmental control rules, adopted to regulate the use and enjoyment of the association's common areas and common facilities and amenities. The rules often take the form of a single document covering all the common areas and amenities, but occasionally a separate set of rules is adopted for each amenity because of the unique characteristics and usage of each amenity or facility.

Like the architectural or environmental control rules, the association rules or amenity rules should be consistent with the underlying governing documents and reflect a fair, reasonable and nondiscriminatory approach to the regulation of the facilities.

An example of an association rule invalidated and held unenforceable by the court because it exceeded the scope of restrictions stated in the association's declaration is found in *Major v. Miraverde Homeowners Association, Inc.*[83] In this case, the association's declaration of CC&Rs provided that all record owners of a condominium in the development were members of the association. The declaration also provided that association memberships could not be transferred except with the sale of the condominium. The declaration then specified that any member could delegate his or her right of enjoyment to the common areas and facilities to members of his or her family, tenants or contract purchasers who reside on the property. The declaration did not address the issue of whether non-resident owners could use the common facilities and amenities. The husband and wife condominium owners moved out of the development and allowed the wife's elderly mother to reside in the condominium. Subsequently, the association adopted new rules which included a rule prohibiting non-resident owners from using the association's facilities, including the tennis court.

The condominium owners, who continued to use the tennis court occasionally, filed a lawsuit seeking an injunction to prevent the association from enforcing its new rule prohibiting non-resident owners from using the common facilities. The court first found that the condominium owners had not delegated their use privileges to the wife's mother and that the mother did not use the tennis court.[84] The court then held that the association rule was invalid and unenforceable because it exceeded the scope of authority granted in the declaration of CC&Rs and discriminated between resident owners and non-resident owners.

In reaching its decision, the *Major* court concluded:

> "When disputes arise between the homeowners and the homeowners' association, the courts will look to the governing instruments for guidance in determining whether the Association has acted within its authority. ... Actions taken in excess of the association's power are unenforceable and courts have granted injunctive relief against associations which have exceeded the scope of their authority. ... [W]e conclude an association may not exceed the authority granted to it by the CC&Rs. Where the association exceeds its scope of authority, any rule or decision resulting from such an ultra vires act is invalid whether or not it is a 'reasonable' response to a particular circumstance. Where a circumstance arises which is not adequately covered by the CC&Rs, the remedy is to amend the CC&Rs. The courts have held homeowners are subject to any reasonable amendment of the CC&Rs properly adopted."

However, where the exercise of the association's rulemaking power is consistent with and within the authority granted in the association's declaration of CC&Rs or bylaws, the courts are likely to uphold the validity of the adopted rule so long as the rule is rationally related to a legitimate purpose or function of the association.[85]

When considering or adopting rules or amending existing association rules, associations should endeavor to ensure that such rules are commensurate with the scope of authority granted to the association in the declaration of CC&Rs and consistent with the covenants and restrictions stated in the declaration.

CHAPTER IV

ENFORCING THE DECLARATION OF COVENANTS, CONDITIONS AND RESTRICTIONS AND OTHER GOVERNING DOCUMENTS

The subject of the validity and enforceability of the declaration of CC&Rs and other governing documents such as architectural control and association rules is discussed at length in Chapter III. The next subject frequently encountered by associations and property owners alike is the methods of enforcement which may be available. A variety of governing document enforcement mechanisms are provided by law. Additional methods may be provided under the association's governing documents themselves.

This Chapter addresses the methods of enforcement and the questions most frequently arising with respect to enforcement issues. Although general statements can be made with respect to the nature, type, variety and procedures of enforcement methods available by law, associations and property owners must carefully examine their particular governing documents before proceeding with any one of the available methods. The terms and provisions of each association's governing documents are an integral part of the enforcement powers prescribed by law and, as a general rule, the association's own internal rules and procedures must be followed before the judicial system can be effectively used in the enforcement process.

ASSOCIATIONS AND PROPERTY OWNERS BOTH MAY ENFORCE THE DECLARATION OF CC&RS

Under Section 1354(a) of the Civil Code, ordinarily the owner of a separate interest or the association, or both, may file a legal action to enforce the covenants and restrictions contained in the declaration.[1]

While an owner may enforce the declaration of CC&Rs,[2] associations bear the legal responsibility for doing so and may be sued for failing or refusing to do so.[3]

METHODS OF ENFORCEMENT

A great variety of legal and internal mechanisms exist for the enforcement of an association's declaration of CC&Rs and other governing documents. Although several enforcement methods are generally available to all associations, as explained below, additional and different methods may be available depending on the specific terms of each association's governing documents.

Ultimately, what an association desires to achieve through enforcement of its declaration of CC&Rs should be the maintenance and preservation of the development, regardless of the methods of enforcement available or the particular method or methods exercised.

INTERNAL DISCIPLINARY MEASURES

Conduct Of Disciplinary Proceeding Must Be In Executive Session If Requested By The Member:

Where a property owner violates the association's governing documents and the association's board of directors intends to exercise any number of disciplinary measures which may be granted to it under the association's governing documents, the disciplinary procedures must be accomplished in an executive (closed) session of a board meeting if the affected member so requests. The member is entitled to attend the board's executive session. Civil Code Section 1363.05(b) reads in part as follows:

> "... The board of directors of the association shall meet in executive session, if requested by a member who may be subject to a fine, penalty, or other form of discipline, and the member shall be entitled to attend the executive session."

The executive session requirement, optional with the affected member, is undoubtedly intended to avoid undue embarrassment for the member and preserve a certain level of confidentiality with respect to matters which may be discussed and acted upon during the disciplinary process.

Suspension Of Membership Rights After Hearing Affording Due Process Safeguards:

Generally speaking a property owner's membership rights in the CID association may be suspended for the property owner's violation of the declaration of CC&Rs or other governing documents.

Most CID associations are either originally created as or are treated by the law as nonprofit, mutual benefit corporations.[4] As nonprofit, mutual benefit corporations, the internal and administrative aspects of associations are governed to a large extent by the association's governing documents, including the articles of incorporation or association and the bylaws, as well as those portions of the California Corporations Code applicable to nonprofit, mutual benefit corporations.[5]

Most declarations of CC&Rs and bylaws typically provide that a property owner's membership rights in the association may be suspended for the property owner's violation of the association's governing documents. Ordinarily, such suspension includes suspension of the property owner's voting rights and rights to use and enjoy the association's common areas and facilities.

Before a property owner's membership rights may be suspended, however, the property owner must be provided with an opportunity for a hearing, usually before the association's board of directors or another hearing body specified in the association's declaration or bylaws.[6] The property owner's right to a hearing arises out of basic procedural due process safeguards. The property owner's membership in a CID association is generally recognized as a property interest, of which the property owner cannot be deprived without first having an opportunity to defend himself or herself.

Membership Suspension Procedures Must Be "Fair And Reasonable":

Under Corporations Code Section 7341, a property owner is entitled to receive advance notice of and attend a hearing at which the suspension of his or her membership rights will be addressed. The property owner is entitled to receive advance written notice of the hearing and an opportunity to present evidence to contest the suspension. Section 7341 permits an association to provide alternative membership suspension procedures so long as they are "fair and reasonable", but when the procedures are specified in the association's articles of incorporation or bylaws, and include the processes specified in the statute, the suspension procedure is presumed to be fair, reasonable and valid.

It must be understood that Section 7341 addresses only the procedural requirements that must be followed in order to effect a legitimate suspension of membership rights. It does not address the substantive or legal basis for a suspension of rights. Compliance with the procedural requirements of Section 7341 will not validate an otherwise unlawful suspension of membership rights.[7]

Because Section 7341 is so important to members and associations alike, the full text of the statute is reproduced here:

> "(a) No member may be expelled or suspended, and no membership or memberships may be terminated or suspended, except according to procedures satisfying the requirements of this section. An expulsion, termination or suspension not in accord with this section shall be void and without effect.
>
> "(b) Any expulsion, suspension, or termination must be done in good faith and in a fair and reasonable manner. Any procedure which conforms to the requirements of subdivision (c) is fair and reasonable, but a court may also find other procedures to be fair and reasonable when the full circumstances of the suspension, termination, or expulsion are considered.
>
> "(c) A procedure is fair and reasonable when:
>
> "(1) The provisions of the procedure have been set forth in the articles or bylaws, or copies of such provisions are sent annually to all the members as required by the articles or bylaws;
>
> "(2) It provides the giving of 15 days' prior notice of the expulsion, suspension or termination and the reasons therefor; and
>
> "(3) It provides an opportunity for the member to be heard, orally or in writing, not less than five days before the effective date of the expulsion, suspension or termination by a person or body authorized to decide that the proposed expulsion, termination or suspension not take place.

"(d) Any notice required under this section may be given by any method reasonably calculated to provide actual notice. Any notice given by mail must be given by first-class or registered mail sent to the last address of the members shown on the corporation's records."

"(e) Any action challenging an expulsion, suspension or termination of membership, including any claim alleging defective notice, must be commenced within one year after the date of the expulsion, suspension or termination. In the event such an action is successful the court may order any relief, including reinstatement, it finds equitable under the circumstances, but no vote of the members or of the board may be set aside solely because a person was at the time of the vote wrongfully excluded by virtue of the challenged expulsion, suspension or termination, unless the court finds further that the wrongful expulsion, suspension or termination was in bad faith and for the purpose, and with the effect, of wrongfully excluding the member from the vote or from the meeting at which the vote took place, so as to affect the outcome of the vote.

"(f) This section governs only the procedures for expulsion, suspension or termination and not the substantive grounds therefor. An expulsion, suspension or termination based upon substantive grounds which violate contractual or other rights of the member or are otherwise unlawful is not made valid by compliance with this section."

An association's membership rights suspension procedures will be presumed to be fair and reasonable and therefore valid by the courts under Section 7341 when three requirements have been satisfied: (1) the procedures have been stated in the association's articles of incorporation or articles of association or bylaws, or copies of such procedures are sent to all of the association's members annually as required by the articles or bylaws (2) the procedures require the association to give the affected member at least 15 days' prior notice of the expulsion, suspension or termination and the reasons for the expulsion, suspension or termination, and (3) the procedures provide the affected member with an opportunity to be heard, orally or in writing, not less than five days before the effective date of the expulsion, suspension or termination by the person or governing body with the authority to decide that the proposed expulsion, termination or suspension should not take place.

Under Corporations Code Section 7341(b), a court is given the discretion to determine that other, alternative membership suspension procedures are fair and reasonable when the full circumstances of the suspension, termination or expulsion are considered. For example, although an association's articles of incorporation and bylaws may not include membership suspension procedures, if the association follows the notice and hearing requirements specified in Section 7341 and publishes the procedures in a newsletter regularly sent to all association members, a court may find that a challenged suspension is in fact fair and reasonable and therefore valid when the facts and circumstances giving rise to the suspension are considered.

With respect to the substantive basis or grounds for a member's suspension, the association and member must look to the specific provisions of the association's governing documents, including the declaration of CC&Rs, architectural control rules, association rules, articles of incorporation or association, and bylaws. The governing documents should specifically state which provisions, or group of provisions, if violated, will subject members to a possible suspension of membership rights.

Possible Availability Of Automatic Suspension Without A Section 7341 Hearing:

Associations may be able to effect automatic suspension of membership rights without affording the affected member an opportunity for a hearing following prior notice in certain limited circumstances and where the association's articles of incorporation or association or bylaws include such authority.

Where the association's articles of incorporation or association or bylaws authorize the automatic suspension of membership rights for violations of the association's governing documents and where the fact and nature of the violation and the identity of the member are not in question, automatic suspension without a hearing is permissible.[8] The most commonly encountered example is where an association's bylaws authorize the automatic suspension of membership rights for a property owner's failure to pay assessments properly levied against the member's property.[9] A more complete and detailed discussion of suspension of membership rights without a hearing is found in Chapter VII.

Recording A "Notice Of Noncompliance" Or "Notice Of Violation":

Where an owner's property or certain conditions existing on the property does not conform with the provisions of an association's declaration of CC&Rs, some associations have recorded in the public land title records a document commonly referred to as a "Notice of Noncompliance".

The notice typically includes a brief statement of the covenant or restriction which has been violated and recitation that the owner has been found to be in violation of the covenant or restriction. The notice is then recorded in the county recorder's records and serves as constructive notice that the subject property does not comply with the association's declaration or other governing documents. Once it has been recorded, the notice creates an encumbrance or "cloud on title" to the subject property and prevents or severely restricts the owner's opportunity to sell the property or obtain financing with respect to the property.

The notice, in effect, attempts to persuade or motivate the owner to comply with the declaration of CC&Rs without the association having to file a lawsuit to compel compliance.

Associations must be cautious in the use of such notices. Where a CID association's declaration of CC&Rs specifically authorizes the recordation of a notice of violation, the notice is probably a recordable document and the association probably has the legal authority to record the notice. The association's authority is somewhat tenuous at this time because the California Supreme Court ordered the only judicial decision addressing the issue not to be published in the Official Reports of cases.[10]

On the other hand, where no such specific authority is granted the association in its declaration of CC&Rs, there is no legal authority for the recordation of such notice and the recording of such notice may give rise to a legal action for slander of title.[11]

Unless the association's declaration of CC&Rs authorizes the use and recording of a Notice of Noncompliance when a property owner violates the declaration, the association should not use such notices as an enforcement mechanism. An improper notice may render the association subject to liability for slander of title and related legal theories.[12]

Monetary Fines And Penalties:

Where an association's governing documents authorize the association to impose monetary fines or penalties against association members for violations of the governing documents, the association has the authority to do so. But, in the absence of such governing document provisions, the authority of the association is highly questionable.[13]

Currently, in the absence of governing document authority, there is no California statutory or case authority conferring power on associations to impose fines or monetary penalties on members who violate the association's governing documents, other than for a failure to pay lawful assessments.

Section 1363(g) of the California Civil Code was made effective on January 1, 1993. Section 1363(g) does not establish the power to impose monetary penalties. It merely states that if the association has a policy of imposing fines or penalties, it must adopt and distribute a schedule of fines and penalties. Section 1363(g) reads in full as follows:

> "If an association adopts or has adopted a policy imposing any monetary penalty, including any fee, on any association member for a violation of the governing documents or rules of the association, including any monetary penalty relating to the activities of a guest or invitee of a member, the board of directors shall adopt and distribute to each member, by personal delivery or first-class mail, a schedule of the monetary penalties that may be assessed for those violations, which shall be in accordance with authorization for member discipline contained in the governing documents. The board of directors shall not be required to distribute any additional schedules of monetary penalties unless there are changes from the schedule that was adopted and distributed to the members pursuant to this subdivision. The board of directors of the association shall meet in executive session if requested by the member being disciplined, and the member shall be entitled to attend the executive session."

Section 1363(i) of the Civil Code then makes it clear that Section 1363 in and of itself neither creates nor reduces the authority to impose monetary penalties. Section 1363(i) provides in full:

> "Nothing in this section shall be construed to create, expand, or reduce the authority of the board of directors of an associa-

> tion to impose monetary penalties on an association member for a violation of the governing documents or rules of the association."

Authority May Be Granted Directly In Declaration Of CC&Rs Or Bylaws Or May Be Instituted Through Rules Adopted By The Association Which Are Consistent With The Declaration And Bylaws:

In light of Sections 1363(g) and 1363(i), and the absence of any contrary case law, it appears that only where an association's governing documents empower the association to impose monetary penalties may the association do so. The authority to impose monetary fines and penalties need not be stated in the declaration of CC&Rs or the association's bylaws. It is enough if the association is granted authority in the declaration of CC&Rs or bylaws to adopt rules and regulations governing land use, use of the common areas and use of the community facilities and amenities and the rules actually adopted by the association are consistent with the underlying governing documents.[14] As recently stated by the California Supreme Court, restrictions on property use are not the only characteristic of common interest ownership:

> "Ordinarily, such ownership also entails mandatory membership in an owners association, which through an elected board of directors is empowered to enforce any use restrictions contained in the project's declaration or master deed and to enact new rules governing the use and occupancy of property within the project."[15]

As an example, many declarations of CC&Rs and association bylaws include language similar to the following: "The board of directors shall have power to adopt and publish rules and regulations governing the use of the common areas and facilities, and the personal conduct of the members and their guests thereon, and to establish penalties for the infraction thereof".

Given that the primary purpose of CID associations is to manage, maintain and preserve the design, environment, harmony and scheme of the development, when rule making authority is granted in the declaration of CC&Rs, articles of incorporation or association, or bylaws, the association has the authority to adopt rules which are consistent with the governing documents and which promote the purposes of the development, including rules which provide for the imposition of monetary fines and penalties.[16]

Executive Session Board Meeting May Be Required:

Where the association's board of directors intends to impose monetary fines or penalties as a disciplinary measure against a member, it must be done in executive session if requested by the affected member, and the member must be allowed to attend the meeting. Civil Code Section 1363(g), quoted in full above, states that:

> "The board of directors of the association shall meet in executive session if requested by the member being disciplined, and the member shall be entitled to attend the executive session."

No Statutory Hearing Required:

An opportunity for a hearing must always be provided to association members before suspension of membership is imposed as a form of discipline. However, unless the association's governing documents require a hearing in accordance with the procedural criteria specified in Corporations Code Section 7341, no such hearing need be provided to a member prior to the imposition of monetary fines or penalties for a member's infraction of the governing documents.[17]

Fines And Penalties Probably Cannot Be Treated As A Lien Against The Member's Property By Which The Property Can Be Sold Following Lien Foreclosure:

Associations frequently seek to enforce monetary fines and penalties by treating the fines and penalties as an assessment and enforcing payment of the amounts due as a lien against the affected member's separate interest by which the member's separate interest may be sold pursuant to foreclosure of the lien. The legitimacy of this practice is highly questionable and probably invalid. Many declarations of CC&Rs do not include provisions by which monetary fines and penalties imposed against members as a disciplinary measure may be enforced as liens against the member's real property. This is most probably due to the fact that when the developer prepares the original governing documents for a CID, the developer is constrained by Department of Real Estate regulations which prohibit the treatment of disciplinary monetary fines and penalties as assessments which may become a lien against the affected member's property.[18]

Adoption And Distribution Of Uniform Schedule Of Penalties:

If the association has the requisite authority to impose monetary fines and penalties, either directly stated in its declaration of CC&Rs or bylaws or through rules adopted consistent with the declaration or bylaws, before imposing any such fines or penalties, the association's board of directors must adopt and distribute to all members, by personal delivery or first-class mail, a schedule of the monetary penalties that may be assessed for each type or category of violations.[19]

LAWSUITS AND ALTERNATIVE DISPUTE RESOLUTION:

Injunctive Relief:

Ordinarily, when a lawsuit is filed to enforce a declaration of CC&Rs, the person or organization filing the lawsuit (the "plaintiff") is seeking a court decision ordering the person against whom enforcement is sought (the "defendant") to do certain things or acts or to refrain from doing certain things or acts. For example, the declaration of CC&Rs may require a property owner to first obtain the association's approval of construction plans before commencing construction. If the property owner fails to submit his or her plans for review, the association might seek a court decision ordering the property owner to submit the plans to the association for review and approval or disapproval and to cease all construction activities until the plan review process is completed.

The court order which is requested in a lawsuit such as the one described above is called an "injunction".[20] Generally speaking there are three types or phases of injunctions. A "temporary restraining order" is an injunction which a court may issue on a very quick basis before all the evidence is presented by the parties, but is of temporary and short duration, ordinarily lasting no more than 22 days.[21] A "preliminary injunction" is an injunction which the court may issue for the duration of the case and until final resolution of the lawsuit.[22] A "permanent injunction" is the injunction which the court may issue at the conclusion of the lawsuit as the final determination of the parties' rights and final court order or judgment.

Declaratory Relief:

A lawsuit involving a declaration of CC&Rs may also involve the association's or a property owner's request that the court review the terms of the declaration at issue and decide what the terms and provisions mean. The parties may also request the court to determine whether and to what extent the provisions may be enforced as between the parties, as well as the parties' respective rights and obligations according to the terms of the declaration. This form of legal relief or remedy is commonly referred to as "declaratory relief".[23] An association is authorized to file and prosecute a lawsuit for declaratory relief with respect to its governing documents.[24]

Of course, a lawsuit seeking an injunction and/or declaratory relief may be combined with other legal theories and remedies sought, including an award of monetary damages. In any lawsuit filed to enforce a declaration of CC&Rs, the party who ultimately prevails in the lawsuit is entitled to recover the attorney's fees and court costs incurred in the lawsuit.[25]

Ordinarily, when a lawsuit is filed seeking an injunction to enforce covenants and restrictions, or declaratory relief to determine the parties' respective rights under the declaration, it must be filed in the Superior Court of the county where the CID is located. The municipal and lower jurisdictional courts of the State of California have no jurisdiction to issue or grant permanent injunctions or to hear general declaratory relief lawsuits.[26]

Association Must Act In Good Faith And Follow Its Own Standards And Procedures:

Before an association can judicially enforce its declaration of CC&Rs against property owner members who are in violation of the declaration, the association must show that it has followed its own standards and procedures in finding a violation has occurred, that its procedures are fair and reasonable, and that its determination that a violation exists was made in good faith and was not arbitrary or capricious.[27]

For example, in *Ironwood Owners Association IX v. Solomon*[28] property owners planted eight date palm trees without submitting proposed landscaping plans to the association for review or obtaining a permit or other approval for the landscaping addition as required under the association's declaration of CC&Rs. The association's declaration required the architectural control committee to review and approve or disapprove lot improvements proposed by the property owners. The association filed a lawsuit seeking an injunction compelling the property owners to remove the trees which had been planted without association approval. The court reached the conclusion that owners had violated the declaration of CC&Rs because they had failed to submit a landscaping plan to the architectural control committee as required by the declaration. The appellate court, however, reversed the trial court's granting of the requested injunction because it found there was no evidence showing the association had followed its own rules and procedures in reaching the determination that the owners had violated the declaration.

ALTERNATIVE DISPUTE RESOLUTION:

Certain kinds of lawsuits related to an association's governing documents may be subject to mandatory arbitration or mediation efforts before proceeding to court. In an effort to provide a dispute resolution method quicker and more cost effective than the court system may offer and to stem the flood of lawsuits clogging our courts involving disputes between associations and members related to the interpretation or enforcement of an association's governing documents, the legislature enacted an alternative dispute resolution ("ADR") statute in 1993. The ADR provisions are now found in Civil Code Section 1354(b)-(j).

The statute is a pre-lawsuit mechanism designed to promote relatively quick resolution of certain kinds of disputes. The intent of the statute is to furnish a forum which can be used more expeditiously and at lower costs than the forum available in our state courts.

Types Of Lawsuits Subject To Mandatory ADR Resolution Efforts:

Unless the applicable statute of limitations would expire within 120 days, before an association or an association member may file a lawsuit seeking only to enforce the governing documents by injunction or declaratory or injunctive relief or declaratory relief together with a claim for monetary damages (other than association assessments) not exceeding $5,000.00, the parties must make diligent efforts to submit their dispute to some form of alternative dispute resolution such as arbitration or mediation.[29]

The definition of "governing documents" in Civil Code Section 1351(j) includes "the declaration and any other documents, such as bylaws, operating rules of the association, articles of incorporation, or articles of association, which govern the operation of the common interest development or association". Under this statutory definition of "governing documents", disputes related to the enforcement of the declaration of CC&Rs, articles of incorporation or association, bylaws, and association rules may first have to be submitted to a form of alternative dispute resolution before a lawsuit is filed.

The alternative dispute resolution process is a "private" one in the sense that it is not a judicial process utilizing the courts to resolve the controversy. Neither is it a public procedure which members of the public may observe, unless the parties and the arbitrator or mediator so desire.

While the parties may choose to submit any dispute to private alternative dispute resolution, the above-described disputes are the only types which the parties must endeavor to resolve through alternative dispute resolution.

The alternative dispute resolution may be binding or nonbinding, at the option of the parties.[30] If the parties choose binding alternative dispute resolution, whether arbitration, mediation or some other mechanism of resolution, the result of the alternative dispute resolution is final and neither party may sue the other in a court on the same dispute. If the parties choose nonbinding alternative dispute resolution, if either party is dissatisfied with the results, either or both parties may then file a lawsuit in an appropriate court.

The statute does not specify the rules of procedure which the parties must follow during the alternative dispute resolution process. Instead, the parties and the arbitrator or mediator must mutually agree on those rules. The rules will ordinarily have to address such issues as the location of the arbitration or mediation, the number of witnesses a party may call, whether or not a party may subpoena or otherwise access the other party's documents prior to the arbitration or mediation, whether "expert" witnesses will be allowed, and the scope of the issues or matters to be submitted.

Initiation Of Alternative Dispute Resolution Procedure:

Any party involved in the dispute may initiate the process by serving on any other involved party a "Request For Resolution" which must include (1) a brief description of the dispute, (2) a request for alternative dispute resolution, (3) a statement that the party receiving the Request has 30 days to respond to it or the notice will be treated as having been rejected.[31] The Request For Resolution must include a copy of Civil Code Section 1354:

The Request For Resolution must be served in the same manner as a claim in a small claims court action by one of the following alternative methods: (1) personal delivery of the Request for Resolution to the other party by a person over the age of 18, but not a party involved in the dispute,[32] (2) by leaving a copy of the Request For Resolution at the other party's dwelling house in the presence of a competent member of the household and then mailing a copy of the Request to the other party at the dwelling house where the copy was left,[33] or (3) by leaving a copy of the Request for Resolution, during usual office hours, at the office of the other party, with a person who is or appears to be in charge of the office and then mailing a copy of the Request to the other party at the place where the copy was left by first-class mail, postage prepaid.[34]

If the Request For Resolution is served by a method other than personal delivery, then service of the Request is not complete until the tenth day after the mailing is made.[35]

Under Sections 1354(b) of the Civil Code and Section 116.340 of the Code of Civil Procedure, personal delivery of a Request for Resolution by a party to the dispute is not valid service of the Request and will not start the running of the 30-day period within which to respond.

Response To Request For Resolution:

Once a Request For Resolution has been properly served on another party to the dispute, that party has thirty days after the date of the service within which to respond to the Request.[36] If no response is made, the request is deemed rejected.[37] Depending on the method of service used, the response deadline may or may not be the thirtieth day following receipt of the Request for Resolution.

If the Request For Resolution does not specify the type of alternative dispute resolution, or if the type specified is not acceptable to the recipient, and the receiving party agrees to submit the dispute to alternative dispute resolution, the response should clearly indicate the type or types of alternative dispute resolution acceptable to the recipient.

Completion Of Resolution Process:

If the party receiving a Request For Resolution accepts the request, the alternative dispute resolution process must be completed within 90 days after the initiating party receives the acceptance.[38] The parties may, however, by a written stipulation signed by all parties, extend the date for completion of the alternative dispute resolution.[39]

Ordinarily, the parties and/or the arbitrator or mediator will have to agree on written rules prescribing the procedures to be followed during the dispute resolution process. Unless all parties consent otherwise, any documents prepared for use in the resolution process are not admissible in evidence in any lawsuit.[40]

The statute prescribes that the costs of the alternative dispute resolution shall be paid by the parties to the dispute.[41] The parties are free to agree on the proportionate sharing of the costs involved, which will ordinarily include the arbitrator's or mediator's fees, and attorney's fees if either or both parties choose to be represented by legal counsel.

Prerequisite To Filing Certain Lawsuits:

As previously mentioned, the submission of certain types of disputes to some form of alternative dispute resolution is a prerequisite to the filing of a lawsuit with respect to such dispute. At the time of filing a lawsuit solely for declaratory relief or injunctive relief or injunctive relief together with a claim for monetary damages (other than association assessments) not exceeding $5,000.00, the party filing the lawsuit must also simultaneously file with the court a certificate stating that alternative dispute resolution has been completed in accordance with Civil Code Section 1354(b).[42]

If the certificate of compliance is not filed, the complaint initiating the lawsuit is subject to dismissal upon the motion of any other party named in the lawsuit, unless the plaintiff files a certificate stating that another party refused alternative dispute resolution, or that alternative dispute resolution is not necessary because the applicable statute of limitations will expire within 120 days after the lawsuit is filed.

CHAPTER V

COMMON AREAS AND COMMUNITY AMENITIES AND FACILITIES

ACCESS TO, USE AND ENJOYMENT OF COMMON AREAS AND FACILITIES

Deciding who may use an association's common areas and facilities is an important issue which may or may not be adequately addressed in an association's governing documents. The association and its members are often legitimately concerned about the depreciation and wearing out of facilities by persons who do not share in the cost of repair, maintenance, operation and replacement of the facilities.

Access to and the use of an association's common areas and community facilities is an issue frequently encountered by associations and property owners. Some associations and property owners want severe restrictions on who can use the common areas and facilities. Others prefer an environment which is more open to use by persons who are not members of the CID association.

In some CIDs the streets and sidewalks may be owned by local governments and in others the streets and sidewalks may be owned and operated by the private association. Each situation raises its own unique questions and legal issues.

Questions may arise from time to time regarding who may use the association's common areas and amenities and facilities.

Prohibiting The Use Of Common Areas And Community Facilities By Non-resident Property Owners:

Membership in a CID association is typically limited by the governing documents to owners of separate interests, whether lots, parcels, units or apartments, in the development. Membership in the association is appurtenant to, and is not transferable separately from, the owner's entire estate in his or her separate interest. Association membership is, of course transferred upon the sale or other conveyance of all of the member's title in the separate interest.[1]

When a member rents or leases his or her separate interest, the member has not transferred all of his or her title to the separate interest. Instead, the owner continues to own a "reversionary interest", which will entitle the owner to full possession and enjoyment of the property once the lease or rental agreement has expired or has been otherwise terminated.

The governing documents of many associations permit the owner to delegate his or her common area and amenity use rights to a tenant or lessee of the owner's separate interest. The question is sometimes raised whether, after such delegation, both the owner and his or her tenant may use the common areas and facilities of the development.

Nonresident property owners who lease or rent their property to lessees or tenants may be lawfully excluded from using the association's common area facilities and amenities, at least where the property owner has delegated his or her use rights to the lessee or tenant and the recorded declaration or rules adopted by the association pursuant to and consistent with the declaration authorize such use prohibitions.[2]

The rationale for the rule is that the added burden from use by nonresident owners in addition to tenants and owner-residents could potentially greatly increase the number of individuals competing for use of the association's facilities, which in turn decreases availability to resident owners and reduces the attractiveness of the development. In addition, use of community facilities by both nonresident owners and their tenants increases wear and tear while the costs of maintenance and repair are borne only by the assessments levied against that separate interest, not all of the users.

On the other hand, associations may not discriminate among their members by prohibiting non-resident members from using and enjoying the common areas, including recreational facilities within the common interest development, solely because the members are not resident members.[3]

Prohibiting The Use Of Common Areas And Community Facilities By Persons Who Are Not Property Owners:

Since the typical association is a private corporation or unincorporated association formed for the benefit of its members, the association's governing documents may properly limit the use and enjoyment of association common areas and facilities to the association members and any other persons the association and its members may wish to allow.

If, however, nonmembers are given access to the development, at least for purposes which may involve the exercise of constitutionally-protected rights, such as freedom of the press, the association cannot discriminate between such nonmembers, permitting some access and denying access to others.[4]

Traffic And Parking Regulation:

Generally speaking, associations which own all of the streets within the development have two methods of regulating traffic and parking of vehicles within the development.

An association may adopt portions of the California Vehicle Code regulating the parking of vehicles in CIDs by petitioning the county in which the development is located to enact an ordinance under Section 21107.7 of the Vehicle Code. If a petition is brought before the county and the county then adopts an ordinance under Section 21107.7 of the Vehicle Code, both the public and members of the association are subject to the provisions of the California Vehicle Code while operating vehicles within the development.

On the other hand, an association may simply adopt its own internal parking rules under authorizing provisions in the association's governing documents. With traffic and parking regulation under association governing documents only, it is only the members of the association who are subject to enforcement of the association's governing documents.

Parking regulations which may be adopted by a CID association may be effectively enforced through the towing of improperly parked vehicles. Under California Vehicle Code Section 22658.2 an association may have improperly parked vehicles removed and towed to the nearest public garage if specified requirements are satisfied. In order to be able to cause the removal and towing of improperly parked vehicles, the association must meet all three of the following statutory requirements:

(1) A sign, at least 17 by 22 inches in size with lettering at least one inch high, must appear at each entrance to the common interest development and must contain: (a) a statement that public parking is prohibited and all vehicles not authorized to park in the development will be removed at the owner's expense; and (b) the telephone number of the local traffic law enforcement agency. The sign may also indicate that a citation may be issued for the violation.

(2) If the identity of the registered owner of the vehicle is known or readily ascertainable, the president of the association, or a designee, must notify the vehicle owner of its removal within a reasonable time by first-class mail. The association must also notify the vehicle owner of the grounds for removal of the vehicle if the owner so requests.

If the identity of the vehicle owner is not known or readily ascertainable, the association president or a designee must, if the vehicle is not reclaimed within 120 hours after the removal, give written notice of the removal to the State Department of Justice, Stolen Vehicle System and to the owner of the public garage at which the vehicle is stored. The notice must include a complete description of the vehicle, the date, time and place from which it was removed, the amount of mileage on the vehicle at the time of removal, and the name of the garage or place where the vehicle is stored.[5]

(3) In all events, the president of the association or a designee must give notice of the removal to the local traffic law enforcement agency immediately after the vehicle has been removed. The notice must include a description of the vehicle, the license plate number, and the address from where the vehicle was removed.

If an association complies with all of the requirements of Vehicle Code Section 22658.2, it is not liable for any damages incurred by the vehicle owner because of the removal of the vehicle or for any damage to the vehicle caused by the removal.[6]

However, the vehicle owner may recover for damage caused by the negligent or intentional acts of the association or any person removing the vehicle. As an example, although the Association would otherwise be immune from liability because of a removal, if its representative negligently struck and dented the vehicle with his or her car during the removal, the Association and/or its representative could be held responsible.

Certain Community Services Districts Have Been Enabled By Special Legislation To Restrict And Limit Access On And Over District-Owned Streets And Roads To Landowners And Residents Of The District:

A community services district is one of several different kinds of "special districts" which can be formed under the provisions of the California Government Code to provide certain types of services to the residents of the special district. Community services districts are usually formed to provide services which we typically expect the government to provide, including police protection, streets and sewers, parks and recreation, and water supply.

By special legislation specifically naming the community services districts benefited by the statute, certain community services districts are authorized to limit and restrict vehicular access to and over streets and roads owned by the district to those landowners and residents of the district.[7]

In the absence of such special legislation however, an association cannot close or otherwise restrict or limit the public's access to or use of streets and roads owned by the public or which have been dedicated to the public use.[8]

MAINTENANCE AND REPAIR OF COMMON AREAS AND COMMUNITY FACILITIES

Routine Maintenance And Repair:

As explained in Chapter I, unless the declaration of CC&Rs delegates the responsibility differently, the CID association is ordinarily responsible for the maintenance and repair of all common areas and common or community facilities and amenities located in the development.[9]

Civil Code Section 1364 allocates the association's and owners' maintenance responsibilities as follows:

> "(a) Unless otherwise provided in the declaration of a common interest development, the association is responsible for repairing, replacing, or maintaining the common areas, other than exclusive use common areas, and the owner of each separate interest is responsible for maintaining that separate interest and any exclusive use common areas appurtenant to that separate interest."

However, depending on the type, design and complexity of the development as well as the language of the governing documents, determining what areas of the development are common areas can be a challenging task. Nevertheless, the determination of what components of the development are part of the common areas as opposed to separate interests or exclusive use common areas is critical in the analysis of maintenance responsibilities and related issues. The reader is referred to the discussion in Chapter I for further detailed discussion.

Responsibility For Damage To The Common Areas:

Most association declarations or rules also include terms which place the responsibility for repairing damage to the common areas and facilities on the property owner or other person who caused the damage. Such terms will ordinarily be binding on the person or persons who cause damage to or destruction of the association's common areas or community facilities.

CONSTRUCTION DEFECTS

Unfortunately, common interest developments are not immune to the problems that sometimes occur in connection with the improvement of real estate with residential dwellings, other buildings, streets, roads, and other improvements and infrastructure ordinarily found in the typical residential setting. Associations and their members may occasionally find themselves struggling with problems arising out of defective workmanship, construction, installation, design, or materials used in the planning and construction of the development's common areas and facilities.

Construction defect claims and litigation can be extremely complicated and intricate. The following is a mere summary of some of the more salient factors involved of which associations and their members should generally be aware. Before an association or property owner embarks on an analysis of, or takes legal action related to, suspected design or construction defects, the advice of experienced legal counsel and other qualified experts including, where appropriate, engineers, architects and contractors, should be sought and considered.

Developer Liability:

If an association encounters defects in the design or construction of the development's common areas or common facilities and amenities, the developer and others participating in the design and construction may be responsible for repairing or replacing the defective or deficient items.

The responsibility of the developer and its architects, engineers and contractors for defective design or construction of common areas and facilities may be premised on a number of different legal theories, including negligence, strict product liability,[10] breach of contract, breach of warranties, fraud, misrepresentation and breach of fiduciary duties. Which legal theories may or may not be appropriate and available to an association will depend on the facts and circumstances of each case. In the event defects in the design or construction of the development or any of its common areas or facilities are discovered or suspected by the association, the association should undertake a diligent investigation of the same with the assistance of qualified professions, including engineers, architects, surveyors and contractors, as the circumstances may indicate.

Association Liability:

As previously discussed, the association ordinarily bears the responsibility for maintaining and repairing the common areas and facilities under the terms of most governing documents. When defective design or construction of the common areas or facilities is discovered, an association may face a dilemma in deciding whether to first repair or replace the defective items at its expense and then seek redress against the developer, or pursue remedies against the developer first and subsequently repair or replace the defective facilities. Associations which bear the common area maintenance responsibilities and fail to take appropriate action to remedy the defects may be held responsible for failing to do so and for damages resulting to the separate interests because of common area deficiencies.[11]

In addition, board members who fail to make reasonable inquiries and investigations regarding damage to or defective design or construction of the common areas and pursue appropriate legal remedies against the responsible parties may be held liable for breach of their fiduciary duties.[12] And, the dominance or control of the board of directors by the developer or its agents may also create conflicts of interest and result in independent breaches of the directors' fiduciary obligations to act in the best interests of the association.[13]

Legal Recourse Should Be Sought With Reasonable Promptness:

If construction or design defects are discovered to exist in an association's common areas or facilities, the association needs to be aware of two kinds of procedural rules which may bar the association from seeking legal relief against the developer in the event the association fails to act with reasonable promptness.[14]

Statutes Of Limitation:

"Statutes of limitation" are procedural rules which govern the time periods within which a lawsuit must be filed after the "cause of action" (the injury or wrong complained of and creating a right to a legal remedy) arises.

Various statutes of limitation may apply to an association's claims against a developer and other persons arising out of defects in the design and/or construction of the development and its components. For example, lawsuits predicated on a developer's alleged negligence which result in personal injuries must be filed within one year of the occurrence of the injury.[15] A lawsuit based on alleged trespass on or injury to real property must be commenced within three years of the trespass or injury.[16] A lawsuit alleging the developer has breached a contract must be filed within four years after a breach of a written contract,[17] and within two years after a breach of an oral contract.[18] A lawsuit against the developer or a director for breach of fiduciary duties is governed by a three-year statute of limitations.[19]

Where the construction or design defects cause permanent and immediate injury to the property and the injury is readily apparent, with the harm to the property actual and appreciable, the applicable statutes of limitation will generally begin to run on the date of the act or occurrence causing the injury.[20]

On the other hand, when the cause of injury or damage to the property is not readily apparent, the applicable statutes of limitation will generally begin to expire on the date when the association acquired, or should have acquired through the exercise of diligence, sufficient knowledge to discover the cause of the damage.[21]

The running of an applicable statute of limitations may be tolled or suspended during the period of time that the developer or the developer's representatives dominate the board of directors and control the affairs of the association. If an association can establish that during the period of developer control of the association, the developer made false representations that defects were corrected or concealed the existence of the defects, the applicable statute of limitations may be tolled.[22]

"Statutes Of Repose":

In addition to statutes of limitation, associations need to be aware of two other important statutes which may cut off their right to seek legal redress against developers and others for the defective design or construction of a development or its components. The two statutes are "statutes of repose". If a cause of action exists, an applicable statute of limitations may prohibit the injured person from asserting it in a lawsuit (even though it does exist) after the expiration of a specified period after the cause of action first arises.

On the other hand, a "statute of repose" typically specifies the time period within which a cause of action can arise at all. In other words, if a cause of action does not arise within the period of time specified in the statute of repose, it can never arise or exist at all. Two statutes of repose have been enacted by the California legislature which specifically govern lawsuits based on alleged defects in the design or construction of improvements to real estate.[23] Which of the two statutes may apply in any given situation depends on whether the defect is "patent" or "latent".

"Patent Deficiencies":

A "patent deficiency" in the design or construction of improvements to real estate is defined as a "deficiency which is apparent by reasonable inspection".[24] A "reasonable inspection" is one that is undertaken and performed with ordinary care and prudence.[25] What constitutes a "reasonable inspection" is a question of fact and a matter that must be determined in light of all the circumstances of the particular case and varies with the nature of the thing to be inspected and the nature and gravity of the harm which is sought to be averted.[26]

"Latent Deficiencies":

A "latent deficiency" in the design or construction of improvements to real estate is defined as a "deficiency which is not apparent by reasonable inspection."[27] As contrasted with a patent defect, a latent defect is one which is hidden and which would not be discovered by a reasonably careful inspection.[28]

An action against developers and other persons for patent construction deficiencies must be commenced within four years after the substantial completion of the improvement.[29] An action against the developer or others for latent construction deficiencies must be commenced within ten years after substantial completion of the development or improvement.[30]

The ten-year statute of repose for latent construction defects, however, does not apply to actions for willful misconduct or fraudulent concealment.[31] If a developer or the developer's agents or employees fraudulently conceal known defects from an association, the developer cannot rely on the ten-year statute of repose as a defense to legal action for construction defects.

"Substantial Completion":

Both the four-year statute of repose stated in Code of Civil Procedure Section 337.1 and the ten-year statute of repose stated in Section 337.15 begin to run upon the "substantial completion" of the improvement. For purposes of the ten-year statute applicable to latent deficiencies, substantial completion is defined to be the earliest of: (1) the date of final inspection of the improvement by the applicable public agency, (2) the date a valid notice of completion is recorded, (3) the date of first use or occupation of the improvement, or (4) one year after termination or cessation of work on the improvement.[32]

Associations must be aware that in multi-structure developments, or developments with multiple common areas, facilities, and amenities, the statutes of repose may expire long before the entire development is completed. The limitations period begins to expire on the date the improvement is substantially completed, not the date the entire development is completed.[33]

An association must be aware of both the statutes of limitation, as well as the patent deficiency and latent deficiency statutes of repose.[34] If a shorter statute of limitations applies to a particular cause of action or legal theory, the time within which an association must file a lawsuit is not extended by a longer statute of repose.[35] For example, if defects in the construction of the common areas of a development are discovered, a cause of action for trespass or injury to real property must be asserted within three years under Code of Civil Procedure Section 338, not within the four years provided in Section 337.1 or the ten years provided in Section 337.15.

Disclosure Of Litigation To Property Owners:

An association's board of directors is obligated to provide written notice to members of the association regarding any civil action filed by the association against the declarant or other developer of a common interest development for alleged damage to the common areas and any other areas or interests that the association is obligated to maintain or repair.[36]

The association's board must also, prior to the commencement of any lawsuit against the declarant or developer, hold a board meeting, to discuss the problems and possible solutions available, which members are entitled to attend. In the event that the applicable statute of limitations will expire before the association files any such lawsuit, the association may give the members notice of the problems and meeting as late as 30 days after the filing of the lawsuit.[37]

Mandatory Alternative Dispute Resolution:

Before an association files a lawsuit against the declarant, developer or other builder of the CID for defective design or construction of the development, in most instances the association must first endeavor to submit the controversy to alternative dispute resolution.[38]

The association must provide a written notice to the declarant, developer or other builder which must include a preliminary written list of defects, a summary of the results of a survey or questionnaire distributed to homeowners to determine the nature and extent of defects, if the survey has been conducted or a questionnaire has been distributed, and either a summary of the results of testing conducted to determine the nature and extent of defects or the actual test results, if such testing has been conducted.[39]

After the association's notice has been delivered to the developer or builder, the association and developer have a period of time, not exceeding 90 days unless the parties agree to an extension of time, during which the association and the developer must either attempt to settle the dispute or attempt to agree to submit the dispute to alternative dispute resolution.[40]

Upon delivery to the developer, the association's notice tolls, or suspends, any further running of all potentially applicable statutes of limitation which could otherwise expire and bar a lawsuit against the developer by the association.[41] At any time, the developer may give the association written notice to cancel the tolling of the statutes of limitation, after which the association is excused from any further obligation to comply with the settlement and alternative dispute resolution requirements and may commence a lawsuit against the developer after satisfying certain membership disclosure requirements.[42]

Within 25 days after the association delivers its notice to the developer, the developer may request in writing to meet with the board of directors of the association, and to inspect the CID and conduct its own testing.[43] If, however, the developer fails to make a timely request to meet and confer with the board of directors of the association, or to conduct inspection and testing, the association is relieved of any further obligations to attempt to meet with the developer and settle the dispute or submit it to alternative dispute resolution.

If the developer fails to respond within 25 days in writing to the association's notice, the association may then file a lawsuit against the developer.[44] The lawsuit may only be filed, however, 30 days after the association sends a written notice to all members specifying (1) the list of defects provided to the developer and information about any other documents the association may have provided to the developer, (2) the options, including civil lawsuits against the developer, which are available to address the problems, and (3) a statement that if 5 percent or more of the members request a special meeting to discuss the matter within 15 days after the notice is mailed or delivered to the members, a special meeting of members will be held.[45]

Certificate Of Merit Required Before Filing Suit Against Architects, Engineers, Surveyors And Contractors:

The legislature has made an effort to dissuade frivolous lawsuits against architects, engineers, land surveyors and contractors for alleged defective design and construction of property and buildings. Statutes currently require the plaintiff's attorney to investigate and review the facts involved and file a certificate attesting to the results of the investigation and review and state a conclusion that the proposed lawsuit has a reasonable basis.

Generally, before anyone, including CID associations and property owners, may file a lawsuit against a licensed architect, engineer or land surveyor for professional negligence, a certificate must be prepared and filed with the court stating that the lawsuit has a reasonable and meritorious basis.[46] With only a few narrow exceptions, the failure to file the certificate may result in the court's dismissal of the lawsuit.[47]

A similar requirement applies when a CID association contemplates filing a lawsuit against a licensed contractor for negligent construction and the construction contract price is $20,000 or more.[48] Before an association may file a lawsuit against a licensed contractor for the negligent construction, repair or improvement of property within the development, the association's attorney must prepare and file with the court a certificate stating that the contractor named as a defendant actually participated in the construction of the property or improvement which is alleged to have been negligently constructed.[49] The failure to file the certificate may result in the court's dismissal of the lawsuit.[50] As of the date of publication of this book, this particular statutory requirement is effective only until January 1, 1997, at which time it is repealed.[51]

Association Has No Duty To Inform Prospective Purchasers Of Separate Interests About Construction Defects:

An association has no legal duty to inform a prospective purchaser of a separate interest about construction defects or the existence of a civil lawsuit against the developer to compel the repair of the defects.[52]

CHAPTER VI

ASSOCIATION STRUCTURE AND GOVERNANCE: GOVERNING DOCUMENTS, LAWS AND REGULATIONS

As briefly described in Chapter I, all CIDs share many common and important characteristics. All have a collection of "governing documents" defining the CID, the association, its powers, authority and responsibilities, as well as those of the property owner members. The scope, complexity and terms and conditions of the governing documents vary from each association to the next. The variation is often a function of each association's environment, for example, a rural as opposed to a metropolitan location, and the developer, who is responsible for the preparation of the original governing documents.

In addition to the governing documents, all CIDs, associations and association members are governed by a relatively large body of statutory and case law and administrative agency regulations.

This Chapter contains a detailed discussion of the association's corporate structure and governance, its governing documents, how they relate to one another, and how they relate to and are affected by the laws and regulations governing CIDs.

CORPORATE STRUCTURE AND GOVERNANCE

Most CID associations are incorporated as nonprofit mutual benefit corporations. Even those associations which are not incorporated and instead operate as unincorporated associations typically have articles of association or a charter which establish a governing board responsible for the management of the association.

The Corporations Code clearly requires that the management of the affairs and activities of a nonprofit mutual benefit corporation be managed by the corporation's board of directors. Corporations Code Section 7210 states in part that:

> "Subject to the provisions of this part and any limitations in the articles or bylaws relating to action required to be approved by the members ..., the activities and affairs of a corporation shall be conducted and all corporate powers shall be exercised by or under the direction of the board. The board may delegate the management of the activities of the corporation to any person or persons, management company or committee however composed, provided that the activities and affairs of the corporation shall be managed and all corporate powers shall be exercised under the ultimate direction of the board."

The power to manage a corporation's affairs is vested in the directors as a collective board, not as individuals.[1] Although the board may appoint officers and delegate the management of the association's activities to any person or persons or committees, all corporate powers must be exercised under the ultimate control of the board of directors.[2]

Ordinarily, and unless the association's articles of incorporation or bylaws provide otherwise, the board of directors, in turn, appoints the officers of the association, all of whom serve at the pleasure of the board of directors.[3]

A detailed discussion of the responsibilities, powers and authority of the board of directors and officers of the association is found in Chapter VIII. Generally speaking, the association's directors and officers are required to respect, accept and comply with the basic principles applicable to corporate governing bodies, the laws which apply to common interest developments and the association's governing documents. The remainder of Chapter VI is devoted to a discussion of these related subjects.

GOVERNING LAWS AND REGULATIONS

Chapter I contains a brief overview of the two primary kinds of laws applicable to CIDs, statutory law and common law or "case law". Statutory law consists of those laws enacted by legislatures, the California

Legislature at the state level and Congress at the federal level. In California the statutes are categorized into various "Codes", groups of statutes organized according to their general substantive content. For example, the Civil Code contains many statutes addressing numerous aspects of civil law, the Insurance Code contains numerous statutes addressing insurance contract or policy issues and the regulation of the insurance industry, and the Corporations Code contains many statutes governing the creation and operation of corporations in the State of California. The bulk of statutory law applicable to CIDs is found in the California Civil Code and Corporations Code.[4]

"Common law" or "case law" is established when state and federal appellate courts render decisions which are authorized for publication in the official reports of judicial decisions. Such cases often arise when a dispute develops between association members or the association and one or more members and the court is called upon to interpret and/or apply a statute and/or a provision in an association's governing documents. The trial court's decision in such cases, while binding on the parties, and possibly binding on all of the association's members whether or not they are parties to the lawsuit,[5] does not establish legal precedent. That is, such decisions do not establish rules of law which can or must be relied on by courts and litigants in other lawsuits.

Instead, legal precedent is established when an appellate court reviews a trial court decision on appeal by one of the parties, and renders a written decision or opinion which is published in the official case reporters.[6] Not all appellate court opinions are published.[7] Those that are not published do not constitute binding legal precedent on persons not involved in the particular lawsuit which produced that unpublished appellate court opinion.[8]

Associations and association members are governed to a great extent by both statutory and common law in the creation, long-range planning and policy making, and daily operation and management of CIDs. In addition, a great many state and federal administrative agencies enact regulations, too numerous to specifically discuss, which may apply to CIDs, associations and property owners. For instance, the California Department of Real Estate has adopted regulations which govern the regulation of CIDs before the developer's ownership is phased out of the development[9] and the Department of Fair Employment and Housing has adopted regulations governing a variety of housing issues, including housing located in CIDs.[10]

The "Davis-Stirling Common Interest Development Act" California Civil Code Sections 1350 Through 1374:

The single most important body of California statutes governing CIDs is commonly referred to as the "Davis-Stirling Common Interest Development Act". This Act was adopted by the legislature in 1985 and first became effective on January 1, 1986.[11] It has been amended numerous times by the legislature since 1985, with modifications of and additions to the original statutes contained in the Act. The Act is now found in Sections 1350 through 1376 of the California Civil Code.

When it was adopted in 1985, the Act consolidated many other existing statutes which were found scattered in California statutes, primarily in the Civil Code and the Business and Professions Code, into one location in the Civil Code and added new statutory provisions applicable to CIDs.[12]

The Davis-Stirling Common Interest Development Act addresses a wide range of subjects including the enforcement of governing documents, the levy and collection of assessments, membership rights and the power and authority of CID associations in general. The Act provides the fundamental framework of statutory law applicable to CIDs.

The Davis-Stirling Common Interest Development Act does not apply to all real estate subdivisions. Instead, the Act is specifically tailored to apply only to real estate subdivisions which have certain characteristics and, as such, qualify as a common interest development as defined in the Act. Civil Code Section 1352 provides the definitive characteristics of a common interest development to which the Act will apply:

> "This title applies and a common interest development is created whenever a separate interest coupled with an interest in the common area or membership in the association is, or has been, conveyed, provided all of the following are recorded:
> "(a) A declaration.
>
> "(b) A condominium plan, if any exists.
>
> "(c) A final map or parcel map, if Division 2 (commencing with Section 66410) of Title 7 of the Government Code requires the recording of either a final map or parcel map for the common interest development."[13]

Generally speaking, under Civil Code Section 1352, a CID is created and the Davis-Stirling Common Interest Development Act applies to that

CID whenever land is subdivided into lots, parcels, areas or units and a lot, parcel, area or unit is sold to a purchaser, together with an interest in common areas either owned in common with the other owners of separate lots, parcels, areas or units or owned by the association, or with a membership in an association, and the required documents have been recorded.

The interest in the common areas which is conveyed with the separate interest to a property owner (see Chapter I for definition of "separate interest") may consist of a fee estate, a life estate, a leasehold interest, or any combination of those estates, or, in the case of a planned development, mutual and reciprocal easement rights.[14]

The California Corporations Code:

Every CID is required by law to be managed by an association, whether it is incorporated or unincorporated.[15] The California Corporations Code contains a vast array of statutes applicable to all forms of business and organizational entities conducting business in California, including nonprofit corporations and unincorporated associations. This Code defines and regulates the creation, existence, operation and management of all corporations formed or conducting business in California.

All CID associations have been or are incorporated as nonprofit corporations or nonprofit, mutual benefit corporations or treated as such by the law,[16] or they are unincorporated associations which are given many of the same powers, authorities and duties as nonprofit, mutual benefit corporations. For example, Civil Code Section 1363(c) provides that:

> "Unless the governing documents provide otherwise, and regardless of whether the association is incorporated or unincorporated, the association may exercise the powers granted to a nonprofit mutual benefit corporation, as enumerated in Section 7140 of the Corporations Code, except that an unincorporated association may not adopt or use a corporate seal or issue membership certificates in accordance with Section 7313 of the Corporations Code.
>
> "The association, whether incorporated or unincorporated, may exercise the powers granted to an association by Section 383 of the Code of Civil Procedure and the powers granted to the association in this title."

In 1978, the California legislature enacted a revised Corporations Code which was reorganized in various chapters, divisions and parts based on the various types of corporations recognized and allowed under California law.[17]

The bulk of the California Corporations Code applicable to all nonprofit, mutual benefit corporations is found in two parts of the Corporations Code. Title 1, Division 2, Part 1, generally referred to as the "Nonprofit Corporations Law" is found in Corporations Code Sections 5000 through 5080 and is applicable to all nonprofit corporations recognized under California law. Title 1, Division 2, Part 3, commonly referred to as the "Nonprofit Mutual Benefit Corporation Law" is found in Corporations Code Sections 7110 through 8910 and is applicable to all nonprofit, mutual benefit corporations.

Unincorporated associations, on the other hand, are governed and controlled by the statutes contained in Title 3, Parts 1, 2, and 4 of the Corporations Code, found in Sections 20000 through 21103 and Sections 21300 through 21310 of the Code. While unincorporated associations are permitted to register their names and insignia with the California Secretary of State and prevent others from using deceptively similar names or insignia, they are not required to do so.[18]

There is not a great deal of law controlling and governing unincorporated associations, and for that reason there is a relatively great degree of uncertainty with respect to legal issues related to such associations. Although both incorporated and unincorporated associations formed to manage CIDS are governed by the Davis-Stirling Common Interest Development Act,[19] there are few statutory guidelines with respect to the internal or administrative affairs of unincorporated associations.

Unincorporated associations may sue and be sued in the association's name.[20] Under Sections 21100 through 21102 of the Corporations Code, members of unincorporated associations are, unless they have assumed such obligations in writing, shielded from personal liability for the debts incurred by the association in connection with the acquisition of land and the purchase or construction of buildings for association purposes. But, beyond these very narrow protections, the personal liability of members of unincorporated associations is open to question and can only be determined on a case-by-case basis. The personal liability of such members often turns on the extent of the individual member's participation in association affairs.

On the other hand, incorporated associations and their members have the advantage of the California Corporations Code, specifically, the Nonprofit Mutual Benefit Corporation Law, which provides a comprehensive set of legal rules and guidelines with respect to such issues, providing a degree of certainty lacking for unincorporated associations and their members.

The scheme of the Corporations Code is one of breadth and flexibility. The Code permits a nonprofit, mutual benefit corporation to choose many of its own corporate characteristics, but also contains many provisions which are mandatory or which cannot be varied by a corporation's articles of incorporation or bylaws.

The Corporations Code grants nonprofit, mutual benefit corporations broad and sweeping powers and authority, limited only by its own articles of incorporation and bylaws and the provisions of the Corporations Code and any other applicable laws, and then explicitly provides that such corporations shall have, in addition to other powers and authority, 12 specifically enumerated powers, including the power to enter into contracts, issue membership certificates, and levy dues and assessments.[21]

> "Subject to any limitations contained in the articles or bylaws and to compliance with other provisions of this division and any other applicable laws, a corporation, in carrying out its activities, shall have all of the powers of a natural person, including, without limitation, the power to: ..."[22]

Chapters I through III illustrate how an association's declaration of CC&Rs and association rules must be read and applied in light of the Davis-Stirling Common Interest Development Act and other statutes and common law affecting the interpretation, validity and application of land use covenants, restrictions and rules. Similarly, the provisions of an association's corporate documents, chiefly its articles of incorporation and bylaws, must be read and applied in light of the Nonprofit Mutual Benefit Corporation Law and common law affecting the interpretation, validity and application of the provisions contained in the articles and bylaws.

An example of the flexibility available to corporations by which they may create and amend their corporate documents to fit their own intended purposes and needs under the Corporations Code is found in Section 7151(c) in which it is stated that:

> "The bylaws may contain any provision, not in conflict with law or the articles, for the management of the activities and

for the conduct of the affairs of the corporation, including but not limited to: ..."

On the other hand, the Corporations Code also contains many provisions which specify certain standards and requirements which cannot be changed or varied by a corporation in its corporate documents or otherwise. One example is stated in Sections 7151(e) and 7222 which deal with the removal of directors without cause from the board of directors. Section 7222(a)(2) states that in a corporation with 50 or members, directors may be removed without cause by the members by a majority of the votes represented and voting at a duly held meeting at which a quorum is present. An association's corporate bylaws cannot validly require a greater vote of the members to remove directors without cause and any such bylaw provision is void and unenforceable because Section 7151(e) specifies that:

"The bylaws may require, for any or all corporate actions (except as provided in paragraphs (1) and (2) of subdivision (a) of Section 7222 ...) the vote of a larger proportion of, or all of, the members ... than is otherwise required by this part."

Other Statutes:

A wide variety of other statutes, both state and federal, may apply to an association, depending on each association's characteristics, functions and purposes. For example, the California courts have held that CID associations are "business establishments" within the meaning of the "Unruh Civil Rights Act", California Civil Code Sections 51 through 53, which statute prohibits a broad range of discriminatory practices.[23]

Many statutes enacted by the legislature are designed to regulate the affairs of California citizens and businesses regardless of location. For example, there are many statutes regulating the validity and enforceability of land use restrictions, whether such restrictions are found in contracts, deeds, declarations or CID association governing documents. As discussed in detail in Chapter III, a significant number of provisions found in the California Health and Safety Code, Government Code and Civil Code, not directly related to CIDs, govern the validity and enforceability of a variety of land use restrictions.

Other state and federal statutes may or may not apply to any particular CID and association, depending on the particular circumstances unique to each association. For instance, if an association has employees, the association, as an employer, will be governed by the California Labor Code. It may, depending on a variety of factors, including the number of employees, also be subject to federal and state statutes governing work conditions, employee grievance procedures, employee family and medical leave entitlements, and wages and salaries. If the association owns or operates a clubhouse including restaurant and lounge facilities, it will in that respect be governed by the statutes and regulations applying to restaurant and lounge operators.

"Common Law" Or "Case Law":

As discussed earlier in this Chapter, common law or case law is established when one or more parties involved in a lawsuit file an appeal from a trial court decision or judgment and a state or federal appellate court review of the trial court decision results in a written opinion published in the official case reporters.[24]

Hundreds of such published opinions have been rendered by California appellate courts since the State was first admitted to the Union. Many of the opinions affect CIDs indirectly by establishing legal rules applicable to incidental features of an association. For example, many principles of liability for "tortious" conduct or activities, that is, conduct or activities which result in personal injury or property damage, are established by the courts and are applicable to all persons and entities engaging in such conduct or activities. Other court opinions have interpreted and/or decided the validity and enforceability of corporate documents or land use restrictions in general. Even though a CID or association may not have been involved in the facts of the cases which produced such opinions, such opinions where otherwise applicable under general principles of jurisprudence will be binding on and affect CIDs, associations and their members.[25]

Other published opinions directly impact CIDs and/or associations because the facts involved in such cases are substantively identical or substantially similar to the facts and circumstances presented by the typical CID and association.

California Department Of Real Estate Regulations:

The California Department of Real Estate and Real Estate Commissioner have no direct regulatory jurisdiction over CIDs which are not controlled by the real estate developer or subdivider. The Department and Commissioner have regulatory jurisdiction over certain persons or entities which are required to be licensed by the Department, such as real estate brokers and agents and real estate subdividers. Nevertheless, the

Department of Real Estate's administrative regulations play an important role in the affairs of CIDs, associations and property owner members.

The California Code of Regulations is a compilation of administrative regulations adopted by the various administrative agencies which make up part of the government of the State of California. Title 10, Chapter 6, Article 12, of the California Code of Regulations contains hundreds of administrative regulations adopted by the Real Estate Commissioner in the California Department of Real Estate addressing real estate subdivisions, including CIDs.[26]

The Department of Real Estate Regulations affect CIDs, associations and property owner members in two fundamental ways. First, the regulations prescribe the mandatory and permissible contents of the initial CID governing documents, including those governing document provisions regulating the rights, duties, responsibilities, powers and authorities of associations and members. So long as the subdivider or developer holds or directly controls one-fourth or more of the votes which may be cast to amend the provisions of the governing documents, no amendment of the governing documents which would materially change the rights of the property owners, either directly or as a member of the association, is valid without the prior written consent of the Department of Real Estate.[27]

Second, after the subdivider or developer ceases to hold or control one-fourth or more of the votes, the association members are free to amend the association's governing documents without approval of the Department of Real Estate. But, as a practical matter, many provisions originally included in the governing documents because they were required under the Department of Real Estate regulations continue to exist in the case of many associations because the members have never amended or deleted such provisions. The Department of Real Estate regulations, therefore, continue to have a "residual" effect on many associations long after the developer has been phased out of the CID.

Among other requirements, the Department of Real Estate Regulations require that an association's governing documents, at least during the period of developer control, include a number of fundamental provisions such as the creation of an association to manage and operate the CID,[28] procedures for calculating and collecting assessments,[29] creation of the association's governing body,[30] specification of the powers and duties of the association's governing body,[31] the voting rights of members,[32] and architectural and design control.[33]

The regulations then contain detailed provisions which prescribe what the Department of Real Estate deems to be "reasonable arrangements" with respect to the operation and management of the CID and association, including procedures governing meetings of members,[34] members' voting rights,[35] elections of the governing body,[36] meetings of the governing body,[37] the powers and limitations of the governing body,[38] and the preparation and review of budgets and financial statements and the distribution of such budgets and financial statements to the association members.[39]

Most, if not all, of the Department of Real Estate regulations are derived from and correlate directly with provisions in the Davis-Stirling Common Interest Development Act and the Nonprofit Mutual Benefit Corporation Law, which statutes are, of course, binding on CIDs, associations and association members. The regulations, however, tend to be more detailed than their statutory counterparts and, even though they are not binding on CIDs which are not controlled by the developer or subdivider, they can provide valuable guidance on certain issues.

Use Of Qualified Legal Counsel:

The expansive body of law which has evolved over the years to govern CIDs is relatively extensive and complex. Attempting to find and apply all of the legal principles involved with respect to any particular issue can be overwhelming. Researching, locating, reading, understanding, analyzing and applying legal principles and rules in the form of statutory, common law, and administrative regulations is the function of legal counsel. The reader is seriously urged to seek the advice and representation of qualified legal counsel experienced in such matters whenever the need may arise.

GOVERNING DOCUMENTS

Section 1351(j) of the Civil Code defines "governing documents" to mean "the declaration and any other documents, such as bylaws, operating rules of the association, articles of incorporation, or articles of association, which govern the operation of the common interest development or association."

An association's governing documents may, for practical purposes, usually be grouped in two broad categories based on the primary function or purpose of the document which for the purposes of this book are referred to generally as: (1) "land use and regulation documents", and (2) "corporate or administrative documents".

Land Use And Regulation Documents:

The Declaration Of Covenants, Conditions And Restrictions:

As we have seen in Chapters III and IV, the declaration of CC&Rs is that document or instrument which is recorded in the public land title records in the Office of the County Recorder of the county in which the CID is located. The declaration typically includes covenants and restrictions binding on all property to which it applies, regulating and controlling the use and occupancy of such land. The reader is referred to Chapters III and IV for a detailed discussion of the declaration and its typical contents.

Occasionally, an association's declaration will overlap with the association's bylaws and include provisions governing the internal, corporate affairs of the association, such as membership voting rights and members' meetings. There is nothing necessarily wrong with this overlapping of provisions, so long as the documents are consistent with one another and do not contain conflicting terms and provisions.

Architectural Or Environmental Control Rules:

Many associations typically have adopted rules which govern and control the use, occupancy and improvement of the properties located within the CID. Much like administrative agency regulations provide detailed provisions addressing the same issues already addressed by broader statutes, the architectural or environmental control rules, as they are frequently called, provide greater detail for and implement the broader provisions of the declaration of CC&Rs.

As pointed out in Chapter III, architectural or environmental control rules are subordinate to the terms of the declaration of CC&Rs, and although they may provide greater detail than the declaration, they must be consistent with the terms of the declaration.

Association Rules:

Some associations, particularly larger associations with many community facilities and amenities, have a separate set of rules which govern the use and enjoyment of the association's facilities. Such rules often contain detailed provisions on such matters as the operating hours of swimming pools and tennis courts, who may use the facilities, and the conduct and behavior that is expected from members and guests using the facilities.

Corporate Or Administrative Documents:

The Articles Of Incorporation Or Articles Of Association:

The articles of incorporation of an incorporated association or the articles of association of an unincorporated association is the name of the written document or instrument which creates, forms and establishes the association in the first instance. It is the charter by and through which the incorporated association comes into existence and is recognized and sanctioned by the State of California. The corporation begins its legal existence as soon as the articles of incorporation have been filed in the Office of the California Secretary of State.[40] A certified copy of the articles of incorporation is conclusive evidence of the formation of the corporation.[41]

A corporation's articles of incorporation are generally extremely broad in nature and contain enabling provisions stating the creation of the corporation, its name, its address and usually a very general statement of its purposes and powers.

The articles of incorporation for a nonprofit mutual benefit corporation must include: (1) the name of the corporation, (2) a statement that, "This corporation is a nonprofit mutual benefit corporation organized under the Nonprofit Mutual Benefit Corporation Law. The purpose of this corporation is to engage in any lawful act or activity for which a corporation may be organized under such law", and (3) the name and address of the corporation's initial agent for service of process (the person or entity authorized by the corporation to receive lawsuits and other legal papers on its behalf).[42]

In addition to the above requirements, the articles of incorporation for any incorporated association filed on or after January 1, 1995 must include a statement that (1) identifies the corporation as an association formed to manage a common interest development, (2) states the business or corporate office of the association, if there is one, and (3) states the name and address of the association's managing agent if the association has one.[43]

The articles of incorporation may also include a number of optional provisions, including a statement limiting the purposes or powers of the corporation,[44] the names and addresses of the initial directors,[45] provisions governing the transfer of memberships in the corporation,[46] if more than one class, the classes of members,[47] and any other provisions for the management of the activities and the conduct of the affairs of the corporation which are not in conflict with applicable law, including any provisions which are authorized to be stated in the corporation's bylaws.[48]

An association's articles of incorporation is considered as the paramount corporate or administrative document of the association. The terms and provisions stated in the articles will prevail and control over any conflicting terms and provisions in subordinate corporate documents such as the bylaws.[49] The fundamental nature of the document is generally considered by the law to constitute a contract between the corporation and the state and between the corporation and its members.

Bylaws:

The association's bylaws contain those administrative and operating rules by which the association operates and conducts its internal business and affairs. Issues such as membership voting rights, the holding of meetings, the qualifications and election of directors, and the appointment and responsibilities of officers are ordinarily addressed in the bylaws. Unless the articles of incorporation contain the provision, the bylaws must contain a statement setting forth the number of directors of the corporation, or a minimum and maximum number of directors of the corporation.[50]

Bylaws are adopted after the corporation is created by the filing of its articles of incorporation with the California Secretary of State. The bylaws may initially be adopted by the person or persons incorporating the corporation and later ratified by the initial directors of the corporation,[51] or by the members of the corporation.[52]

The association's bylaws may include any number of provisions governing the corporate affairs and operation of the association, so long as such provisions are not in conflict with applicable law or the articles of incorporation. Corporations Code Section 7151(c) specifies that:

> "The bylaws may contain any provision, not in conflict with law or the articles, for the management of the activities and for the conduct of the affairs of the corporation, including but not limited to:
>
> "(1) Any provision referred to in subdivision (c) of Section 7132 [optional provisions which may be stated in the articles of incorporation]

"(2) The time, place and manner of calling, conducting and giving notice of members', directors' and committee meetings, or of conducting mail ballots.

"(3) The qualifications, duties and compensation of directors; the time of their election; and the requirements of a quorum for directors' and committee meetings.

"(4) The appointment of committees, composed of directors or nondirectors or both, by the board or any officer and the authority of any such committees.

"(5) The appointment, duties, compensation and tenure of officers.

"(6) The mode of determination of members of record.

"(7) The making of reports and financial statements to members.

"(8) Setting, imposing and collecting dues, assessments, and admission and transfer fees."

In addition to the provisions outlined above, the association's bylaws may provide for the manner of admission, withdrawal, suspension, and expulsion of members, so long as such procedures meet certain statutory standards,[53] and may require, with certain exceptions, that any or all corporate actions be approved by a greater number of members than is otherwise required under the Nonprofit Mutual Benefit Corporation Law.[54]

Generally speaking, the law views the bylaws, in an elementary or fundamental way, as a contract between the corporation and its members. A violation of the terms of the bylaws may give rise to a legal right of action for monetary damages or some sort of equitable remedy such as injunctive or declaratory relief by the courts.

Board Of Directors Resolutions And Policies:

Corporations Code Section 7210 specifies that the business and activities of a nonprofit mutual benefit corporation shall be exercised by the board of directors:

"... the activities and affairs of a corporation shall be conducted and all corporate powers shall be exercised by or under the direction of the board. The board may delegate the management of the activities of the corporation to any person or persons, management company, or committee however composed, provided that the activities and affairs of the corporation shall be managed and all corporate powers shall be exercised under the ultimate direction of the board."

Corporations Code Section 7211(a)(8) then provides that:

"... every act or decision done or made by a majority of the directors present at a meeting duly held at which a quorum is present is the act of the board. ..."

Association boards of directors ordinarily take action at board meetings through the adoption of resolutions or policies addressing the wide variety of business issues which may come before the association. Such resolutions and other board decisions and actions should be recorded in the minutes of the meeting and made a permanent part of the association's records.[55]

Certified copies of such minutes and resolutions constitute proof of the corporate action taken. Corporations Code Section 7215 reads as follows:

"The original or a copy of the bylaws or of the minutes of any incorporators', members', directors', committee or other meeting or of any resolution adopted by the board or a committee thereof, or members, certified to be a true copy by a person purporting to be secretary of the corporation, is prima facie evidence of the adoption of such bylaws or resolution or of the due holding of such meeting and of the matters stated therein."

Rules Of Parliamentary Procedure:

Civil Code Section 1363(d) requires that all meetings of association members be conducted in accordance with some recognized system of parliamentary procedure or parliamentary procedures adopted by the association.[56] In addition, some associations have adopted, in their bylaws or elsewhere, a requirement that meetings of the board of directors be conducted in accordance with some system of parliamentary procedure.

Probably the most frequently encountered rules of parliamentary procedure are called "Robert's Rules of Order". Rules of order or parliamentary procedure are intended to provide rules by which meetings of collective bodies may progress in an orderly fashion. They are not intended to supplant or replace an association's governing documents, and they should not be used for such purposes. The author has, in his professional representation of CID associations, witnessed a number of occasions where directors or members deliberately attempted to misuse, abuse and misapply rules of parliamentary procedure in an attempt to avoid the applicable provisions of the association's governing documents for the purpose of achieving some preconceived political agenda, frequently a thinly veiled quest to usurp control of the association in clandestine fashion.

Various editions of rules order and parliamentary procedure are available commercially. Many have model form bylaws and suggested bylaw provisions. However, when associations already have their own bylaws, ordinarily they should not adopt or use any system of parliamentary rules for any purpose other than to facilitate the smooth and orderly progression of meetings. The borrowing of suggested interpretations of hypothetical bylaw provisions which do not in fact exist can be perilous and yield confusing results completely contrary to those intended by the association's governing documents.

Parliamentary procedure has its proper place in helping to conduct expeditious and productive meetings. The rules ordinarily provide valuable guidance on a variety of procedural matters, including how motions should be made, seconded, discussed, and acted upon during meetings of members. However, such rules of procedure should never be relied upon as a substitute for the association's governing documents.

RELATIONSHIP BETWEEN GOVERNING DOCUMENTS AND APPLICABLE LAWS

An association's declaration of CC&Rs must be considered and treated as the association's preeminent land use control and regulation document. The declaration will generally prevail and control over other documents, such as architectural or environmental control rules. Ordinarily, the declaration is the only association land use control document which is recorded in the public land title records of the County Recorder in which the CID is located. Once recorded, the declaration imparts "constructive notice" to all the world of its contents, whether or not any of those persons have ever actually seen the declaration.[57]

The association's articles of incorporation, or articles of association in the case of an unincorporated association, and bylaws, must be considered the chief and paramount administrative governing documents. That is, other rules, board policies, resolutions of the board of directors and the members must be within the scope of, consistent and not in conflict with the articles and bylaws.

An association's governing documents cannot accurately be read and applied without reference to, and a clear understanding of, applicable law. Nor can the applicable law be read and applied without reference to the association's governing documents. The law frequently permits a relatively wide degree of latitude in the terms and provisions associations may place in their governing documents. The law also permits varying levels of discretion to be exercised by associations in the operation and management of CIDs. The governing documents and the applicable law must, therefore, be read and applied together.

For example, even though Corporations Code Section 7151(c)(7) permits an incorporated association's bylaws to specify the procedures for the making of reports and financial statements to the members, if an association's bylaws do contain such provisions and the provisions do not comply with the financial disclosure requirements of Section 1365 of the Civil Code, Civil Code Section 1365 must nevertheless be followed in preparing and distributing financial statements and reports to the association members. The bylaw provisions would, to that extent, be superseded by the Civil Code and could not be relied upon by the association in meeting its reporting obligations.

Another example is found in Civil Code Section 1366(b) which confers a great deal of discretion on an association's board of directors to increase regular assessments. Section 1366(b) limits the amount by which the board of directors may increase regular assessments without membership approval. But, Section 1366(b) also permits the board of directors to impose, without approval by the members, regular assessments up to twenty percent greater than the regular assessment for the preceding fiscal year, even if the declaration or other governing documents contain provisions with more stringent limitations on regular assessment increases, so long as the association has complied with the financial disclosure requirements of Civil Code Section 1365. For instance, if the association's declaration provides that the association cannot, without prior approval of the owners or members, increase regular assessments by more than ten percent, despite this governing document limitation, under Civil Code Section 1366(b) the board may increase the regular assessment by as much as twenty percent without the owners' approval, if the association has met the financial disclosure criteria in Civil Code Section 1365.[58] Section 1366(b) reads in part as follows:

> "Notwithstanding more restrictive limitations placed on the board by the governing documents, the board of directors may not impose a regular assessment that is more than 20 percent greater than the regular assessment for the association's preceding fiscal year ... without the approval of owners ..."

It should, therefore, be readily observable to associations, boards of directors and property owners that the association's governing documents can only be read, understood and applied in light of current applicable law. The advice and representation of qualified legal counsel experienced in such matters should be sought whenever the need may arise.

AMENDING THE GOVERNING DOCUMENTS

Because the association's governing documents play such a critical role in the lives and property rights of the association members, virtually all governing documents, at least those most directly affecting the members, require that the members approve of any amendments to the documents. In order to avoid potential abuse and the possibility of amendments being passed by a bare majority of property owners, frequently the governing documents require that amendments be approved by some percentage of the owners significantly greater than a simple majority.

Amendments During Period of Developer Control:

During the period of time that the developer owns or controls 25 percent or more of the votes entitled to be cast, the governing documents cannot be amended without the review and approval of the Department of Real Estate.[59] Once the developer ceases to own or control 25 percent of the votes, the governing documents may be amended without the approval of the Department of Real Estate.

Amendment of Declaration Of Covenants, Conditions And Restrictions:

With only one narrow exception, only the property owner members of the CID association have the authority to amend the declaration of CC&Rs.[60] Other than amendments to delete obsolete terms in the declaration designed solely to help the developer complete and market the development, an association's board of directors has no authority to amend the declaration. Safeguards against a developer's potential abuse of authority are also prescribed in the Department of Real Estate Regulations. The Regulations ensure that during the period of time the developer continues to own separate interests in the CID, a majority of all property owners other than the developer must approve any amendments of the declaration.

The Department of Real Estate Regulations specify a range of membership approval required to amend the association's declaration of CC&Rs. The real estate subdivider or developer prepares the original declaration of CC&Rs which must be submitted to and approved by the Department of Real Estate.[61] The Department of Real Estate Regulations permit the developer to specify a range of voting requirements necessary to amend the declaration within prescribed minimum and maximum proportions. The declaration itself ordinarily includes at least one clause which specifies the percentage or proportion of owners, within the parameters specified in the Department of Real Estate Regulations, which must approve any amendments.

Unless the declaration is amended after the developer ceases to own or control 25 percent or more of the votes to change the amendment voting requirements specified in the Department of Real Estate Regulations, such requirements will still be found in the declaration of CC&Rs. The voting requirements specified in the declaration within the criteria specified in the Regulations must be satisfied (unless a petition to reduce the required voting requirements is filed with and granted by the court as discussed in following paragraphs) in order for members to adopt amendments of the declaration.[62]

The Department of Real Estate Regulations require that amendments to the declaration of CC&Rs be approved by at least a majority of the total voting power of the association which is at least a bare majority and not more than 75 percent and at least a bare majority of the votes of members other than the developer.[63] Title 10 California Code of Regulations Section 2792.24(a) specifies the voting requirements as follows:

> "In a single-class voting structure, amendments of the CC&Rs may be enacted by requiring the vote or written assent of members representing both:
>
> "(1) A majority of the total voting power of the Association which is at least a bare majority and not more than 75%; and
>
> "(2) At least a bare majority of the votes of members other than the subdivider.
>
> "The percentage of the voting power necessary to amend a specific clause or provision shall not be less than the percentage

of affirmative votes prescribed for action to be taken under that clause. For example, if the CC&Rs expressly state that 75% of the voting power must agree to an increase in the maximum annual assessment, then 75% of the voting power is necessary to amend this provision regardless of the percentage prescribed in the general provision pertaining to amendments of the CC&Rs."

Civil Code Requirements Governing Amendment Of The Declaration Of CC&Rs:

The Davis-Stirling Common Interest Development Act contains a number of provisions governing the amendment of an association's declaration of CC&Rs. As mentioned above, whether or not the amendment voting requirements specified in the Department of Real Estate Regulations continue to apply after the developer no longer owns or controls 25 percent or more of the votes depends on whether the declaration has been amended to alter those voting requirements.

On the other hand, the Davis-Stirling Common Interest Development Act requirements will always govern and control the amendment of the declaration of CC&Rs. Section 1355 of the Civil Code governs the amendment of declarations in general and provides that the declaration can only be amended by the approval of the percentage of property owners required by the terms of the declaration or other governing documents.

Amendment Of Declarations Which Specify The Required Level Of Approval By Owners:

Most declarations of CC&Rs will include one or more clauses or paragraphs specifying the number, percentage or proportion of owners required to approve amendments of the declaration. In order to avoid potential abuse by a simple majority of property owners, frequently the governing documents require that amendments be approved by some percentage of the owners significantly greater than a bare majority. Such increased approval requirements are often referred to as "supermajority" vote requirements.

When the declaration does include such voting requirements, including supermajority vote requirements, they must ordinarily be satisfied in order for the declaration to be amended. In addition, the fact of approval of an amendment by the owners must be certified in writing and the amendment and certification must be recorded in the County Recorder's Office of the county where the CID is located.[64] Civil Code Section 1355(a) governs the amendment of declarations which contain provisions specifying the required ownership approval and states:

> "The declaration may be amended pursuant to the governing documents or this title. Except as provided in Section 1356, an amendment is effective after (1) the approval of the percentage of owners required by the governing documents has been given, (2) that fact has been certified in a writing executed and acknowledged by the officer designated in the declaration or by the association for that purpose, or if no one is designated, by the president of the association, and (3) that writing has been recorded in each county in which a portion of the common interest development is located."

Amendment Of Declarations Which Do Not Specify The Required Level Of Approval By Owners:

As mentioned above, occasionally a declaration of CC&Rs, particularly older declarations, fails to include provisions specifying how the declaration may be amended or the required ownership approval of amendments. In such cases, so long as the declaration does not expressly state that it cannot be amended in whole or in part, the declaration may be amended at any time after the proposed amendment(s) have been distributed to all of the owners for their review and have been approved by owners representing more than 50 percent of the separate interests in the development or such greater percentage of owners as may be specified in the declaration.[65] Section 1355(b) of the Civil Code specifies that:

> "Except to the extent that a declaration provides by its express terms that it is not amendable, in whole or in part, a declaration which fails to include provisions permitting its amendment at all times during its existence may be amended at any time. For purposes of this subdivision, an amendment is only effective after (1) the proposed amendment has been distributed to all of the owners of separate interests in the common interest development by first-class mail postage prepaid or personal delivery not less than 15 days and not more than 60 days prior to any approval being solicited; (2) the approval of owners representing more than 50 percent, or any higher percentage required by the declaration for the approval of an amendment to the declaration, of the separate interests in the common interest development has been given, and that fact has been certified in writing, executed and acknowledged by an officer of the association; and (3) the amendment has been

recorded in each county in which a portion of the common interest development is located. A copy of any amendment adopted pursuant to this subdivision shall be distributed by first-class mail postage prepaid or personal delivery to all of the owners of separate interests immediately upon its recordation."

In order to adopt valid and effective amendments of a declaration of CC&Rs, the association must follow all of the steps specifically described in the statute. All of the owners must be provided with copies of the proposed amendment(s) between 15 and 60 days before any solicitation of the amendment(s) is sought, by first-class mail with the postage prepaid or personal delivery. Property owners representing at least a simple bare majority of the separate interests, or any higher percentage required by the declaration, must approve the amendment(s). The approval by the required percentage of owners must be certified in writing by an officer of the association. The amendment(s) and certification of approval must be recorded in the County Recorder's Office of the county in which the development is located. A copy of the amendment(s) must be delivered to all property owners by first-class mail with postage prepaid or personal delivery.

Amendments To Delete Provisions Related To Developer's Completion Of Marketing Of Development:

In order to make it easier to amend a declaration of CC&Rs to remove obsolete provisions which may be in an association's declaration solely for the purpose of facilitating the developer's completion of the development and marketing activities, the legislature adopted Civil Code Section 1355.5 which permits the board of directors to adopt such amendments with the approval of a simple majority of the association members.

Petition To Reduce Membership Voting Requirements To Amend The Declaration Of CC&Rs:

Where an association's declaration requires owners holding more than 50 percent of the votes in the association to vote in favor of amending the declaration, the association or any owner may petition the Superior Court for an order reducing the percentage of votes required to amend the declaration.[66]

For example, if an association's declaration specifies that it can be amended only upon the approval of 60 percent of the owners and attempts to amend the declaration have failed due to lack of quorums at membership meetings or an insufficient number of affirmative votes, the association may request that the Superior Court reduce the quorum requirements and/or the number of affirmative votes required to approve amendments.

Under Section 1356 of the California Civil Code, a petition may be filed with the Superior Court for an order reducing the percentage of affirmative of votes of members necessary to amend the declaration, when past efforts to obtain membership approval of an amendment have proved futile.

In order to have the petition granted and obtain the court order, the petitioner must, among other things, provide satisfactory evidence of efforts made to solicit approval of the members in accordance with the terms of the declaration, including copies of solicitation materials, ballots, etc., establishing that balloting on the proposed amendment was conducted in accordance with all applicable provisions of the association's governing documents. Most importantly, the petitioner must be able to show that the proposed amendment was approved by owners holding more than 50 percent of the votes in the association.[67]

If the court grants the petition, the court may, in its discretion, order that the amendment has been validly approved on the basis of the affirmative votes actually received during the balloting period or the court may dispense with any quorum requirements or requirements related to the number or percentage of votes needed for approval of the amendment.[68]

Amendment Of Articles Of Incorporation:

Generally speaking amendments of an association's articles of incorporation require the approval of the association's members, as well as the approval of the board.[69] Once memberships are issued by the association, with only a few narrow exceptions, the board of directors acting alone cannot amend the articles of incorporation. Corporations Code Section 7812 reads in relevant part that "amendments may be adopted if approved by the board and approved by the members ... and approved by such other person or persons, if any, as required by the articles."[70]

If an association's memberships are divided into two or more classes, then the approval of each class of members is ordinarily required in order to adopt any amendments of the articles of incorporation which would materially affect the rights of the members or affect the rights of each class differently.[71]

Amendment Of Bylaws:

In many instances, either the board of directors acting alone, or the members acting alone, may adopt amendments to an association's bylaws.

So long as the association's articles of incorporation or bylaws do not prohibit or restrict the board from adopting or amending bylaws, the board has authority to do so.[72] Under Section 7150(a) of the Corporations Code, the board of directors may adopt bylaw amendments unless the amendments would (1) materially and adversely affect the rights of members as to voting, dissolution of the association, or transfer of memberships, (2) increase or decrease the number of authorized memberships, (3) result in an exchange, reclassification or cancellation of memberships, or (4) authorize a new class of memberships.[73]

Section 7150(b) of the Corporations Code grants the association members the power to adopt and amend bylaws. The members' authority is separate and may be exercised independently from the board's authority to adopt and amend bylaws. Generally speaking, if amendments adopted by the members will materially and adversely affect the rights of a class of members, then each class so affected must also approve the amendments.[74]

Majority Voting Requirements:

Frequently, the percentage of membership approval for the amendment of bylaws is specified as a simple majority of the members or votes of the association in the bylaws or the Corporations Code. For example, many provisions of the Corporations Code refer to "approval of the members (Section 5034)". This reference to Section 5034 of the Corporations Code is a reference to one of two very different types of membership approval requirements. Section 5034 approval of the members, simply means approval or ratification by the affirmative vote of a simple majority of the votes represented and voting at a meeting at which a quorum is present.[75]

On the other hand, a reference in the bylaws or the Corporations Code to "approval by (or approval of) a majority of all members" or a reference to Section 5033 of the Corporations Code, means approval by an affirmative vote of a majority of all membership votes entitled to be cast.[76] This requirement generally means that a majority of all eligible votes, or members eligible to vote, in the association (those whose membership or voting rights have not been suspended) must approve the proposed bylaw amendment.

Supermajority Voting Requirements:

Sometimes the bylaws or other governing documents will specify that amendments (or some other action by the members) be approved by some percentage of the members significantly greater than a bare majority. Such increased approval requirements are often referred to as "supermajority" vote requirements.

If the bylaws contain a supermajority voting requirement for certain action by the members, the directors or the association, such requirements are generally valid and must be satisfied. In addition, any such bylaw provision requiring a supermajority vote cannot be amended to reduce or otherwise alter the voting requirements, unless such amendment or alteration is approved by the same or greater number of required votes.[77]

For example, if the bylaws require the approval of 70 percent or more of the members to adopt an amendment of the bylaws, the requirement that 70 percent or more of the members approve of the amendments cannot itself be amended to reduce the required percentage unless 70 percent or more of the members approve.

Petition To Reduce Membership Voting Requirements To Amend The Articles Of Incorporation And Bylaws:

Sometimes associations are unable to achieve a quorum or acquire a sufficient number of votes to adopt amendments to their bylaws and/or articles of incorporation. Whether low voter turnout is due to voter apathy, a high percentage of absentee property owners who cannot attend meetings and who do not timely return proxy forms, or some other reason, the association's predicament can be a serious one. There is a remedy available for those associations which may encounter this problem.

Similar to the mechanism under Civil Code Section 1356 by which the association may petition the Superior Court for an order reducing the number or percentage of votes necessary to amend the declaration of CC&Rs, an association may likewise petition the Superior Court for an order reducing the voting requirements necessary to amend the articles of incorporation or bylaws.[78]

The petition may be filed by any director, officer or member of the association[79] and it may request the court to alter any number of voting or other consent requirements, including quorum requirements and a reduction in the number or percentage of votes which may otherwise be required by the articles of incorporation or bylaws.[80]

The alternative methods available to associations to amend their declarations of CC&Rs, articles of incorporation and bylaws by petitioning the court are potential resources which should not be overlooked. These alternatives may be invaluable for those associations where voter apathy, a high percentage of absentee property owners and/or a remote development location have made it impractical or futile to amend the governing documents through the more conventional membership meeting or balloting processes.

DURATION OF THE ASSOCIATION:

As long as there is any lot, parcel, unit, area or apartment for which the association is responsible to provide management, maintenance, preservation or control, the association cannot be terminated or dissolved without the approval of 100 percent of the association members. Nor can an association sell or otherwise transfer all or substantially all of its property or assets without the approval of 100 percent of the members if there is any lot, parcel, unit, area or apartment for which the association is responsible to provide management, maintenance, preservation or control.[81]

CHAPTER VII

THE ASSOCIATION MEMBERS

It is often said that the "enlisted man is the backbone of the navy". The same statement can be applied to the members of CID associations. Without the property owners, who are the association members, there would be no need for an association in the first place. Association members are a key and integral part of every association. The members' interests are best served when they adopt an active role in the governance of their planned communities. In this Chapter we will survey the rights, duties, interests and responsibilities of the association members and the methods by which they can become involved in their associations.

MEMBERS

Definitions of Member and Membership:

Not all persons who reside in a CID and who may enjoy the common areas, community facilities and other benefits the CID may offer are members of the CID association. In addition to the association members, tenants, lessees and guests of property owners may reside in the CID. An association member may generally be defined as a person who, in accordance with the association's governing documents, has the right to vote for directors of the association and to approve or disapprove changes to the association's governing documents.

CID association membership is ordinarily limited, either in the declaration of CC&Rs, the articles of incorporation or the bylaws, to the owners of property within the development.[1]

A "member" of a nonprofit mutual benefit corporation is a person who, pursuant to a provision in the association's articles of incorporation or bylaws, holds the right to vote for the election of directors, or vote to approve or disapprove a disposition of all or nearly all of the association's assets, or vote to approve or disapprove the association's merger or dissolution. "Member" also includes any persons designated as members in the association's articles of incorporation or bylaws and who holds the right to vote on proposed changes to the articles or bylaws.[2]

A "membership" refers to the rights a member has according to a nonprofit mutual benefit corporation's articles of incorporation and bylaws and the Nonprofit Mutual Benefit Corporation Law.[3]

Which Persons Are Entitled To Be Members:

Generally speaking, a nonprofit mutual benefit corporation may determine in its articles of incorporation or bylaws which persons shall be admitted as members of the corporation.[4]

Typically, an association's declaration of CC&Rs and bylaws both include provisions requiring that all owners of property within the CID be members of the association. A covenant in a recorded declaration making membership in the association mandatory for all property owners is valid and enforceable.[5] Sometimes, the governing document provisions specify that "all owners of record are members of the association", or similar language.

Some governing document provisions go even further and state that only those owners of record under a "grant deed" are members of the association. Since forms of conveyance of title to land other than grant deeds are commonly used, it is doubtful that such limiting provisions are enforceable. For instance, people may own title to property under "quitclaim deeds", "warranty deeds", and real property sales contracts. These forms of conveyance generally convey all the incidents of ownership to the purchaser, including the right to use and enjoy the property and the obligation to pay taxes and assessments which may be levied against the property.[6]

Associations are, however, entitled to require that proof of ownership be furnished to the association before a person is entitled to exercise the rights of membership, including the right to vote and to use and enjoy the association's common areas and facilities.

Multiple Memberships:

Although an association may, in its governing documents, permit property owners to hold a separate membership for each separate interest owned in the development, no fractional memberships are permitted.[7] In addition, two or more persons may hold an indivisible interest in a single membership, as where a husband and wife or other multiple owners own property as cotenants or joint tenants.[8]

Membership Certificates:

A membership certificate is a written document showing that a member has a transferable property interest in the nonprofit mutual benefit corporation.[9] An association may issue membership certificates to its members, but it is not required to do so unless the governing documents impose such a requirement.[10] If membership certificates are issued, they must include certain required disclosures including a statement that the corporation is a nonprofit mutual benefit corporation and any restrictions on the transferability of memberships.[11]

A membership certificate, as defined above, should not be confused with a membership identity card or member facility or amenity use card which many associations use to restrict amenity use to authorized persons only.

RESPONSIBILITIES

Close community living necessarily involves some compromise on the part of all property owners in order to achieve and preserve the desired living environment planned by the subdivider and for which the association and all of its members are responsible to maintain. When a person purchases property located in a CID, he or she should be prepared to give up some degree of autonomy and independence in the enjoyment of his or her property rights in exchange for the benefits of community living. Certain activities and conduct which might be entirely legal and acceptable in typical detached single-family residential neighborhoods may be restricted for the common good and benefit of all owners in a CID.

For example, an individual's subjective tastes and preferences in architectural style, exterior paint colors, and landscaping may be lawfully restricted and limited by the association's governing documents. In addition, other activities such as the playing of loud music, the keeping of noisy dogs, late-night workshop activities and generally any other conduct likely to interfere with the neighbors' enjoyment of their own properties or the common areas are frequently prohibited or curtailed in the association's governing documents. Although such activities may not be annoying to others in different circumstances, they often result in substantial interference with other owners' rights in the CID.

Persons contemplating the purchase of property located in a CID should be prepared to be responsible members of the CID association and comply with the enforceable provisions of the association's governing documents. The regulation of the conduct and activities of association members, their families and guests, and the conditions of the members' properties is an inherent component of common interest communities. As detailed in Chapters III and IV, all owners of property subject to a recorded declaration of CC&Rs are required by law to comply with the reasonable covenants and restrictions set forth in the declaration, as well as other rules and regulations adopted by the association commensurate with the authority granted to the association in the declaration and other governing documents. Those who are not willing to give up some degree of freedom in exchange for the benefits of community living, probably should not purchase property in the CID environment.

Property owners must also be willing to "roll up their sleeves" and participate in the democratic and political process of governing and operating their association and community. Active participation in community politics, whether serving on the board of directors, a committee or some other important volunteer position, gives the individual member an opportunity to shape and mold the character of the association for the common benefit of all association members.

POWERS AND AUTHORITY

The essence of a member's power and authority lies in the member's right to vote for the election of directors to the association's board of directors, remove directors from the board, amend the association's governing documents, and certain other important issues. The association's members ultimately control the association, its business and the path or direction the association takes through their exercise of their political rights of voting on such issues and serving on the governing board and committees.

SPECIFIC RIGHTS

As defined in the Nonprofit Mutual Benefit Corporation Law, persons holding a membership in a nonprofit mutual benefit corporation have those membership rights described in the corporation's articles of incorporation and bylaws and the Nonprofit Mutual Benefit Corporation Law.[12] In addition, CID association members also have certain other rights which are specified in the Davis-Stirling Common Interest Development Act and a number of court decisions. Some of the more important rights of CID property owners and association members are discussed individually in the following sections.

Election Of Directors:

Although a nonprofit mutual benefit corporation's articles or bylaws may provide for the designation or selection of up to one-third of the directors by means other than election by the members,[13] such a provision in a CID association's articles or bylaws would be extremely unusual. And so long as a majority of the association's voting power is held by the developer of the CID, the governing documents must specify that no less than twenty percent of the directors serving on the board must be elected solely by owners other than the developer.[14]

Ordinarily, the association members elect the directors at a meeting of the members. Corporations Code Section 7510(b) provides for the regular holding of members' meetings for this purpose:

> "A regular meeting of members shall be held on a date and time, and with the frequency stated in or fixed in accordance with the bylaws, but in any event in each year in which directors are to be elected at that meeting for the purpose of conducting such election, and to transact any other proper business which may be brought before the meeting."

However, so long as the members are not authorized to vote "cumulatively" (see definition below) for the election of directors, members may also select directors by conducting a mail ballot without holding an actual meeting of members.[15]

"Cumulative voting" for the election of directors is the description of that election process where each association member may cast a number of votes equal to the number of votes to which the member is entitled (ordinarily one vote per separate interest owned) multiplied by the number of directors to be elected.[16] The member may also distribute the number of votes which he or she may cast among the candidates as he or she chooses. For example, assume that each association member is entitled to one vote for each condominium unit or lot owned. Further assume that there are three vacancies to be filled on the board of directors and member Doe owns two lots and member Roe owns one lot. Cumulative voting permits member Doe to cast a total of six votes and distribute them among the candidates in any manner member Doe may choose, while member Roe has three votes which he or she may distribute in whatever manner he or she may choose.

Under the Department of Real Estate Regulations, cumulative voting is mandatory for all elections in which more than two positions on the board of directors are to be filled during the period of time that the developer owns or controls 25 percent or more of the votes entitled to be cast.[17] The Department of Real Estate Regulations are designed to guard against the developer's abuse of the political process by ensuring that the association's board of directors is not monopolized entirely by the agents of the developer or other persons elected solely by reason of the developer's control.

Other than the circumstance described above, where the developer owns or controls 25 percent or more of the votes, cumulative voting by association members is available only if the association's articles of incorporation or bylaws explicitly authorize cumulative voting.[18]

After the developer ceases to own or control 25 percent or more of the voting power, many associations amend their articles of incorporation and bylaws to delete the cumulative voting authority. To determine whether or not cumulative voting is permitted, associations and members must look to the language of the association's articles of incorporation and bylaws.

Removal Of Directors:

Generally speaking, directors elected by the members can only be removed from the board without cause by the members. The directors have no power or authority to oust a fellow director without cause.

Association members have alternative mechanisms to cause the removal of directors from the board in the event the need for such action arises. Removal of directors, popularly referred to as a "recall", is a severe remedy and can cause great division between association members and disharmony in the community. It is a remedy which should be used sparingly, only after other less extreme efforts to resolve problems have proved fruitless. Nevertheless, the power of association members to remove renegade, insurgent or troublemaking directors is an important right conferred on the members by law which cannot be overlooked.

Directors may remove a director from his or her position on the board in summary or expedited fashion for good cause only as defined by law. The summary removal of a director by the board of directors occurs where the board declares a director's position vacant either because: (1) a director is declared by a court order to be of unsound mind, (2) a director has been convicted of a felony, (3) a director has been found by a court to have breached his fiduciary duties in a corporation holding assets in charitable trust, or (4) the association's bylaws specify that a director may be removed for missing a specified number of board meetings and the director fails without legitimate excuse to attend the specified number of meetings.[19]

No such summary removal procedure is available to the association members. Instead, association members may remove directors from the board with or without cause through one of two alternative methods: (1) with the majority vote of either all of the members or those members attending a meeting, depending on the size of the association, at a regular or special meeting of the members,[20] or (2) a lawsuit filed in the Superior Court based on the director's fraudulent or dishonest acts or gross abuse of authority or discretion with reference to the association.[21]

The two methods of removal mentioned above and described in detail in the following paragraphs are the only two methods by which association members may remove directors from the board.[22] No other actions taken by the members can cause the removal of directors from their offices.

Removal Of Directors By Vote Of The Members:

Under Section 7222 of the Corporations Code the association members may remove any or all of the directors without cause at any time by majority vote of either all of the members, or a majority vote of the members represented in person or by proxy and voting at a regular or special meeting of the members, depending on the size of the association. Section 7222(a) of the Corporations Code reads in relevant part as follows:

> "Subject to subdivisions (b) and (f) of this section, any or all directors may be removed without cause if:
>
> "(1) In a corporation with fewer than 50 members, such removal is approved by a majority of all members (Section 5033).
>
> "(2) In a corporation with 50 or more members, such removal is approved by the members (Section 5034)."

In associations having fewer than 50 members, the members may successfully vote or cast written ballots for the removal of any or all directors so long as at least a majority of all members of the association eligible to vote approve the removal.[23]

In associations having 50 or more members, the members may successfully vote or cast written ballots for the removal of any or all directors so long as at least a majority of members represented and voting at the members' meeting, in person or by proxy, or pursuant to written ballot action, approve the removal.[24]

The Nonprofit Mutual Benefit Corporation Law includes a number of statutes specifying the proportion or percentage of members which must approve certain corporate actions. Associations are free, however, to adopt bylaws which require a greater proportion or percentage of membership approval of almost all corporate actions, except the voting requirements for the removal of directors, the effects of cumulative voting where such voting is permitted, and voluntary dissolution of the association.

Any association bylaws which purport to require a greater proportion of the members to approve a removal of directors than is specified in Corporations Code Section 7222(a)(1) or 7222(a)(2) are invalid and unenforceable.[25]

Additional Requirements Where Cumulative Voting Is Authorized Or Where The Members Of A Designated Class Are Entitled To Elect One Or More Directors:

If an association's articles of incorporation or bylaws authorize cumulative voting for the election of directors, additional requirements are imposed for the removal of directors by a vote of the members. When cumulative voting is authorized, no individual director can be removed (unless the entire board is removed) if the votes cast against removal would be sufficient to elect the director using cumulative voting.[26]

If the association's articles of incorporation or bylaws divide membership into two or more classes and permit the members of any class, voting as a class, to elect one or more directors, any director so elected can only be removed by the applicable vote of the members of that class.[27]

Removal Of Directors By Lawsuit Filed In Superior Court:

A lawsuit seeking a court order removing a director from the board of directors and barring his or her reelection for the director's fraudulent or dishonest acts or gross abuse of authority or discretion is available to the association members and other directors under the Nonprofit Mutual Benefit Corporation Law.[28]

Any such lawsuit must be filed by one or more association directors or by a group of association members. If the lawsuit is filed by members of the association, the number of members must equal twice the "authorized number" of members or 20 members, whichever is less, in associations where the total number of votes entitled to be cast for a director is less than 5,000, or twice the "authorized number" of members or 100 members, whichever is less, in associations where the total number of votes entitled to be cast for a director is 5,000 or more.[29] "Authorized number" of members is defined as: (1) 5 percent of the voting power of the association, or (2) where the total number of votes entitled to be cast for a director (disregarding cumulative voting) is 1,000 or more, but less than 5,000, 2 1/2 percent of the voting power but not less than 50, or (3) where the total number of votes entitled to be cast for a director (disregarding cumulative voting) is 5,000 or more, 1/20th of 1 percent of the voting power but not less than 125.[30]

Section 7223 of the Corporations Code which provides the mechanism for removal of a director by a lawsuit reads in relevant part as follows:

> "(a) The superior court of the proper county may, at the suit of one of the parties specified in subdivision (b), remove from office any director in case of fraudulent or dishonest acts or gross abuse of authority or discretion with reference to the corporation or breach of any duty arising as a result of Section 7238 [corporation holding assets in charitable trust] and may bar from reelection any director so removed for a period prescribed by the court. The corporation shall be made a party to such action.
>
> "(b) An action under subdivision (a) may be instituted by any of the following:
>
> "(1) A director.
>
> "(2) In the case of a corporation where the total number of votes entitled to be cast for a director is less than 5,000, twice the authorized number (Section 5036) of members,[31] or 20 members, whichever is less.
>
> "(3) In the case of a corporation where the total number of votes entitled to be cast for a director is 5,000 or more, twice the authorized number (Section 5036) of members, or 100 members, whichever is less."

As of the date of this writing, there are no published court cases interpreting or applying Section 7223 or explaining what acts, conduct or omissions by a director are sufficiently egregious to constitute "fraudulent or dishonest acts or gross abuse of authority or discretion" or to support a court order of removal. Section 304 of the Corporations Code, applicable to regular stock corporations, contains removal language virtually identical to the language of Section 7223. But, in the case of Section 304 there is unfortunately very little case law available to be of help. The few published cases addressing Section 304 all involved a director's alleged financial mismanagement or fraudulent or dishonest taking of corporate funds or property. None of the reported judicial decisions have involved other types of director behavior or conduct unrelated to financial affairs.

Amendment Of Governing Documents:

Association members generally have the power and authority to amend the association's governing documents.[32] This power and authority is another means by which the members can influence or control the course and policy direction of the association.

The procedures which must be followed, and the ease with which governing documents may be amended, depends on the type of governing document involved, the language of the particular governing document, and a variety of other factors, including the percentage of separate interests which may still be owned by the developer and the classes of membership if there are more than one.

A detailed discussion on the various methods by which the governing documents may be amended and the requirements which must be satisfied to effect valid amendments is found in Chapter VI.

Approval Of Assessment Increases:

The association's board of directors, without the approval of members, generally has the authority to increase regular assessments by as much as 20 percent greater than the prior fiscal year's regular assessments so long as the board has complied with certain financial disclosure requirements with respect to the fiscal year for which an assessment increase is proposed.[33]

Before the board of directors can increase the association's regular assessments without the approval of the members, the board must prepare and distribute to all association members a pro forma operating budget which must include a statement of estimated revenue and expenses on an accrual basis, a summary of the association's reserves, a statement as to whether the board has determined or anticipates the need for one or more special assessments, and a statement explaining the procedures used to calculate and establish reserves.[34] If more stringent financial disclosure requirements are required under the association's governing documents, the board must comply with those requirements.[35] The operating budget must be distributed to all members annually, not less than 45 days and no more than 60 days prior to the beginning of the association's fiscal year.[36]

On the other hand, where the regular assessment is proposed to be increased by more than 20 percent greater than the regular assessment levied for the association's preceding fiscal year, the property owners, by a majority of the votes cast at a meeting or election of the association at which a quorum is present, must approve the proposed increase.[37]

Similarly, special assessments which in the aggregate exceed 5 percent of the budgeted gross expenses of the association for the fiscal year in which the special assessments are proposed, must be approved by a majority of the votes at a meeting or election of the association.[38]

Attendance At Board Meetings:

All association members have the right to attend meetings of the association's board of directors, except when the board adjourns to executive session to consider litigation, matters related to the formation of contracts with third parties, personnel matters, and when the board meets in executive session to consider disciplinary action against a member when executive session is requested for this purpose by the affected member (the disciplined member may attend the executive session).[39]

Whether or not association members are entitled to speak or raise issues during meetings of the board of directors is not addressed by current law. Instead, the right of a member to speak or address the board of directors is determined by the association's governing documents, board policies and historical practices.

"Common Interest Development Open Meeting Act":

Beginning on January 1, 1996 associations and their boards of directors are subject to the "Common Interest Development Open Meeting Act". The Act was adopted by the legislature during 1995 and is intended to prohibit and discourage secret board meetings or gatherings of directors where authority may be abused by preliminary deliberation and decision making in the absence of board meetings for which the association members have been given notice and an opportunity to attend.[40] The Act is somewhat similar to, but less stringent than, the "Ralph M. Brown Act", which applies to meetings of local government bodies.

Parts of the Act are merely a reorganization of prior statutory law. The crucial substance of the Act is its relatively broad definition of board "meeting". Section 1363.05(f) of the Civil Code defines board "meeting" to include a gathering of a majority or greater number of the directors to hear, discuss or deliberate certain business of the association:

> "As used in this section, 'meeting' includes any congregation of a majority of the members of the board at the same time and place to hear, discuss, or deliberate upon any item of business scheduled to be heard by the board, except those matters that may be discussed in executive session.

All meetings of the board, except "emergency meetings", where timely notice to the members is impracticable, must be preceded with written notice posted, delivered or published in accordance with the Act. For purposes of the Act, "emergency meetings" are those which may be called by the president of the association, or by any two members of the board other than the president, "if there are circumstances that could not have been reasonably foreseen which require immediate attention and possible action by" the board, "and which of necessity make it impracticable to provide notice" to the members as required by the Act.[41]

Rights To Inspect And Copy Association Books And Records:

All association members are entitled to inspect and copy certain specified association records, books and documents.[42]

The documents that must be made available for member inspection and copying are:

(1) The record of all the members' names, addresses and voting rights;[43]

(2) A list of the names, addresses and voting rights of those members entitled to vote for the election of directors;[44]

(3) The accounting books and records of the association;[45]

(4) The minutes of proceedings of the members (members' meetings, actions and ballots taken without a meeting);[46]

(5) The minutes of proceedings of the board and committees of the board;[47]

(6) The association's articles of incorporation and bylaws, as amended;[48]

(7) All of the association's governing documents, including the declaration of CC&Rs, upon written request of a member.[49]

(8) A statement prepared by the association specifying the enforceability of restrictions limiting occupancy of a separate interest on the basis of age, if any exist, upon the written request of a member;[50]

(9) A copy of the most recent pro forma budget and financial and other documents prepared in accordance with Civil Code Section 1365, upon the written request of a member;[51]

(10) A statement prepared by an authorized representative of the association specifying the current regular and special assessments, the amount of assessments levied against the requesting member's separate interest, and the amount of assessments and other charges which are or may be made a lien on the date of the statement;[52]

(11) The association's application for tax-exempt status filed with the Internal Revenue Service and the corporation's annual return filed with the IRS.[53]

The minutes of board meetings, minutes proposed for adoption that are marked as draft status, or a summary of the minutes, of any meeting of the board, other than an executive session, must be available to the members within 30 days of the meeting and must be distributed to any member upon request and upon reimbursement of the association's costs in making that distribution.[54]

Members of the association must be notified in writing at the time the pro forma budget required under Civil Code Section 1365 is distributed, or at the time of any general mailing to the entire membership, of their right to have copies of the minutes of meetings of the board of directors and how and where copies of the minutes may be obtained.[55]

Members' Inspection Rights Include The Right To Make Copies:

The association members' rights of inspection and copying include the right to make photocopies (at a reasonable charge) of the documents within the above-described categories subject to inspection and copying. An agent or attorney of the member may exercise the right of inspection on behalf of the association member.[56]

Time Of Inspection And Copying:

The accounting books and records of the association and minutes of member and director meetings must be available for inspection upon a member's written demand "at any reasonable time," and the minutes of meetings must be made available to members within 30 days after the meeting.[57]

The articles of incorporation and bylaws must be available for inspection by members "at all reasonable times during office hours."[58]

If an association member requests in writing a copy of the association's governing documents, a statement specifying the enforceability of restrictions limiting occupancy of a separate interest on the basis of age, a copy of the pro forma budget and other financial documents prepared in accordance with Civil Code Section 1365, and/or a statement of the association's current regular and special assessments and the amount of assessments levied against the requesting member's separate interest on the date of the statement, the association must provide the requested information or documents within 10 days after the request is mailed or delivered.[59]

Limitations On Members' Inspection Rights:

The association member's rights to inspect and copy the association's accounting books and records must be for a purpose reasonably related the member's interests as a member of the association.[60]

Other than the minutes of board meetings, financial, governing, and corporate documents discussed above, the association is under no legal obligation to provide copies or permit member inspection and copying of any additional materials. However, an association may choose, as a matter of administrative policy, to permit the inspection and copying of additional documents.[61]

Association's Options When Member Demands List Of Names And Addresses Of Members Eligible To Vote For Directors:

When a member, by written demand, requests from the association a list of the names, addresses and voting rights of those members entitled to vote for the election of directors, the association may provide the requested list or permit the inspection and copying demanded by the member within five business days after receiving the demand.

On the other hand, if the association reasonably believes that the request is made not for a purpose reasonably related to the member's interests as a member of the association the association may deny the member access to the list,[62] or within ten business days after receiving the demand, the association may deliver to the member a written offer of a reasonable alternative method of achieving the purpose identified in the demand without providing access to or a copy of the membership list.[63]

Alternatively, within ten business days after receiving the demand (or a written rejection of the alternative method offered by the association), the association may petition the Superior Court for an order setting aside the demand, where the association believes, in good faith and with substantial basis, that the membership list demanded will be used for a purpose not reasonably related to the demanding person's interest as a member.[64]

In any legal action brought to enforce or set aside an inspection demand, if the court finds the association, without justification, failed to comply with a proper inspection demand, it may award reasonable attorney's fees to the demanding member.[65]

The association cannot insist that it be permitted to review the materials a member intends to distribute as a condition to permitting a member to inspect and copy the association's membership list.[66]

It is the member's legal obligation, however, to ensure that an association membership list is used only for purposes reasonably related to that person's interests as an association member. An association's membership list is the association's property. Without the consent of the board of directors, neither the membership list nor any part of it may be used for any purpose which is not reasonably related to the member's interest as a member of the association.[67]

The association may obtain an injunction to restrain the misuse of its membership list and may obtain money damages, including punitive damages, as well as court costs and attorney's fees against any person who misuses a membership list.[68]

MEMBERSHIP PROTECTIONS

General Requirements With Respect To Notice And Delivery Of Information To Members:

Unless another statute in the Corporations Code or the Davis-Stirling Common Interest Development Act specifies the type and delivery of notice which must be provided by an association, the general rules set forth in the Corporations Code will apply. There are many statutes which do include more specific notice and delivery requirements and those statutes will govern those specific situations. The following are merely the general rules which will apply in the absence of more specific rules.

Except as otherwise specifically required, any reference in the Corporations Code to the "mailing" of notices or other information means first, second, or third-class mail, postage prepaid, unless registered mail is specified. Registered mail includes certified mail.[69]

Except as otherwise specifically stated, any reference in the Corporations Code to the time a notice is given or sent means the time a written notice by mail is deposited in the United States mails, postage prepaid, or the time any other written notice is personally delivered to the recipient or is delivered to a common carrier for transmission, or actually transmitted by the person giving the notice by electronic means, to the recipient, or the time any oral notice is communicated in person or by telephone or wireless, to the recipient or to a person at the office of the recipient who the person giving the notice has reason to believe will promptly communicate it to the recipient.[70]

A notice or report mailed or delivered as part of a newsletter, magazine or other publication regularly sent to the members constitutes written notice pursuant to the Nonprofit Mutual Benefit Corporation Law when it is addressed and mailed or delivered to the member, or in the case of members who are residents of the same household and who have the same address on the books of the corporation, when addressed and mailed or delivered to one of such members, at the address appearing on the books of the corporation.[71]

Discipline In Executive (Closed) Session Of Board Meetings:

Any member who is subject to being disciplined by the association, including those occasions when the association intends to impose monetary fines or penalties or suspend membership rights, may request that the board of directors meet in executive session to consider or accomplish any such disciplinary action. If the member being disciplined makes the request, the board must meet in executive session for that purpose and the disciplined member has the right to attend that portion of the executive session during which the disciplinary action is considered, discussed or taken.[72]

Suspension Of Membership Rights:

The governing documents of most CID associations include provisions under which association members' membership rights may be suspended. In fact, the Department of Real Estate Regulations which govern the contents of the governing documents as originally prepared by the declarant or developer of the CID require that such provisions be included in the governing documents.[73]

The courts have long provided for the protection against unreasonable or unfair terminations of membership rights in organized societies and associations by insisting that a certain minimum level of fairness be provided to affected members. The fairness, or due process, required includes at a minimum that the affected member be given notice of the charges against him or her which may lead to termination or suspension and an opportunity to refute those charges in front of the governing body holding the authority to make the decision.

Under Section 7341 of the Corporations Code, generally speaking no member of an association may be expelled or suspended, and no membership may be terminated or suspended, except according to the procedures satisfying Section 7341.[74] The fundamental requirements which must be met are that any expulsion or suspension "must be done in good faith and in a fair and reasonable manner". Section 7341 then specifies a fair and reasonable procedure, but also states that a court may find other, alternative, procedures to be fair and reasonable when the full circumstances of the expulsion or suspension are considered. In other words, Section 7341 contains a membership suspension, termination or expulsion procedure which is deemed to be fair and reasonable, but the statutory procedure is not necessarily exclusive.

The Section 7341 procedure which is deemed to be fair and reasonable requires that[75]:

(1) The provisions of the procedure are contained in the association's articles or bylaws, or copies of the provisions are sent annually to all the association members as required by the articles or bylaws;

(2) The procedure provides the giving of 15 days' prior notice to the affected member of the expulsion, suspension or termination and the reasons for the discipline; and

(3) The procedure provides an opportunity for the member to be heard, orally or in writing, not less than five days before the effective date of the expulsion, suspension or termination by a person or body authorized to decide that the proposed expulsion, termination or suspension not take place.

The notices which may be required under Section 7341 may be given by any method reasonably calculated to provide actual notice to the member. Any notice given by mail must be given by first-class or registered mail sent to the last address of the member shown on the association's records.

Section 7341 of the Corporations Code addresses only the procedural fairness and reasonableness of a membership suspension, expulsion or termination. It does not govern or address the substantive grounds for any such disciplinary action.[76] Even though an association's procedures for suspending or terminating a membership may be procedurally fair and reasonable and consistent with the requirements of Section 7341, a disciplinary action based on substantive grounds which violate contractual or other rights of the member or which are otherwise unlawful are not validated simply because Section 7341 is complied with.[77]

Section 7341 contains a one-year statute of limitations. Any legal action challenging an expulsion, suspension or termination of membership, must be commenced within one year after the date of the expulsion, suspension or termination.[78]

Where fair procedures in suspending or terminating membership rights are not provided or not followed, the courts appear to presume that such failure is prejudicial to the aggrieved member and the termination or suspension decision is subject to being reversed by the courts.[79]

Ordinarily, decisions made by the association's board of directors are reviewed by the courts applying the "business judgment" rule, under which the courts will not disturb or "second guess" the board so long as the board has acted in good faith and with a view consistent with the best interests of the association and all of its members.[80] Where, however, a membership association allegedly fails to provide an aggrieved member with a minimum level of due process before suspending or terminating the member's membership rights, the courts will examine whether the contested decision is substantively rational and procedurally fair.[81] The courts will interfere with an association's decision to expel a member if the rules of the association governing expulsion or suspension have not been followed or if the accused member has not been afforded those rudimentary rights which will give him a reasonable opportunity to defend against the charges made.[82]

No Notice Or Hearing May Be Necessary For Suspension For Failure To Pay Assessments Where Bylaws Provide For Automatic Suspension:

Where an association's bylaws specifically permit the suspension of membership rights without a hearing because of a member's failure to pay assessments, or some other violation for which the fact of the violation and the identity of the member are not seriously in question, the membership rights may be suspended without providing the member with an opportunity for a hearing on the matter.[83]

Suspension Of Membership Rights When Member Owns More Than One Separate Interest:

Sometimes a question may arise concerning the effect of membership suspension when the member owns more than one lot, unit, parcel or apartment in the development. For example, if an owner owns three lots and has failed to pay assessments levied on one lot, does a suspension of membership rights based on that default effectively terminate or suspend the owner's membership rights attached to the remaining two lots?

Just like many other issues considered in this book, the answer depends to a great extent on the language of the association's governing documents.

If the association's governing documents establish that a property owner holds one membership for each separate interest owned, suspension of membership rights with respect to one separate interest may not effectively result in total suspension with respect to all of the separate interests owned.[84] Conversely, if the governing documents do not address the issue or if they specify that a property owner holds one membership in the association, regardless of the number of separate interests he or she owns, a suspension arising out of the owner's default with respect to one property will effectively suspend his or her membership rights with respect to all separate interests he or she may own.

The controlling statute is found in Section 7312(d) of the California Corporations Code which prohibits multiple memberships, unless the association's articles of incorporation or bylaws provide otherwise. Section 7312(d) reads as follows:

> "No person may hold more than one membership, and no fractional memberships may be held, provided, however, that:
>
> "(d) In the case of membership in an owners association, (as defined in Section 11003.1 of the Business and Professions Code, and created in connection with any of the forms of development referred to in Section 11004.5 of the Business and Professions Code) the articles or bylaws may permit a person who owns an interest, or who has a right of exclusive occupancy, in more than one lot, parcel, area, apartment, or unit to hold a separate membership in the owners association for each such lot, parcel, area, apartment, or unit."

Although Corporations Code Section 7312(d) permits a CID association to provide for an owner to hold one association membership for each separate interest owned, such multiple membership is not required. If the association's articles of incorporation and bylaws are silent on this issue, Section 7312(d) effectively prohibits such multiple memberships. In that event, a suspension arising out of the owner's default with respect to one property will effectively suspend the membership rights, regardless of the number of properties he or she may own.

Members Cannot Be Disciplined For Exercising Their Rights To Seek Judicial Redress:

Associations cannot discipline members who prosecute lawsuits in good faith against the association, even if the lawsuit is unsuccessful, simply because the member resorted to litigation.[85] When a person has a legitimate claim to seek redress for the violation of his or her rights, he or she must have access to our judicial system. The courts have protected this access by holding that a member cannot be expelled or suspended from an association simply because he or she prosecutes litigation against the association. If the rule were otherwise, the threat of membership suspension or expulsion could have a "chilling" effect on a member's civil rights to seek redress in our courts.

MEETINGS AND VOTING

Probably the most important aspect of association government is active membership involvement. Without membership involvement, it is frequently difficult for the board of directors to have an accurate sense or assessment of membership needs, goals and desires. As elected governing board members, the directors should make every reasonable effort to represent their constituents, the association members, while fulfilling their legal responsibilities and duties to the association.

While there are many valuable ways for association members to contribute to the community, including volunteering for committees and various community works projects, perhaps the most effective participation is through the exercise of the member's voting power. Unfortunately, in the author's professional experience, many associations suffer from such extensive voter apathy that they cannot even establish a quorum of members at many annual meetings of members. Without a quorum of members present at such meetings, no business may be conducted and no directors may be elected.

While voter apathy may indicate that a larger proportion of members are satisfied with the status quo, it can also indicate a widespread feeling of dissatisfaction and hopelessness, or simply a general uncaring attitude. Regardless of the cause of voter apathy, it is generally not healthy for any community, including a CID. Associations and their boards of directors and managers should take all reasonable steps available to encourage membership participation in the association's governing processes. An extremely important way of encouraging such participation is through education and a good fundamental understanding of the processes by which the association is governed. The remainder of this Chapter is devoted to that subject with the hope that members and directors alike will have a fuller understanding of the political and legal processes which are an integral part of association government.

Prior to and during any meeting of members of an association, whether the meeting is a regular annual meeting or a special meeting, a wide variety of issues must be dealt with and handled properly in order for the meeting to run smoothly and comply with applicable legal requirements. Candidates for the board of directors must be sought and nominated, notices of meetings and agendas must be prepared and distributed, and proxy and ballot forms must be prepared.

A thorough discussion of the requirements governing the nominations of candidates and elections of directors is found in Chapter VIII.

Time And Conduct Of Regular Meetings:

The first meeting of the association members must be held within 45 days after the close of escrow of the sale of the separate interest (lot, parcel, unit or apartment) representing the 51st percentile interest authorized for sale in developments with 50 separate interests or more, but no later than six months after the close of escrow of the sale of the first separate interest in all developments regardless of the number of separate interests.[86]

Ordinarily, at the time the first meeting of members is to be held, the developer will still control the voting power of the association and its governing body and the developer will be responsible for the proper meeting notices to be given to all other association members.

Regular meetings of association members must be held with the frequency and on the dates and times stated in the association's bylaws.[87] Regardless of whether or not regular meeting dates and times are prescribed in the association's bylaws, regular meetings of members must be held in each year in which directors are to be elected at such a meeting.[88]

Membership meetings must be held at the location specified in the association's bylaws or, if no location is specified, the meetings must be held at the association's principal office.[89]

All meetings of members must be conducted in accordance with some recognized system of parliamentary procedure, such as Robert's Rules of Order, or some other form of parliamentary procedures adopted by the association.[90] This statutory requirement is intended to encourage order and decorum at membership meetings in order to facilitate membership participation and the transaction of meaningful business in an efficient manner.

Time And Conduct Of Special Meetings Of Members

In addition to the regular meetings of association members, frequently held only annually, special meetings of members for any lawful purpose may also be called and held. Special meetings of members may be called by:[91] (1) the board of directors; (2) the chairman of the board; (3) the president; or (4) such other persons, if any, as specified in the bylaws. In addition, special meetings of members for any lawful purpose may be called by 5 percent or more of the members.

Notice Of And Date Of Special Meeting Of Members:

Upon written request to the chairman of the board, president, vice-president, or secretary by any person (other than the board) entitled to call a special meeting of members, the officer receiving the written request must promptly cause notice of the meeting to be given to all members entitled to vote.[92]

The notice of special meeting must state that a special meeting will be held on a date determined by the board but not less than 35 days nor more than 90 days after receipt of the written request.[93]

If the notice of special meeting is not given within 20 days after the officer's receipt of the written request for the holding of the meeting, the persons entitled to call the special meeting may give the notice of meeting or petition the Superior Court to summarily order the giving of the notice.[94]

CONTENTS AND DELIVERY OF NOTICE OF MEETINGS OF MEMBERS

All meetings of members, whether regular or special, must be preceded with a written notice of meeting. The notice of meeting must contain certain information required by law, be delivered to all members entitled to vote at the meeting within certain prescribed times in advance of the meetings, and be delivered to the members in a required manner.

Section 7511(a) of the Corporations Code requires that the following criteria be satisfied with respect to notices of regular and special meetings of members:

(1) Written notice of the meeting must be given no less than 10 days and no more than 90 days before the date of the meeting to each member entitled to vote as of the record date for notice of the meeting, provided the notice is mailed by first-class, registered or certified mail;

(2) If the written notice is mailed, but is not mailed by first-class, registered or certified mail, the written notice must be given not less than 20 days before the meeting;[95]

(3) The written notice of meeting must state the place, date and time of the meeting;

(4) In the case of regular meetings, the notice must also state the general nature of those matters which the board, at the time the notice is given, intends to present for action by the members. However, except where meetings with less than a 1/3 quorum are authorized and conducted, any proper matter may be presented at the meeting for the action;

(5) In the case of special meetings, the notice must also state the general nature of the business to be transacted, and no other business may be transacted.

(6) A written notice of any meeting at which directors are to be elected must include the names of all persons nominated at the time the notice is given.

In addition, if any of the nine following special business matters are intended to be acted upon by the members at a meeting of members, the general nature of those matters must be stated in the notice of meeting:[96] (1) removal of a director without cause;[97] (2) filling vacancies on the board of directors resulting from the removal of directors;[98] (3) approval of contracts or transactions between the corporation and a director with a material financial interest therein;[99] (4) amendment of the articles of incorporation or the bylaws repealing, restricting, creating or expanding proxy rights;[100] (5) certain specified amendments of the articles of incorporation, primarily prohibiting the amendment of any provision of the articles requiring approval of the members for a particular corporate action;[101] (6) disposition of all or substantially all of the association's assets;[102] (7) a merger of the corporation with another corporation;[103] (8) amendment of any agreement of merger;[104] (9) dissolution of the corporation;[105]

Quorum:

A majority of the voting power, held by association members, represented in person or by proxy, constitutes a quorum at a meeting of members. The bylaws may, however, set a different quorum. If an association's bylaws permit a meeting of members to be held with a quorum of less than 1/3 of the voting power, the only matters which may be voted on at any regular meeting actually attended, in person or by proxy, by less than 1/3 of the voting power are those matters the general nature of which was described in the notice of meeting.[106]

VOTING AT MEETINGS OF MEMBERS

Number of Votes: Distribution Of Voting Power Between Developer And Other Members:

The Department of Real Estate Regulations permit the subdivider or developer to prepare governing documents providing for two classes of membership, "Class A" members who are all owners other than the subdivider and a "Class B" member who is the developer. Class A members are entitled to one vote for each separate interest owned in the development. The regulations permit the Class B member, the developer, to hold up to a maximum of three votes for each separate interest owned.[107]

The Department of Real Estate Regulations then provide a mandatory plan by which Class B membership is irreversibly converted to Class A membership (thus reducing the developer's voting power) upon the happening of specified events during the time the developer's interests in the development are phased out through sales of the separate interests.[108]

General Voting Power Rules:

With the exception of the developer's voting power prior to the conversion of Class B to Class A membership, the general rule applicable in most CIDs is the "one vote per member" rule.

Except as may otherwise be provided in an association's articles of incorporation or bylaws or except in the case of "cumulative voting", each member is entitled to one vote on each matter submitted to a vote of the membership.[109] In most mutual benefit corporations no person may hold more than one membership. However, a special rule for CID associations is found in the Corporations Code which authorizes the articles of incorporation or bylaws of the association to permit a person to hold a separate membership for each separate interest owned by that person.[110] In addition, no fractional memberships are permitted in a nonprofit mutual benefit corporation.[111]

In a true "one lot - one vote" setting, a member is entitled to one vote on each matter presented to the members for action at the meeting. If the election of directors is considered as one matter, then each member should be entitled to only one vote for the election, regardless of the number of vacancies on the Board.

On the other hand, if, as is the more common practice, each vacancy on the board is considered to be a separate "matter" for purposes of voting, then each member is entitled to a cast one vote for each vacant seat on the board. For example, under most governing documents each member is entitled to a number of votes equal to the number of lots or units owned by him or her multiplied by the number of vacancies on the board.

Voting Jointly-Owned Property Votes:

Where the ownership of a lot, parcel, or unit is legally titled in the names of two or more persons, for example joint tenants or tenants in common, a vote by one owner binds all owners, unless the secretary of the corporation is given advance written notice to the contrary.[112]

The association's bylaws themselves may constitute such notice to the secretary and if they provide that all joint owners of a property must sign a ballot or proxy or otherwise jointly vote the membership attributable to that property, all must vote and a vote by one joint owner alone is not a valid vote and cannot be counted.[113]

Cumulative Voting:

"Cumulative voting" is a voting mechanism that applies only to the election of directors. It does not apply to any other business matters transacted by the association members. Cumulative voting, where it is authorized, permits a member to cast a total number of votes equal to the number of memberships held multiplied by the number of vacancies on the board of directors. Cumulative voting also permits the member to cast all of his or her votes for one candidate or to distribute his or her votes among the various candidates in whatever manner the member chooses.

Members of CID associations incorporated as nonprofit mutual benefit corporations are entitled to cumulate their votes for the election of directors only if the association's articles of incorporation or bylaws authorize cumulative voting.[114]

Even where cumulative voting is authorized in the association's articles of incorporation or bylaws, no member can cumulate votes for a candidate or candidates unless the candidates' name(s) have been placed in nomination prior to the voting.[115] In addition, no member is entitled to cumulate votes until at least one member has given notice at the meeting of his or her intention to cumulate votes. If any one member has given notice of such intention to cumulate votes, all members may cumulate their votes.[116]

Use Of Proxies By Association Members:

Members of California nonprofit mutual benefit corporations have the right to vote by proxy at all meetings of members, unless such right is withdrawn, limited or restricted by the articles of incorporation or the bylaws. The proxy rights are conferred on members by statute.[117] The statutory right to vote by proxy may not be eliminated, restricted or expanded unless such alteration is done by amendment of the articles of incorporation or bylaws approved by the members.[118]

Frequently, the association itself prepares forms of proxies which are then distributed to the association members for their use. In preparing a form of proxy, the association needs to ensure that the form meets all of the legal requirements which may apply, keeping in mind that the requirements may vary according to the size of the association. A member's use of a proxy form prepared by the association is not mandatory, so long as the form of proxy used by the member also complies with all of the applicable requirements with respect to form and content.

Commonly, both stock and nonprofit corporations prepare their proxy forms designating or naming the board of directors, or a majority of them, as the proxyholder, that is, the person who will actually exercise the proxy on behalf of the absent member. This practice is in widespread use.[119] When the proxies are undirected, meaning the voting member has not specified a choice as to how he or she wishes his or her votes cast, the proxyholder may cast the votes in any manner the proxyholder determines.

Where proxy forms designate or name the board of directors, or any other group of persons, as the proxyholder, the persons so designated are to determine by an act of the majority how to cast the votes represented in the proxy.[120]

Use Of Proxies, Ballots, Or Memberships Of Suspended Members For Purposes Of Determining Presence Of Quorum:

The membership, proxy, ballot or vote of members whose rights to vote have been suspended or otherwise terminated cannot be used or counted for purposes of determining a quorum at a meeting of members.[121]

Use Of Ballots/Proxies With Votes For Directors Marked Withheld:

Where a proper written ballot or proxy is marked by the member to indicate the member's desire to withhold votes for the election of directors, the ballot or proxy may still be counted for purposes of determining whether a quorum of members is present at the annual meeting.[122]

Distinctions Between Proxy And Ballot:

A "proxy" is defined by the California Nonprofit Corporation Law as:

> "[A] written authorization signed by a member or the member's attorney in fact giving another person or persons power to vote on behalf of such member."[123]

The word "signed" as used in the context of a proxy means the placing of the member's name on the proxy, whether by manual signature, typewriting, telegraphic transmission or otherwise, and includes facsimile transmission.[124]

Simply put, a "proxy" is a written document giving a person or persons the power to vote on behalf of a member. Other than the requirements that it be in writing and be signed (as defined by the statute) by the member, there is no requirement that the proxy be in any particular form. However, a form of proxy to be valid must describe the general nature of certain matters that are to be voted upon. In addition, for California nonprofit mutual benefit corporations with 100 or more members, the form of proxy must contain certain other specified matters.

"Proxyholder" means the person or persons to whom a proxy is given by the member.[125] A member may give an unlimited and unrestricted proxy to his or her proxyholder by conferring all authority to vote on behalf of the member but not specifying how the member desires to vote (a "blank check"). Or, the member may designate in his or her proxy how the votes are to be cast (a "directed proxy"). Where the member specifies in the proxy form how his or her votes are to be cast, the proxyholder is legally obligated to cast the votes in the manner specified.[126]

A "ballot", on the other hand, is a document used to cast or register a vote by the vote holder/member. There is no third party involved, and no intermediary, agent or proxyholder is voting or casting the vote on behalf of the member.

Unless Prohibited In The Association's Articles Of Incorporation Or Bylaws, Members May Take Action At Meetings Of Members Or By Written Ballot Without A Meeting:

In California there are two primary ways by which associations may solicit and take action by their members: (1) a meeting of members attended by the members in person or by proxy and at which members may cast their votes in person or by proxy, and (2) a written ballot procedure where there is no actual meeting of members and members are given a specified period of time to complete and return their ballots to a specified place for counting.

A third method by which association members may take action is by "unanimous written consent". If all members, either individually or collectively, consent in writing to take the action, any action permitted or required to be taken by the members may be taken without a meeting.[127] The requirement of unanimity, however, will in most cases make this form of membership action impracticable except in the smallest of associations.

Unless an association's articles of incorporation or bylaws prohibit members from taking action by written ballot without a meeting, any action which members may take at a regular or special meeting (except the election of directors by cumulative voting) may be conducted by written ballot without a meeting of members.[128]

As used in the California Nonprofit Corporation Law, "written ballot" does not include a ballot distributed at a special or regular meeting of members.[129] In other words, wherever used in the statutory provisions applicable to nonprofit mutual benefit corporations, "written ballot" refers to ballots which are solicited from the members for membership action without a meeting of the members. For example, at any meeting of members, where the election of directors is conducted with secret written ballots distributed at the meeting, such ballots are not "written ballots" within the meaning prescribed by the California Nonprofit Corporation Law.

Directors may be elected by "written ballot" of the members without a meeting where such action is authorized by the articles of incorporation or bylaws, except that election by "written ballot" may not be authorized where the directors are elected by cumulative voting pursuant to Corporations Code Section 7615.[130]

Form, Content and Use of Proxies:

The general rule prescribing the contents of proxies used by corporations with 100 or more members is found in Corporations Code Section 7514(a):

"Any form of proxy or written ballot distributed to 10 or more members of a corporation with 100 or more members shall afford an opportunity on the proxy or form of written ballot to specify a choice between approval and disapproval of each matter or group of related matters intended, at the time the written ballot or proxy is distributed, to be acted upon at the meeting for which the proxy is solicited or by such written ballot, and shall provide, subject to reasonable specified conditions, that where the person solicited specifies a choice with respect to any such matter the vote shall be cast in accordance therewith."

Corporations Code Section 7514(b) then mandates that certain proxies not be voted for the election of any director:

"In any election of directors, any form of proxy or written ballot in which the directors to be voted upon are named therein as candidates and which is marked by a member "withhold" or otherwise marked in a manner indicating that the authority to vote for the election of directors is withheld shall not be voted either for or against the election of a director."

Finally, Corporations Code Section 7514(c) specifies the effect of using proxies which fail to comply with Section 7514:

"Failure to comply with this section shall not invalidate any corporate action taken, but may be the basis for challenging any proxy at a meeting or written ballot and the superior court may compel compliance therewith at the suit of any member."

Duration of Proxies:

All forms of proxies expire and are of no further force or effect 11 months after the date of the proxy, unless the proxy itself states that it is to endure for a longer period of time. However, the maximum duration of any proxy is three years from the date it is signed.[131]

Revocability Of Proxies:

All proxies are revocable by the member signing the proxy, unless the proxy itself states that it is irrevocable and meets other requirements to make it irrevocable. Every proxy continues in full force and effect until it expires or until it is revoked by the person executing it, prior to the proxy being exercised by the casting of the votes represented by the proxy.[132] If the person giving the proxy desires to revoke it, it must be revoked prior to the time it is exercised by the proxyholder.

A proxy is not revoked by the death or mental or physical incapacity of the member making the proxy or the termination of a membership as a result of such death or incapacity unless, before the vote is counted, written notice of such death or incapacity is received by the association.[133]

Three methods are available to members to revoke a previously issued proxy: (1) a revocation in writing delivered to the association stating that the proxy is revoked; (2) a subsequent proxy executed by the person executing the prior proxy and presented to the meeting (the dates contained on the forms of proxy presumptively determine the order of execution, regardless of the postmark dates on the envelopes in which they are mailed); or (3) as to any meeting, by the attendance of the member signing the proxy at such meeting and voting in person.[134]

Irrevocable Proxies:

Proxies may sometimes in limited circumstances be made irrevocable, that is, not susceptible to being changed or canceled. In nonprofit mutual benefit corporations proxies may be made irrevocable only if the proxy is given to one of three specified categories of persons, and, even then, it remains irrevocable only until the happening of certain events.

Unless otherwise provided in the association's articles or bylaws, the proxy of a member which states that it is irrevocable is irrevocable for the period specified in the proxy when it is held by any of the following persons: (1) a person who has purchased or who has agreed to purchase the membership; (2) a creditor or creditors of the corporation or the member who extended or continued credit to the corporation or the member in consideration of the proxy if the proxy states that it was given in consideration of such extension or continuation of credit and the name of the person extending or continuing the credit; or (3) a person who has contracted to perform services as an employee of the corporation, if the proxy is required by the contract of employment and if the proxy states that it was given in consideration of such contract of employment, the name of the employee and the period of employment.[135]

In addition to the above three circumstances, a proxy may be made irrevocable if it is given to secure the performance of a duty or to protect a title, either legal or equitable, until the happening of events which, by its terms, discharge the obligations secured by it.[136]

In spite of the period of irrevocability which may be specified in the proxy, the proxy becomes revocable when the agreement to purchase is terminated, the debt of the corporation or the member is paid, or the period of employment provided for in the contract of employment has terminated.[137]

Other Matters Which Are Required To Be Stated In The Proxy Form Or Written Ballot:

Corporations Code Section 7514(a) requires that any form of proxy or written ballot "afford [the member] an opportunity on the proxy or form of written ballot to specify a choice between approval or disapproval of each matter or group of related matters ... intended to be acted upon at the meeting ..."

In addition to the above requirements, any form of revocable proxy covering the following matters is not valid as to such matters unless the proxy form sets forth the general nature of the matter to be voted on:[138]

(1) Removal of a director without cause;[139]

(2) Filling vacancies on the board of directors resulting from the removal of directors;[140]

(3) Approval of contracts or transactions between the corporation and a director with a material financial interest therein;[141]

(4) Amendment of the articles of incorporation or thebylaws repealing, restricting, creating or expanding proxy rights;[142]

(5) Certain specified amendments of the articles of incorporation, primarily prohibiting the amendment of any provision of the articles requiring approval of the members for a particular corporate action;[143]

(6) Disposition of all or substantially all of thecorporation's assets;[144]

(7) A merger of the corporation with another corporation;[145]

(8) Amendment of any agreement of merger;[146]

(9) Dissolution of the corporation;[147]

Association Should Not Cast Votes Attributable To Association Owned Properties:

An association may sometimes acquire title to separate interests in the development, whether through foreclosure of a delinquent assessment lien, deed in lieu of foreclosure, or otherwise. The board of directors of an association should not, at a meeting of the members or written ballot of the members, attempt to cast votes attributable to association properties. There is currently no law directly addressing this issue in the context of CIDs or other types of nonprofit mutual benefit corporations. However, because the association is not a "member" of itself, it would appear that it cannot vote or take action as a member. Furthermore, the law governing stock corporations prohibits the stock corporation from voting shares of stock that it may own.[148] This rule was developed by the courts to prevent incumbent boards of directors from perpetuating themselves in office. The logic of the rule would appear to apply equally as well to nonprofit mutual benefit corporations.

Inspectors Of Election:

In advance of any meeting of members, the association's board of directors may appoint inspectors of election to perform certain acts at the meeting. If appointed, the inspectors of election are to determine the number of memberships, the voting power of each, the number of members represented at the meeting, the existence of a quorum, the authenticity, validity and effect of proxies, receive votes, ballots or consents, hear and determine all challenges and questions in any way arising in connection with the right to vote, tabulate all votes or consents, determine when the polls shall close, determine the results of the election or vote, and do such other acts as may be proper to conduct the election or vote with fairness to all members.[149]

The number of inspectors of election must be either one or three.[150] If inspectors are to be appointed, the association should ensure that either one or three are appointed in order to avoid subsequent challenges to the validity of an election based on the assertion that an improper number of inspectors were appointed.

In the event the board of directors fails to appoint inspectors of election, or if any of the persons so appointed fail to appear or refuse to act, the chairman of any meeting of members may, and on the request of any member or member's proxy shall, appoint inspectors of election.[151]

The inspectors of election are required to act impartially and in good faith to the best of their abilities and as expeditiously as practical.[152]

If there are three inspectors of election, they are to act by majority decision. The decision, act or certificate of a majority of them is the decision, act or certificate of all.[153]

Members' Eligibility To Cast Votes At Meetings Of Members Or Written Ballots Conducted By The Association

Record Date For Giving Notice Of Meeting Of Members:

The association's bylaws may provide a date or method of fixing a date as the "record date" for determining the members entitled to receive notice of any meeting of members. If the bylaws do not include any such date or method of fixing the date, the board of directors may fix, in advance of the meeting, the record date for determining the members entitled to receive notice of any meeting of members.[154]

Whether the record date is specified in the association's bylaws or determined by the board of directors, the record date cannot be more than 90 days nor less than 10 days before the date of the meeting.[155]

If no record date is specified in the bylaws or set by the board of directors, in advance of the meeting, all members at the close of business on the business day preceding the day on which the notice of meeting is given are entitled to receive notice of the meeting.[156]

Record Date For Voting At Meeting Of Members:

The association's bylaws may specify a date or method of determining a date as the "record date" for determining the members entitled to vote at a meeting of members. In the absence of such a bylaw provision, the board of directors may fix, in advance of the meeting, the record date for determining the members entitled to vote at a meeting of members.[157]

Whether the record date is specified in the association's bylaws or determined by the board of directors, the record date cannot be more than 60 days before the date of the meeting.[158]

In the event the meeting of members is adjourned for any reason, the record date previously specified or determined shall also apply in the case of an adjournment of the meeting unless the board of directors fixes a new record date for the adjourned meeting.[159]

If no record date is specified in the bylaws or set by the board of directors, in advance of the meeting, all members on the day of the meeting who are otherwise eligible to vote are entitled to vote at the meeting of members.[160]

Record Date For Written Ballots:

Where, instead of a meeting of members, an association plans to take action by written ballot of the members, the association's bylaws may provide a date as the "record date" for determining the members entitled to cast written ballots. In the absence of such a bylaw provision, the board of directors may fix, in advance, a date as the record date for determining the members entitled to cast written ballots.[161]

Whether the record date is specified in the association's bylaws or determined by the board of directors, the record date cannot be more than 60 days before the day on which the first written ballot is mailed or solicited.[162]

If no record date is specified in the bylaws or set by the board of directors, in advance of the balloting, all members on the day the first written ballot is mailed or solicited who are otherwise eligible to vote are entitled to cast ballots.[163]

Delegation Of Common Area And Amenity Use Rights By Members To Tenants And Lessees

Ordinarily, the membership in a CID association is appurtenant to (or tied together with) ownership of a separate interest in the development and is not transferable, except upon the sale or other conveyance of all of the member's title in the separate interest. Civil Code Section 1358 provides that when an owner's "entire estate" is transferred by conveyance, judicial sale or other voluntary or involuntary transfer, the transfer also conveys the owner's membership interest in the association.[164]

When a member rents or leases his or her separate interest, the member has not transferred his or her "entire estate" within the meaning of Civil Code Section 1358. Instead, the member continues to own and hold a "reversionary interest", which will entitle the owner to full possession and enjoyment of the property once the lease or rental agreement has expired or has been otherwise terminated.

The governing documents of many associations do permit the owner of a separate interest to delegate his or her common area and amenity use rights to a tenant or lessee of the owner's separate interest. The question is sometimes raised whether, after such delegation, both the owner and his or her tenant may use the common areas and facilities of the development.

Recently, the California Court of Appeal ruled that nonresident property owners who lease or rent their property to lessees or tenants may be lawfully excluded from using the association's common area facilities and amenities, at least where the property owner has delegated his or her use rights to the lessee or tenant and the recorded declaration or rules adopted by the association pursuant to and consistent with the declaration authorize such use prohibitions.[165]

The Court's rationale was that the added burden from use by nonresident owners in addition to tenants and owner-residents could potentially greatly increase the number of individuals competing for use of the association's facilities, which in turn decreases availability to resident owners and reduces the attractiveness of a the development.

On the other hand, a CID association may not discriminate among its members by prohibiting nonresident members from using and enjoying the common areas, including recreational facilities within the development, solely because the members are not resident members.[166]

Limited Liability Protection For Members - Minimum Insurance Requirements:

Several California cases have allowed personal injury claimants to sue the members, as well as the association, for personal injuries sustained in the common areas of the development.[167] The cases have involved developments in which the common areas were owned in common by the members, not the association.

In order to provide CID association members with protection against such claims, the California Legislature enacted Section 1365.9 of the Civil Code. Section 1365.9 protects the association members from being sued merely because they own the common areas as co-tenants in undivided fractional interests if the association maintains a certain level of general liability insurance.[168]

The statute requires that such lawsuits be brought only against the association if the association has procured and maintained, for the type of claim asserted, one or more policies of insurance which include coverage for general liability of the association. In order for the protection to be available, the insurance coverage must be in the following minimum amounts: (1) at least $2,000,000 if the development consists of 100 or fewer separate interests, or (2) at least $3,000,000 if the development consists of more than 100 separate interests.[169]

CHAPTER VIII

DIRECTORS, OFFICERS AND MANAGEMENT

The success of a common interest development rests to a large extent on a cooperative team effort between the property owners, the directors and the management personnel. Depending on the size, complexity and location of the development, the task of properly operating and maintaining the development for the enjoyment of all owners can be substantial. We have examined the rights and responsibilities of the association members in Chapter VII. This Chapter examines the duties and responsibilities of association directors, officers and management. In addition to the regular observance of the laws and regulations which govern CIDs, directors, officers and managers should have a keen working knowledge of their developments, the purposes and goals of the association, and the needs and desires of the property owners.

DIRECTORS

Elected Officials:

The authority to conduct the business and affairs of the CID association is vested in the association's governing body, usually called a board of directors. The members of the board of directors are elected by the association members.[1]

The directors of a CID association constitute a collective governing body, exercising their authority and power as a group on behalf of the association. The power to manage a corporation's affairs is vested in the directors as a board, not as individuals.[2] In the absence of some special delegation of authority from the board to an individual director, no individual director has any legal capacity to make decisions for, act on behalf of, or otherwise bind or commit the association.

Corporations Code Section 7210 expresses the general power and authority of the board of directors in the following manner:

> "Subject to the provisions of this part and any limitations in the articles or bylaws relating to action required to be

approved by the members ..., the activities and affairs of a corporation shall be conducted and all corporate powers shall be exercised by or under the direction of the board. The board may delegate the management of the activities of the corporation to any person or persons, management company or committee however composed, provided that the activities and affairs of the corporation shall be managed and all corporate powers shall be exercised under the ultimate direction of the board."

Although the board of directors may delegate the power and authority to conduct the association's business and activities to others including officers and employees of the association, committees of directors and members, and property managers, the board is required to retain the ultimate governing authority.[3]

In all CID associations, the property owners, who constitute the members of the association, vote for the election of directors.[4] While the holding of meetings of members and elections of directors are in large part governed by the association's governing documents, the California Corporations Code also includes many procedures which must be followed, or at least permitted, in connection with the election of directors.

Each member of the association, other than the developer, is entitled to one vote for each separate interest owned.[5] If a separate interest is owned by more than one person, each person is a member of the association, but there is only one vote attributable to each separate interest.[6]

The Department of Real Estate regulations authorize two classes of membership in a CID association, with the developer or subdivider being designated the "Class B" member and all other property owner members being designated "Class A" members.[7] The developer or subdivider may have as many as three votes for each separate interest owned by the developer, if the association's governing documents so provide.[8]

Typically, when the developer initially begins selling the separate interests in a CID development, the developer, as the owner of all the separate interests, and his or her employees and agents constitute the full board of directors. As the developer continues to sell separate interests, each owner of a separate interest becomes a voting member of the association and the developer's control of the board of directors is gradually phased out as the developer and his or her agents are replaced on the board by other property owners who have been elected by their fellow property owner members.

If the Department of Real Estate's public report for the CID authorizes the sale of 50 or more separate interests, the first meeting of members of an association must occur within 45 days after the closing of the sale of the separate interest representing the 51st percentile separate interest authorized for sale.[9] But, in any event, the first meeting must be held no later than six months after the closing of the sale of the first separate interest sold in the development.[10]

Nomination Of Candidates:

Every association must provide its members with reasonable procedures for the nomination and election of directors which may vary according to the size, nature and operations of the association.[11] The procedures must include: (1) a reasonable means of nominating candidates, (2) a reasonable opportunity for nominees to communicate his or her qualifications and reasons for candidacy to the association members, (3) a reasonable opportunity for all candidates to solicit the votes of the members, and (4) a reasonable opportunity for all members to choose among the nominees.[12]

In associations with 500 or more members, any qualified person may be nominated as a candidate for election as a director by: (1) any method authorized in the association's bylaws, or if no method is specified in the bylaws by any method authorized by the board of directors, or (2) by a written petition delivered to any officer of the association and signed, within 11 months preceding the next time directors will be elected, by members holding two percent of the association voting power in associations with fewer than 5,000 members or one-twentieth of one percent of the association voting power, but not less than 100 votes, in associations with 5,000 or more members.[13]

In the case of associations with 5,000 or more members, the association's articles of incorporation or bylaws must specify a date for the close of nominations for candidates to be elected as directors. The date cannot be less than 50 nor more than 120 days before the date of the election. No candidates may be nominated after the date set for the close of nominations.[14]

If an association with 500 or more members publishes any material soliciting a vote for any candidate nominated for election as a director in any publication owned or controlled by the association, the association must make available to all other nominees in the same issue of the publication an equal amount of space, with equal prominence, to be used by the nominees for purposes reasonably related to the election.[15]

If a nominee requests in writing that the association mail election materials to the association members and the nominee pays for the reasonable costs of the mailing, including postage, the association shall, within 10 business days after the request, mail the materials as requested.[16] Alternatively, the association may at the association's option, within five business days after the nominee's request, make the association's list of the names, addresses and voting rights of members available to the nominee.[17]

Where a nominee for election as a director requests that the association publish or mail materials reasonably related to the election, unless the association first obtains a court order relieving it from the obligation to publish or mail the materials or provide the list of members to the nominee on the ground that the association will be exposed to liability arising out of the materials, the association cannot decline to mail or publish the materials on the basis of its contents.[18]

Neither the association nor any of its agents, officers, directors or employees may be held criminally responsible or liable for negligence or other damages on account of any materials supplied by a nominee and which the association publishes or mails pursuant to the nominee's request.[19] However, the nominee may be held liable and the nominee must indemnify and hold the association and its agents, officers, directors and employees free and harmless from all demands, legal costs, claims and damages arising out of the materials or their mailing or publication.[20]

After more people are nominated to be elected as directors than can be elected to the board, the association cannot expend any association funds to support a nominee without the express authorization of the board of directors.[21]

Prior to any meeting of members, the board of directors may appoint inspectors of election to act at the meeting. If the board fails to appoint inspectors of election, the chairman of the members' meeting may make such appointment. If such an appointment is requested by any member attending the meeting in person or by proxy, the chairman must appoint inspectors of election.[22]

When they are appointed, there must be one or three inspectors of election.[23] If three inspectors of election are appointed, the decision, act or certificate of a majority of them is effective for all purposes as the decision, act or certificate of all the inspectors.[24] Any report or certificate made by the inspectors is presumed to be a correct statement of the facts recited in the report or certificate and is presumed to be valid.[25]

The duties of the inspectors of election are to determine: (1) the number of outstanding memberships and the voting power of each, (2) the number of memberships represented at the meeting, (3) the existence of a quorum, and (4) the authenticity, validity and effect of proxies. In addition, the inspectors of election are to receive the votes, ballots or consents cast or given by the members, hear and determine all challenges or questions arising in connection with the right to vote, count and tabulate all votes and consents, determine when the polls shall close, determine the results of the meeting and election, and perform such other acts which may be proper to conduct the election or vote with fairness to all members.[26]

In carrying out their duties, the inspectors of election are bound to perform impartially, in good faith, to the best of their abilities and as expeditiously as practical.[27]

Any director or member of the association has the right to file a lawsuit in the Superior Court challenging the validity of the election or appointment of a director of an association.[28] As a general rule, any such lawsuit must be filed in the Superior Court of the county where the association's office is located.[29] Ordinarily, an expedited hearing is set by the court,[30] and the court may, in its discretion, determine the person entitled to the office of director, order a new election or appointment to be held, determine the right of persons to vote in the election of directors and determine any other matters in order to assure fair and equitable results in the election or appointment of directors.[31]

Any legal action challenging the validity of any election, appointment or removal of a director or directors must be commenced within nine months after the election, appointment or removal. If no such action is commenced, in the absence of fraud, any election, appointment or removal of a director is conclusively presumed valid nine months thereafter.[32]

Qualifications:

The association's bylaws may include a provision setting forth the qualifications required of persons to serve as directors.[33] Association bylaws frequently include the qualification that persons nominated and elected to serve as directors must be owners of record of property within the development and members in good standing of the association.

As long as the articles of incorporation or bylaws do not prohibit it, compensated employees of an association can probably serve on an association's board of directors. However, potential conflicts of interest may arise in the area of personnel matters and the formation of contracts with third persons.[34]

Policy Makers:

The grant of authority to boards of directors under the Corporations Code includes the authority to govern the day-to-day business affairs of an association as well as the power to adopt and ensure the implementation of broader business and management policy. However, in many associations, particularly large associations in which there are many time demanding tasks, the boards of directors customarily delegate the daily operation and management activities to one or more officers, managers or employees, leaving the board free to consider and act upon larger policy issues and long-range planning.

Decision Making And The "Business Judgment" Rule:

Association business decisions reached by the board of directors in good faith and with the objective of preserving or advancing the best interests of the association are given a wide latitude of respect and significant protection by the courts under the "business judgment" rule. Fundamentally, this rule provides that neither the courts nor members of the association can substitute their judgment on matters of business for that of the board of directors where the board has acted in good faith and with a view as to the best interests of the association and all of its members.[35]

The "business judgment" rule is premised on the notion that those to whom the management of a corporation has been entrusted, and not the courts, are best able to judge whether a particular act or transaction is one which is helpful to the conduct of corporate affairs or expedient for the attainment of corporate purposes.[36]

The "business judgment" rule applies to a wide variety of circumstances to protect the board of directors' decisions regarding association affairs from collateral attack by dissident members, directors or persons not affiliated with the association. The rule also applies to protect the board's interpretation of corporate governing documents such as the bylaws, where the interpretation of the document is reasonable and not arbitrary.[37]

The "business judgment" rule will not, however, generally be applied by the courts to insulate a decision by the association to suspend or expel members where the association fails to provide the affected member with due process in connection with the suspension or expulsion (please see the detailed discussion in Chapter VII). Instead, in the case of membership suspensions, the courts will look beyond the business judgment of the board to determine whether the decision is substantively rational and procedurally fair.[38]

Fiduciaries:

Generally speaking, directors of CID associations are said to be "fiduciaries" of the association and all of its members. A fiduciary is generally defined as a person who occupies the position of a trustee with respect to a trust. A fiduciary must respect the confidence reposed by others and adhere to the scrupulous good faith, honesty and candor which the position requires.[39]

A fiduciary is generally required to meet high standards of honesty, integrity, undivided loyalty and diligence with respect to the corporation and all of its members. The director, who is a fiduciary, must exercise his or her power and authority in a manner consistent with those standards.[40]

In order to fulfill their lawful duties and discharge the obligations for which they have been elected by the members, directors of CID associations must respect, accept and abide by the basic principles applicable to corporate governing bodies and the laws which apply to common interest developments and their managing associations.

Responsibilities:

As the association's highest governing authority, the board of directors is generally responsible for the management of the association as well as the administration of all of its functions including land use control and the operation and maintenance of the common areas. One or more of these responsibilities may be delegated to others, including committees, officers, employees, and employee and contract managers.

Depending on the size and configuration of the association, the board's management responsibilities may encompass a wide range of activities. Typically, the board will be involved directly or indirectly with employment and personnel matters, management of the association's common areas and amenities, enforcement of the association's governing documents, maintenance of the association's books, records, minutes of meetings and other important papers, discipline of members, collection of assessments and other fees, organization of properly held membership meetings, and interaction with governmental agencies, the surrounding or neighboring communities, vendors, contractors, and other persons who have business or legal relationships with the association.

The responsibilities and powers of the board of directors are frequently stated in express terms in the association's articles of incorporation, bylaws and declaration of CC&Rs. The governing document provisions are typically consistent with the powers and duties specified in the Department of Real Estate Regulations[41] and include enforcing the governing documents, paying taxes and assessments which could become a lien on the common areas, contracting for insurance on behalf of the association, delegating powers to committees, officers and employees in a manner consistent with law and the governing documents, preparing budgets and financial statements, formulating and adopting rules for the operation and use of common areas and other association property, disciplining members, electing officers, filling vacancies on the board of directors, and entering on separate interests in the development for construction, repair and maintenance purposes consistent with the governing documents.

In addition to the usual business activities for which one would expect an association's board of directors to be responsible, the board of directors has a number of specific fiscal or financial responsibilities imposed by law, including regular periodic review of all of the association's funds, revenues, expenses and accounts. In addition, the board must also regularly prepare, or cause to be prepared, certain financial documents for distribution to the association members.

A detailed discussion of the association's and the board of directors' responsibilities for the preparation and distribution of financial and related documents is found in Chapter IX. Some of the more important requirements are summarized in the following paragraphs.

The board of directors has a number of important duties related to the review of the association's financial condition and the preparation and distribution of certain financial statements and documents so that all association members are kept informed.[42] Although the association's duty of disclosure is owed to the property owner members, some of the provisions are also designed to provide financial information disclosure to prospective purchasers of separate interests.[43]

The association must prepare a "pro forma" operating budget each fiscal year.[44] A "pro forma" budget is one which may or may not accurately reflect the complete financial position of an association because by its very nature it includes assumed and projected facts and figures. Although the Civil Code does not specify which association members are responsible for preparation of the budget, most CID associations' declarations of CC&Rs and/or bylaws specify that the board is to prepare and adopt the budget in accordance with the criteria specified in those governing documents. Ordinarily, the preparation of the budget is performed by the board of directors, although the advice of committees, officers, management, the members, accountants and property managers may be sought and considered.[45]

The Davis-Stirling Common Interest Development Act explicitly places the responsibility for the maintenance, management and use of reserve funds on the board of directors. Reserve funds are those funds identified by the board for use in paying for the future repair, replacement, or additions to, the major components which the association is obligated to maintain.[46]

Unless the association's governing documents require more rigorous reviews, the board of directors must review current reconciliations of the association's operating accounts and reserve accounts at least quarterly during each fiscal year of the association. The board must also review the current fiscal year's actual reserve revenues and expenses compared to the budget for that year, and review an income and expense statement for the operating and reserve accounts, on at least a quarterly basis.[47] The board must also review all of the latest account statements prepared by the financial institutions where the association maintains its operating and reserve accounts.[48] Finally, for any fiscal year in which the association's gross income exceeds $75,000.00, the association must cause to be prepared a review of the association's financial statement by a licensed accountant.

The board must also ensure that the signatures of at least two persons are required for the withdrawal of money from the association's reserve accounts. Both persons authorized to sign for the withdrawal of reserve funds must be members of the board of directors or, alternatively, one person may be an association officer who is not a member of the board so long as the other person is a member of the board.[49]

Although limited exceptions are available, generally speaking, the board of directors cannot use reserve funds for any purpose other than to pay for the repair, restoration, replacement, or maintenance of the major components of the development for which the association is obligated to provide such services.[50] However, where short term cash flow requirements or other expenses necessitate the borrowing of money from reserve funds, the board of directors may authorize a temporary transfer of money from reserve funds if certain criteria are satisfied.[51] Please see Chapter IX for a detailed discussion of reserve fund borrowing.

In the event the board of directors decides to use reserve funds (including temporary borrowing) to pay for litigation, additional requirements must be met, including notification to the association members of that decision and the availability of an accounting of litigation expenses.[52]

Standard Of Care:

The basic rule with respect to the status and capacity of association directors is that such directors are fiduciaries who are required to exercise their powers in accordance with the duties of the Corporations Code.[53] A director's duties include the obligation to act in good faith and in a manner the director believes to be in the best interests of the association and with such care, including reasonable inquiry, as an ordinarily prudent person in a similar position would use under similar circumstances.[54]

In addition to the foregoing duty of care, a director's fiduciary duty includes a duty of undivided loyalty to act in the best interests of the corporation and all of its members, including the members of minority factions, to administer their powers for the common benefit of all members.[55] The duty of undivided loyalty also means the placing of the association's and members' interests ahead of the director's interests. Directors cannot make decisions that benefit their own interests at the expense of the association and its members.[56]

Corporations Code Section 7231(a) is the statutory expression of the directors' fiduciary obligations and it reads as follows:

> "A director shall perform the duties of a director, including duties as a member of any committee of the board upon which the director may serve, in good faith, in a manner such director believes to be in the best interests of the corporation and with such care, including reasonable inquiry, as an ordinarily prudent person in a like position would use under similar circumstances."

As mentioned in Corporations Code Section 7231(a), in fulfilling their responsibilities directors have a duty of inquiry to investigate matters and seek out the true state of affairs when making business decisions on behalf of the association. In doing so, directors are entitled to solicit and rely on the advice and opinions of experts. Section 7231(b) of the Corporations Code provides directors with a certain layer of insulation against liability by permitting directors to rely on the advice of certain specified persons or entities.

> "In performing the duties of a director, a director shall be entitled to rely on information, opinions, reports or statements, including financial statements and other financial data, in each case prepared or presented by:
>
> "(1) One or more officers or employees of the corporation whom the director believes to be reliable and competent in the matters presented;
>
> "(2) Counsel, independent accountants or other persons as to matters which the director believes to be within such person's professional or expert competence; or
>
> "(3) A committee of the board upon which the director does not serve, as to matters within its designated authority, which committee the director believes to merit confidence, so long as, in any such case, the director acts in good faith, after reasonable inquiry when the need therefor is indicated by the circumstances and without knowledge that would cause such reliance to be unwarranted."

And Section 7231(c) of the Corporations Code provides for protection for directors who fulfill their duties in accordance with the criteria specified in Sections 7231(a) and (b):

> "A person who performs the duties of a director in accordance with subdivisions (a) and (b) shall have no liability based upon any alleged failure to discharge the person's obligations as a director, including, without limiting the generality of the foregoing, any actions or omissions which exceed or defeat a public or charitable purpose to which assets held by the corporation are dedicated."

Committees:

The conduct of association business and affairs in a wise and prudent manner is a serious responsibility and frequently involves a heavy workload year round. Often, an association's bylaws will establish one or more committees composed of members, or members and directors, to help carry out the business of the association. In addition to any committees which may be established under an association's bylaws, the association's board of directors is authorized by law to appoint various "executive" or board committees, consisting of one or more directors, for a number of different purposes.

Distinctions Between Board ("Executive") Committees And "Advisory" Committees:

There is an important distinction between "advisory" committees and board committees ("executive" committees), although the foregoing labels are not uniformly used in the law. A board ("executive") committee is a committee appointed by the board of directors which consists of two or more directors, which serves at the pleasure of the board. Persons who are not directors cannot be members of a board committee.[57]

The creation of board committees must be accomplished by a resolution of the board of directors adopted by a majority of the directors at a meeting at which a quorum of directors is present or under the express terms of the association's bylaws.[58]

With the exception of eight specified areas of decision-making authority, any board committee, has the full authority of the board of directors to the extent provided in the board resolution creating the committee and to the extent such committee authority is not in conflict with law or the association's the articles of incorporation or bylaws.[59]

The board cannot delegate to any committee, including a board committee, the authority to: approve any actions which also require the approval of members under the Corporations Code, fill vacancies on the board or any committee which has the authority of the board, fix compensation of the directors, amend or repeal bylaws or adopt new bylaws, amend or repeal any resolution of the board which by its express terms is not so amendable or repealable, appoint committees of the board or members of such committees, expend corporate funds to support a nominee for director after there are more people nominated for director than can be elected, and with respect to any assets held in charitable trust, approve any self-dealing transaction.[60]

"Advisory" Committees:

An "advisory" committee is a committee appointed by the board of directors which consists of either directors, nondirectors, or both, under the authority of Section 7151(c)(4) of the Corporations Code.

In addition to the "executive" or "board" committees discussed above, an association's bylaws may also provide for the creation of "advisory" committees, or committees which do not have the authority of the board of directors, and the appointment of the members of such committees.[61] Corporations Code Section 7151(c)(4) provides the following general rule:

> "The bylaws may contain any provision, not in conflict with law or the articles, for the management of the activities and for the conduct of the affairs of the corporation, including but not limited to:
>
> "(4) The appointment of committees, composed of directors or nondirectors or both, by the board or any officer and the authority of any such committees."

Corporations Code Section 7210 then delineates the general powers of the board of directors to delegate authority to committees, but makes it clear that the board of directors cannot delegate its ultimate authority to others:

> "Subject to the provisions of this part and any limitations in the articles or bylaws relating to action required to be approved by the members ... the activities and affairs of a corporation shall be conducted and all corporate powers shall be exercised by or under the direction of the board. The board may delegate the management of the activities of the corporation to any person or persons, management company, or committee however composed, provided that the activities and affairs of the corporation shall be managed and all corporate powers shall be exercised under the ultimate direction of the board."

Although an association's bylaws may establish particular committees of the association such as a finance committee, nominating committee, a recreation committee, or an audit committee, if such committees are not board ("executive") committees, composed solely of directors, such committees are advisory in function and capacity only. The board of directors retains ultimate authority and responsibility for the activities and conduct of such committees.

Although no California judicial decisions exist addressing the limitations on the delegation of board authority to committees in the context of nonprofit mutual benefit corporations, the courts have consistently held that the boards of directors of stock corporations cannot delegate their responsibilities to govern the business and affairs of the corporation, unless and to the extent such delegation is permitted by statute.[62]

Directors' Rights:

Notice Of Meetings:

Unless a director signs a written waiver of notice of a directors meeting in advance of the meeting, each director is entitled to receive notice of every special meeting of the board which may be called.[63] In addition, if the time and place of regular board meetings are not fixed in the association's bylaws or by the board, each director is entitled to notice of each regular meeting.[64]

Filling Vacancies:

With respect to vacancies on the board created by some event other than the removal of directors, the general rule is that the directors remaining in office may fill such vacancies with an otherwise qualified person or persons of their choice.[65] If the directors fail to fill a vacancy, the members may elect a director at any time to fill the vacancy.[66]

Unless the association's articles of incorporation or bylaws include a provision authorizing the board to fill vacancies created by the removal of directors, such vacancies can only be filled by the members.[67]

Right To Resign:

Any director may resign from the board of directors at any time during his or her term. A director may resign by giving written notice of the resignation to the chairman of the board, the president, the secretary or the board of directors. The resignation is effective immediately, unless the notice of resignation specifies a later effective date.[68]

Removal From The Board:

Directors may remove other directors from office only "for cause" as narrowly defined in the Corporations Code. This summary removal of a director by the board occurs when the board declares a director's position vacant either because: (1) a director is declared by a court order to be of unsound mind, (2) a director has been convicted of a felony, (3) a director has been found by a court to have breached his fiduciary duties in a corporation holding assets in charitable trust, or (4) the association's bylaws specify that a director may be removed for missing a specified number of board meetings and the director fails without legitimate excuse to attend the specified number of meetings.[69]

Directors elected by the members (as opposed to directors appointed by the remaining directors to fill a vacancy) can only be removed from the board without cause by the members. The directors have no power or authority to oust a fellow director without cause.

On the other hand, association members have alternative mechanisms to cause the removal of directors from the board with or without cause. The members may remove directors either: (1) with the majority vote of either all of the members or those members attending a meeting, depending on the size of the association, at a regular or special meeting of the members,[70] or (2) a lawsuit filed in the Superior Court based on the director's fraudulent or dishonest acts or gross abuse of authority or discretion with reference to the association.[71]

"Absolute" Inspection Rights:

In order for directors to fulfill their management responsibilities to the association and its members and meet the high standards of conduct imposed by law, directors must have relatively free and unfettered access to all of the association's books, records and property.

As distinguished from a member's rights of inspection and copying (see Chapter VII), a director's inspection rights are not limited by statute. Section 8334 of the Corporations Code provides an "absolute" inspection right for directors:

> "Every director shall have the absolute right at any reasonable time to inspect and copy all books, records and documents of every kind and to inspect the physical properties of the corporation of which such person is a director."

In order for directors to fulfill their responsibilities as fiduciaries, it is necessary that they be given virtually unlimited access to all of an association's books and records. In order to discharge his or her duties adequately, a director must be kept well informed about the association's business affairs and activities.[72] As discussed below, however, despite the use of the word "absolute" by the legislature in the statute, the courts have crafted certain limitations on a director's right of inspection.

Oral Request To Inspect Books, Records And Property Is Sufficient:

Unlike a member's demand for inspection which the corporation may require be in written form, a director need not make his or her demand in writing.[73]

Limitations On Directors' Inspection Rights:

The 'absolute right' to inspect documents is the general rule in California. However, where the corporation determines that an unfettered inspection will result in a wrongful act against the corporation, it may decline the request for inspection and the director may seek enforcement of his or her inspection rights by court action.[74]

Although a director's rights of inspection are unqualified and unlimited by statute, when inspection by a director involves clear conflicts of interest, the likely disclosure of information or use of corporate information in violation of the director's fiduciary duties to the corporation and its members as a whole, the board of directors should seek the advice of legal counsel on whether the director should be given access to the documents. There are certain circumstances in which it may be proper to deny a director access to or copies of certain association documents, as for example, where the director has announced his or her intentions to violate his or her fiduciary duties by misusing corporate information or where the director has filed a lawsuit against the association and seeks to inspect or copy documents related to the lawsuit.[75]

Where a director's inspection rights conflict with the legitimate privacy interests or other constitutionally protected rights of other persons, the director's rights may be subordinated to and precluded by the others' privacy interests.[76]

For example, in *Chantiles v. Lake Forest II Master Homeowners Association*,[77] a director who had been successfully elected for ten consecutive years, was most recently elected as part of a minority faction of the board. Believing that he had been improperly shorted by 800 to 1,300 proxy votes, the director asserted that he had an absolute right to inspect and copy the proxy ballots which had been cast by members in the association's election. The association refused to permit the inspection and copying. The director filed suit to compel the association to permit his inspection and copying of the proxy ballots. The trial court concluded that the proxies were the type of record to which a director had a right of inspection under Corporations Code Section 8334, but that the association members had a legitimate expectation of privacy in their proxies against which the inspection rights must be balanced. The court permitted the director's attorney, but not the director, to inspect but not copy the proxies.[78]

The appellate court affirmed the trial court's ruling and stated:

> "We reject [the director's] assertion because section 8334 gives him an 'absolute right' to inspect, this right need not yield to any other right, not even a constitutional right. ... We hold that homeowners' association members have a constitutional privacy right in their voting decisions, even when conducted by proxy ballot. A homeowners' association director's statutory right to inspect the records of the association must be balanced against this privacy right."

The courts of other states have denied corporate directors the exercise of inspection and copying rights where the director sought to exercise such rights for purposes not consistent with the corporation's best interests. The rulings in these cases, while not binding in California, may be instructive and are therefore discussed in the accompanying chapter note.[79]

Exercise Of Inspection Rights By Agent Probably Not Proper:

A director of a nonprofit mutual benefit corporation probably cannot delegate his or her inspection and copying rights to an attorney or other agent of the director. Corporations Code Section 1602 governs regular stock corporations and expressly provides that: "Such inspection by a director may be made in person or by agent or attorney and the right of inspection includes the right to copy and make extracts." Section 1602 was enacted in 1975 and became effective in January, 1977. On the other hand, Section 8334 of the Corporations Code, governing nonprofit corporations, enacted in 1978, does not include the right of the director to exercise inspection through an agent or attorney.[80]

MEETINGS AND BOARD ACTION:

As discussed at the beginning of this Chapter, the directors of an association constitute a collective governing body. This means the board must act as a collective group, usually by majority vote or other action.[81] Such action is ordinarily taken at regular or special meetings of the board of directors. Unless there is some special delegation of authority sufficient to bind the association to third persons, an individual director has no authority with respect to the association's business and affairs.

Subsections (a)(7) and (a)(8) of Section 7211 of the Corporations Code specify the authority of the board in the following manner:

> "(7) A majority of the number of directors authorized in the articles or bylaws constitutes a quorum of the board for the transaction of business. The articles or bylaws may not provide that a quorum shall be less than one-fifth the number of directors authorized in the articles or bylaws, or less than two, whichever is larger, unless the number of directors authorized in the articles or bylaws is one, in which case one director constitutes a quorum."
>
> "(8) ... every act or decision done or made by a majority of the directors present at a meeting duly held at which a quorum is present is the act of the board. The articles or bylaws may not provide that a lesser vote than a majority of the directors present at a meeting is the act of the board. A meeting at which a quorum is initially present may continue to transact business notwithstanding the withdrawal of directors, if any action taken is approved by at least a majority of the required quorum for that meeting, or a greater number required by this division, the articles or bylaws."

The directors of other types of nonprofit mutual benefit corporations may conduct corporate business without a meeting by "unanimous written consent".[82] However, because CID associations are required to provide the members with notice of board meetings and because members are specifically authorized to attend board meetings under the "Common Interest Development Open Meeting Act", except when the board adjourns to executive session,[83] it is unclear whether association boards can conduct business by unanimous written consent. The "Common Interest Development Open Meeting Act" which became effective on January 1, 1996 appears to leave little room for board action by unanimous consent without a meeting. However, the Department of Real Estate Regulations, which are applicable during the period of developer control of the development, explicitly permit governing body action by unanimous consent without a meeting.[84]

In order to avoid potential legal challenges to board action, it is recommended that association boards now take action only through properly noticed meetings whenever practicable. If board action is taken without a meeting because exigent circumstances make a meeting impracticable, it is recommended that the board post a written explanation of the action taken in a prominent place or places within the association's common areas within three days after all of the unanimous written consents have been obtained. This notice posting is consistent with the requirements of the Department of Real Estate Regulations discussed above.

Unless the association's articles of incorporation or bylaws provide otherwise, meetings of the board may be called by the chairman of the board, the president or secretary of the association, or any two directors.[85]

Directors may attend and participate in meetings of the board in person or by conference telephone, electronic video screen, or other communications equipment, so long as all directors can communicate with the other directors concurrently, each director is able to propose or object to proposed action, and the association has some means of verifying that persons communicating by telephone or other electronic means are in fact directors authorized to participate in the meeting.[86]

The Corporations Code rules applicable to meetings of the board of directors generally also apply to meetings of committees of the board.[87]

Association Members Are Entitled To Attend All Meetings Of The Board Of Directors:

"Common Interest Development Open Meeting Act":

During the 1995 legislative session, the California Legislature enacted the "Common Interest Development Open Meeting Act". Effective January 1, 1996, the Act requires that association members be given notice of and the opportunity to attend all board meetings, except when the board adjourns to executive session. The Act is found in Section 1363.05 of the Civil Code and it reads in full as follows:

> "Section 1363.05. (a) This section shall be known and may be cited as the Common Interest Development Open Meeting Act.
>
> "(b) Any member of the association may attend meetings of the board of directors of the association, except when the board adjourns to executive session to consider litigation, matters relating to the formation of contracts with third parties, member discipline, or personnel matters. The board of directors of the association shall meet in executive session, if requested by a member who may be subject to a fine, penalty, or other form of discipline, and the member shall be entitled to attend the executive session.

"(c) Any matter discussed in executive session shall be generally noted in the minutes of the board of directors.

"(d) The minutes, minutes proposed for adoption that are marked to indicate draft status, or a summary of the minutes, of any meeting of the board of directors of an association, other than an executive session, shall be available to members within 30 days of the meeting. The minutes, proposed minutes, or summary minutes shall be distributed to any member of the association upon request and upon reimbursement of the association's costs for making that distribution.

"(e) Members of the association shall be notified in writing at the time that the pro forma budget required in Section 1365 is distributed, or at the time of any general mailing to the entire membership of the association, of their right to have copies of the minutes of meetings of the board of directors, and how and where those minutes may be obtained.

"(f) As used in this section, 'meeting' includes any congregation of a majority of the members of the board at the same time and place to hear, discuss, or deliberate upon any item of business scheduled to be heard by the board, except those matters that may be discussed in executive session.

"(g) Unless the time and place of meeting is fixed by the bylaws, or unless the bylaws provide for a longer period of notice, members shall be given notice of the time and place of a meeting as defined in subdivision (f), except for an emergency meeting, at least four days prior to the meeting. Notice may be given by posting the notice in a prominent place or places within the common area, by mail or delivery of the notice to each unit in the development, or by newsletter or similar means of communication.

"(h) An emergency meeting of the board may be called by the president of the association, or by any two members of the governing body other than the president, if there are circumstances that could not have been reasonably foreseen which require immediate attention and possible action by the board, and which of necessity make it impracticable to provide notice as required by this section."

Although all association members are entitled to receive notice of and attend meetings of the board of directors, the members are not entitled to participate in the board meetings, unless the board chooses to provide for such participation.[88] As a practical matter, many association boards invite comments from the members at a designated point during the board meeting, but limit the time each member can speak in order to ensure the meetings are not stretched into sessions which are unreasonable or unmanageable in length.

Meetings of the board of directors may be held at any location within the state, but ordinarily the meetings are held within the development unless a meeting room or hall of sufficient size is not available in the development.[89]

Under the terms of the Common Interest Development Act, every member of an association is entitled to attend the meetings of the board of directors, except when the board adjourns to executive session to consider litigation, matters relating to the formation of contracts with third parties, member discipline, or personnel matters.

The definition of "meeting" in Civil Code Section 1363.05(f) is quite broad and undoubtedly was deliberately drafted that way by the Legislature in order to ensure association members have the widest possible access to the proceedings of the boards of directors. Boards need to become accustomed to the Common Interest Development Open Meeting Act and the broad definition of "meeting" and take whatever practical steps may be necessary to comply with the Act's requirements.[90]

Occasionally, questions may arise concerning the types of business which fall within the categories qualifying for executive session treatment. For example, whether or not the directors may, in executive session, appoint a person to fill a vacancy on the board or remove a director for cause may be a question which arises from time to time. The question is whether an appointment to fill a vacancy or a removal of a director is a "personnel matter" within the meaning of the Common Interest Development Open Meeting Act.

There is no published California legal authority controlling the issue. However, by analogous reasoning under the "personnel exception" to the open meeting requirements under the Bagley-Keene Open Meeting Act,[91] applicable to state governmental bodies, and the Ralph M. Brown Act,[92] applicable to local government agencies, the board of directors probably cannot meet in executive session to appoint or remove a director.

The question has been addressed in a number of opinions by the California Attorney General in the context of "state bodies" under the Bagley-Keene Open Meeting Act and "local agencies" under the Ralph M. Brown Act. In a series of published opinions, the Attorney General has concluded that, generally speaking, any person who does not receive compensation for his services, other than per diem and reimbursement of ordinary and necessary expenses, in the service of a state body or local agency is not an "employee" and the "personnel exception" to the Open Meeting Act requirements does not apply. The opinions further conclude that an "employee" for purposes of the Open Meeting Acts, does not include any person elected to office or appointed to office by the state body or local agency (other than a few very narrow exceptions).[93] The Attorney General cites numerous cases in which the courts have distinguished between public "employees" and noncompensated public "officers" on the basis that officers occupy a position of public trust after being elected to the position by the public and the public is entitled to full disclosure as to their appointment and removal.

California Attorney General Opinions are not law. Nor are such legal opinions considered persuasive with the California courts, although they may be considered in a court's analysis of legal issues. Neither are common interest development associations "state bodies" or "local agencies" subject to the open meeting requirements set forth in the Bagley-Keene Open Meeting Act or the Ralph M. Brown Act. However, the enactment of the Common Interest Development Open Meeting Act demonstrates the California Legislature's intent to restrict the subject matter appropriate for executive session board meetings in order to provide association members with the fullest possible access to the affairs and governance of the association.

On the other hand, it may be permissible for less than a majority of the directors, or a committee of directors appointed by the board consisting of less than a quorum, to meet to discuss, consider and otherwise "screen" a candidate's personal qualifications for appointment to the board.[94] The actual appointment, however, should be done in a meeting open to the members.

Board Action:

As we have seen, boards of directors typically consider association business and affairs and take action on such matters at board meetings by majority vote of the directors. Consistent with good corporate policy and parliamentary procedure, the substance and language of all motions and the votes for and against any motion should be recorded in the minutes of board proceedings.

As mentioned earlier, directors may attend board meetings in person, or through conference telephone, electronic video screen or other forms of communication equipment by which each director can communicate with all other directors concurrently.[95] Participation in meetings through one of the electronic media authorized by the statute constitutes personal presence so long as the association follows procedures to ensure that the person so appearing is in fact a director.[96] Directors cannot, however, vote or otherwise participate in meetings of the board through the use of proxies. There is no authority for directors to participate in meetings of the board through the use of proxies.

The authority of the board of directors is exercised at meetings of the board by action of a majority of the directors attending meetings at which a quorum is present.[97] A quorum is defined as a majority of the number of directors authorized in the association's articles of incorporation or bylaws or, if the articles or bylaws specify, a smaller number, but no less than one-fifth of the number of authorized directors or two, whichever is greater. For example, if the articles of incorporation authorize seven directors, a quorum is four, unless the articles or bylaws specify a smaller number no less than two.[98]

Once a sufficient number of directors to constitute a quorum have appeared at a board meeting, the board may continue to transact business even if some directors leave the meeting so that a quorum is no longer present. But in that event any action taken must approved by at least a majority of the required quorum for that meeting, or any greater number of directors which may be required under the terms of the association's the articles of incorporation or bylaws.[99]

For example, if an association's board of directors consists of five directors, then unless the articles of incorporation or bylaws provide otherwise, three directors must attend a meeting of the board in order for a quorum to be established. If only four directors initially attend the meeting and one director later withdraws or leaves the meeting, leaving three directors in attendance, then action can be taken by a majority of those remaining, or two directors (a majority of the original three-director quorum).

Ordinarily an association's bylaws will provide that the chairman of the board, or if there is no chairman, the president of the association, will preside at all meetings of the board.

Associations are required to record and maintain written minutes of all meetings of the directors.[100] In recording the board's actions in the minutes at a minimum the following information should be recorded: (i) the names of all directors and any other persons present, (ii) the names of any directors absent, (iii) the fact that a quorum is or is not established, (iv) the names of any directors abstaining from the voting on any business matter or issue, (v) the number of directors favoring any action brought to a vote of the directors, (vi) the number of directors opposing any action brought to a vote of the directors, and (vii) at least a summary statement or description of each matter brought or introduced for the purposes of board action.

Ordinarily, matters are brought to a vote of the directors by one or more directors making a motion that certain action be taken, followed by a second, discussion and the voting. Although it is required that associations conduct their meetings of members in accordance with some recognized form of parliamentary procedure or any parliamentary procedures which may be adopted by the association,[101] there is no similar requirement for meetings of the board. However, associations may adopt bylaws, or the board may enact a resolution, requiring that directors conduct meetings of the board in accordance with some form of parliamentary procedure. Even if the board does not ordinarily follow rules of parliamentary procedure in conducting its meetings, if action is to be taken on controversial issues or matters which might later be questioned, it is good practice to follow at least the basic rules of parliamentary procedure.

From time to time, the meaning of the language in resolutions adopted by the board of directors may be brought into question by the directors, the members or third parties. The minutes of board meetings are merely a record of what transpired at a meeting and that record may or may not be accurate for a variety of reasons. The meaning and interpretation of corporate resolutions are not governed solely by the written language. Instead, primary weight is given to the parties' intent in adopting the resolution.[102]

A majority of the directors present at a meeting may adjourn any meeting of the board, whether or not a quorum is present.[103]

Limited Immunity From Tort Liability For Certain Volunteer Directors And Officers:

Both volunteer directors and volunteer officers of CID associations are afforded limited protection from liability for personal injury and property damage claims which may be asserted against them, if certain important conditions are satisfied.

Generally, a volunteer director or officer is one who receives no compensation from the association for his or her services as a director or officer, other than payment for actual expenses which may be incurred by a director or officer in carrying out his or her duties.[104]

In addition, other persons may not qualify as "volunteer" directors within the meaning of the liability protection statute. An officer or director who, at the time of the act or omission giving rise to the liability claim, was a declarant or who received direct or indirect compensation as an employee from a declarant, or from a financial institution that purchased a separate interest in the development at a judicial or nonjudicial foreclosure of a mortgage or deed of trust, is not a "volunteer" for the purposes of the statute and does not qualify for its protections.[105]

Under Section 1365.7 of the Civil Code if all of the requirements of the statute are satisfied, volunteer directors and officers of associations which manage exclusively residential developments, cannot be held personally liable in excess of the coverage of insurance maintained by the association in accordance with the requirements of the statute, to any person who suffers injury, bodily injury, emotional distress, wrongful death, or property damage or loss as a result of the acts or omissions of the directors or officers.[106]

In order for directors and officers to have the benefit of the liability protection afforded by the statute, all of the following conditions must be met: (i) the director's or officer's act or omission was performed within the scope of his or her association duties, (ii) the act or omission was performed in good faith, (iii) the act or omission was not willful, wanton, or grossly negligent, (iv) the association maintained and had in effect at the time the act or omission occurred and at the time a claim is made one or more policies of insurance including coverage for general liability of the association and individual liability of officers and directors of the association for negligent acts or omissions with both types of coverage in the minimum amount of at least $500,000 if the common interest development consists of 100 or fewer separate interests, and at least $1,000,000 if the development consists of more than 100 separate interests, and (v) the volunteer director or officer is a tenant of a separate interest in the development or is an owner of no more than two separate interests in the development.[107]

While the statute affords protection to volunteer directors and officers if all of the specified criteria are satisfied, the statute does nothing to limit the liability of the association for negligent acts or omissions by the association or any of its officers or directors.[108]

Other statutes which generally apply to various types of nonprofit corporations may also afford additional protections to volunteer directors and officers of CID associations. However, given the general and technical nature and application of such statutes, they should not be relied on until competent legal advice has been sought with respect to the particular facts and circumstances of any given case.[109]

The separate but related topic of an association's authority to protect or "indemnify" its directors, officers and agents from lawsuits and liabilities is discussed at the end of this Chapter.

OFFICERS

Every incorporated association is required to have a chairman of the board or a president or both, a secretary, and a chief financial officer.[110] An association may also have any other officers with such titles and duties as may be stated in the association's bylaws or as determined by the board.[111]

Unless the association's articles of incorporation or bylaws provide otherwise, the president, or the chairman of the board if there is no president, is the general manager and chief executive officer of the association.[112] Unless the articles of incorporation or bylaws provide otherwise, any number of offices may be held by the same person.[113] As a practical matter, however, many banks, other lending institutions, and large contractors and vendors ordinarily expect the signatures of two different persons on promissory notes and contracts entered into by an incorporated association.

The association's bylaws will typically specify at least the general nature of each officer's duties, responsibilities and powers. If the bylaws do not contain any such provisions, then the board of directors may specify those matters.[114]

Generally speaking, officers are chosen by the board of directors and serve in office for such periods of time as the board may determine. The general rule is subject to differing provisions which may exist in the association's articles of incorporation and bylaws and the rights an officer may have under a contract of employment.[115]

MANAGEMENT

Most associations, at least those with 50 or more members, typically find the need of a manager who attends to the daily property management and business affair needs of the association commensurate with the authority delegated to him or her by the association's board of directors or officers. In many cases, the daily and routine management and business matters simply require more time than many volunteer directors can contribute.

Depending on the size and the character, and the nature and specific needs of the association, the manager may be a full-time or part-time employee of the association, or an independent contract property manager.

The Department of Real Estate regulations applicable to CID associations during the period of time the developer owns or controls 25 percent or more of the association voting power prescribe the terms and conditions of an association's governing documents which are acceptable to the Department of Real Estate. Among other criteria, the regulations specify that an association's governing body shall, without the approval of the members, ordinarily be prohibited from entering into a contract with a third person for the provision of goods or services to the association for a term longer than one year.[116] The prohibition applies to all types of contracts for goods or services, including property management contracts. Two exceptions to the general prohibition are available for management contracts which have been approved by the Federal Housing Administration or the Veterans Administration[117] and contracts not exceeding three years in duration which include a term permitting the association to terminate the contract without cause after no longer than one year without any penalty or other obligation.[118]

There are at present no general legal requirements for the licensing of property management agents.[119] Nor are there any general requirements that management contracts be in written form, unless the management agent's duties will include entering into, on behalf of an association, the types of contracts which are themselves required to be in writing.[120] For example, contracts for the purchase and sale of real estate and for the leasing of real estate for a period in excess of one year are required to be stated in writing.[121] And, if an agent is to be given the authority to enter into such contracts, the authority must be stated in writing.[122]

Two very important statutory requirements govern association managing agents who are not also full-time employees of the association.[123] For purposes of both statutes with certain narrow exceptions, a "managing agent" is defined as "a person or entity, who for compensation or, in expectation of compensation, exercises control over the assets" of a common interest development or an association.[124]

Management Agent's Pre-Contract Disclosure Requirements:

Managers who are not full-time employees[125] of the association are required to provide a written disclosure statement to the association before entering into a management agreement with the association.[126] The disclosure statement is intended to provide the association with some fundamental information regarding the basic qualifications and licensing status of the management agent.

The disclosure statement must be provided to the association as soon as practicable before a management contract is entered into, but no earlier than 90 days before the contract is made. The disclosure must include: (1) the names and business addresses of the owners or general partners of the managing agent or, if the managing agent is a corporation, the names and business addresses of the directors and officers and shareholders owning more than 10 percent of the shares of the corporation, (2) a statement as to whether or not any relevant licenses such as architectural design, construction, engineering, real estate, or accounting have been issued by the State of California and are currently held by the management agent owners, partners, directors, officers or shareholders, as the case may be, and (3) if such licenses are held, (i) what license is held, (ii) the status of each such license, and (iii) the name of the licensee appearing on each license.[127]

In addition, the agent's disclosure must include a statement as to whether or not any relevant professional certifications or designations such as architectural design, construction, engineering, real property management, or accounting are currently held by any of agent's owners, partners, directors, officers or shareholders, including, but not limited to, those of certified property manager or professional association manager. If any such certification or designation is held, the statement must also include the following information: (i) what the certification or designation is and what entity issued it, (ii) the status of each certification or designation, and (iii) the names in which the certification or designation is held.[128]

Management Agent's Maintenance, Accounting And Disposition Of Association Funds:

Management agents who are not full-time employees of the association[129] who accept or receive funds belonging to an association must deposit all such funds into an escrow account with a bank, savings association or credit union or an account controlled by the association or a trust fund account maintained by the agent in a bank, savings association or credit union located in California. If the agent deposits association funds into a trust fund account maintained by the agent, the account must be maintained with a financial institution located in California and insured by the federal government.[130]

If the association's board of directors makes a written request, the funds received or accepted by the managing agent on behalf of the association must be deposited into an interest-bearing account in a bank, savings association, or credit union in this state, but only if all of the following requirements are satisfied: (1) the account is in the name of the managing agent as trustee for the association or in the name of the association, (2) all of the funds in the account are covered by federal agency insurance, (3) the funds are kept separate, distinct, and apart from funds belonging to the managing agent or to any other person or entity for whom the agent holds funds in trust (the funds of various associations may be commingled in one account if additional requirements as discussed below are satisfied), (4) the managing agent discloses to the association's board of directors the nature of the account, how interest will be calculated and paid, whether service charges will be paid to the depository and by whom, and any notice requirements or penalties for withdrawal of funds from the account, and (5) no interest earned on funds in the account shall inure directly or indirectly to the benefit of the managing agent or the agent's employees.[131]

Finally, the managing agent must maintain a separate record of receipt and disposition of all association funds received or accepted by the agent, including any interest earned on the funds.[132]

The Managing Agent Cannot Commingle association Funds Without The Written Permission Of The Association And Satisfaction Of Other requirements:

A managing agent cannot commingle in one account funds belonging to an association with the agent's own money or with the money of others, unless all of the following requirements are met: (1) the agent commingled the funds of various associations on or before February 26, 1990, and has obtained a written agreement with the board of directors of each association that the agent will maintain a fidelity and surety bond in an amount that provides adequate protection to the associations as agreed upon by the managing agent and the board of directors of each association, (2) the agent discloses in the written agreement whether the agent is deriving benefits from the commingled account or the bank, credit union, or savings institution where the moneys will be on deposit, (3) the written agreement with each association's board of directors includes the name and address of the fidelity and surety bonding companies, the amount of the bonds, and the expiration dates of the bonds, (4) if there are any changes in the bond coverage or the companies providing the coverage, the managing agent discloses that fact to the board of directors of each affected association as soon as practical, but in no event more than 10 days after the change, (5) the required fidelity and surety bonds assure the protection of the association and provide the association at least 10 days' notice prior to cancellation, and (6) completed payments (funds received which clearly identify the account to which the funds are to be credited) on the behalf of the association are deposited within 24 hours or the next business day and do not remain commingled for more than 10 calendar days.[133]

Legal Relationship Between Association And Managing Agent:

The employment or retention of a property manager by an association creates a legal relationship known as "agency" in which the agent or property manager is employed to perform certain tasks and functions for the benefit and on behalf of the "principal", the association.[134]

Generally speaking, the contract creating the agency relationship may be oral or written. However, where the agency is intended to include authority for the agent to enter into contracts on behalf of the association which must by law be in writing, the agency contract must generally also be in writing.[135]

Scope Of Managing Agent's Authority:

Typically, when associations employ or retain a managing agent, the agent performs many valuable services for which the association's board of directors may not have the time or expertise. Such services typically include the collection of assessments, paying accounts payable, managing, or supervising the management and operation of, the association's common areas and community amenities, procuring contracts with vendors for goods and services provided to the association, and formulating meeting agendas for the meetings of the association's members and board of directors.

Ordinarily, the association and managing agent will enter into an express management contract which should be in written form in order to clarify the parties' relationship and define the agent's areas of responsibility and scope of authority. A written management agreement will provide the parties with a point of reference in dealing with one another as well as third parties, reduce the likelihood of disputes and generally provide for more efficient operation of the association.

The authority conferred on an agent may be given expressly, either orally or in writing, or impliedly, by the conduct of the principal indicating his intention to confer it or causing the agent to believe that he possesses it.[136] Agency may also be established by "ratification",[137] where the agent purports to act on behalf of the principal[138] and the principal accepts the benefits of the acts of the purported agent.

Agency is either actual or "ostensible".[139] Agency is ostensible when the principal intentionally or negligently causes or permits a third person to believe that another person is his agent when that is not in fact the case. Ostensible agency cannot be established merely by the conduct or representations of the purported agent. Instead, the acts, statements or conduct of the principal must be of such nature as to cause the third party to believe that the agency does in fact exist.[140] Actual authority, on the other hand, is the authority the principal intentionally confers on the agent or through negligence allows the agent to believe that he possesses.[141]

Issues of ostensible agency may arise and result in a variety of problems for an association. For example, if the board of directors is not regularly engaged in the exercise of its ultimate governing authority and supervising its officers and managers appropriately, officers, employees and/or managers may exceed the scope of their actual authority by entering into contracts or making other commitments on behalf of the association. The association could be legally bound by and responsible for such "unauthorized" acts, if the other contracting party reasonably believes the errant officer or manager has the authority to be making the contract or other commitment.

Prudent agents, whether officers, employees or independent contract managers will be careful not to exceed the scope of their authority as defined by the association. An agent cannot exceed the limits of the agent's actual authority as defined by the Civil Code statutes governing agency.[142]

The Civil Code statutes governing agency set forth a number of general rules defining and limiting the scope of an agent's authority, subject to the terms of the contract or other instrument appointing the agent, which may further limit and narrow the agent's authority.[143] Where the authority granted to an agent is partially general and partially specific in its terms, the general authority confers no higher powers on the agent than those powers which are specifically described.[144] In addition, even where the contract or other document establishing the agency grants broad authority to the agent, the agent has no power to define the scope of the agency.[145]

The Civil Code also provides that an agent may be authorized to do any acts which the principal might do, except those acts to which the principal is obligated to give his personal attention.[146] The agent has such authority as the principal actually or ostensibly confers upon the agent.[147] An agent has authority to do everything necessary or proper and usual, in the ordinary course of business, for effecting the purposes of the agency. An agent may also exercise a certain amount of discretion to disobey instructions in circumstances where it is clearly in the best interests of the principal that he do so, and there is no time to communicate with the principal.[148]

Property managers and other agents of an association are fiduciaries of the association and cannot lawfully do anything contrary to the best interests of the association. The agent's obligations of diligent and faithful service are the same as those of a trustee.[149]

The property manager, as an agent, is required to disclose to the association all information which the agent has relevant to the subject matter of the agency.[150] The agent has a duty to use reasonable care, diligence and skill in performing his services and carrying out the purposes of the agency.[151]

The fiduciary relationship between an agent and his principal requires that the agent exercise the utmost good faith and undivided loyalty to the principal when the agent is acting for the principal.[152] Part of the agent's duty of undivided loyalty means in turn that an agent's duties include the obligation not to act as an agent for a person whose interests conflict with those of the principal and not to compete with the principal in matters connected with the subject matter of the agency.[153]

The successful management and operation of a common interest development can frequently be a task of substantial proportions. In order to establish a successful working team for the management, operation and preservation of the development, it is critical that the association's board of directors and any property manager retained or employed maintain thorough and open communications and a solid working relationship based on mutual trust and respect.

The requisite relationship begins with dedicated directors and capable managers who can complement one another's contributions and talents, always keeping the primary purposes of the association in mind: the operation, management and preservation of the development for the common benefit and enjoyment of all of the property owners and members.

INDEMNIFICATION OF DIRECTORS, OFFICERS AND AGENTS:

"Indemnification" generally means to hold another person free and harmless from or provide protection against lawsuits, liabilities, judgments, claims, expenses and legal costs. An association which is incorporated as a nonprofit mutual benefit corporation may "indemnify", or protect, its directors, officers and agents from lawsuits and other legal proceedings which may brought against those persons in their capacities as such.[154] In circumstances where the director, officer or agent successfully defends the legal proceeding, the association may be required to indemnify him or her, whether or not the governing documents require or permit indemnification.[155]

To encourage participation in community affairs and governance, most associations have included provisions in their governing documents permitting or requiring the associations to indemnify their directors, officers and/or agents from legal proceedings. However, an association's power or obligation to indemnify its directors, officers and agents is strictly controlled by Section 7237 of the Corporations Code and cannot be changed by any contrary provisions in the association's governing documents.[156]

The nature and extent of an association's power or obligation to indemnify and defend its directors, officers and agents depends on a number of related elements, including the nature of the legal proceeding, the conduct of the director, officer or agent, the outcome of the legal proceeding, and the association's approval of the indemnification.

To be entitled to indemnification by the association, the director, officer or agent must have acted in good faith and in a manner he or she believed to be in the best interests of the association.[157] If the lawsuit is brought by an association member seeking to obtain a judgment in favor of the association, then, the director, officer or agent must also have acted with such care, including reasonable inquiry, as an ordinarily prudent person in a similar position would use under similar circumstances.[158]

Generally speaking, if a legal proceeding against the association's directors, officers, or agents is brought by a nonmember, the association may indemnify the defendant directors, officers and agents and provide them with a defense and pay any costs, expenses, judgments, fines, claims or settlements on their behalf.[159]

On the other hand, if an association member sues the association's directors, officers or agents on behalf of the association to obtain a judgment in favor of the association, the association cannot indemnify the directors, officers or agents (1) if the court determines that the defendant is liable to the association in the performance of his or her duties, unless the court determines that, in spite of such liability, the defendant is under all the circumstances still entitled to indemnification, or (2) for money paid in settling or otherwise disposing of a threatened or pending legal proceeding with or without court approval, or (3) for expenses incurred in settling or otherwise disposing of threatened or pending legal action without prior court approval.[160]

Required Indemnification:

If a director, officer or agent successfully defends a lawsuit against him or her on the merits of the case, the association is generally obligated to indemnify that person for the actual and reasonable expenses incurred in defending the proceeding.[161]

Approval Of Permissible Indemnification:

In all other circumstances, indemnification requires a determination that the director, officer or agent has acted in good faith and in a manner he or she believed to be in the best interests of the association, and the indemnification is approved by either a majority of quorum of directors who are not parties to the proceeding or by a majority of the association members (excluding any members who may be parties to the proceeding).[162] For example, if an association has a board of five directors and three are sued, a majority of the members will have to approve the association's indemnification of the directors.

Advancement Of Defense Expenses:

The expenses incurred by a director, officer or agent in defending any legal proceeding may be advanced by the association, prior to the conclusion of the proceeding, so long as the director, officer or agent agrees in writing to repay the expenses in the event it is ultimately determined such person was not entitled to indemnification.[163]

Contractual Indemnity Not Affected For Agents Other Than Director And Officers:

Section 7237 of the Corporations Code does not negate or otherwise affect any right to indemnification to which persons other than directors and officers may be entitled by contract or otherwise.[164]

The Association's Authority To Procure Insurance Is Not Affected By Restrictions On Indemnification:

Regardless of whether or not an association has the power to indemnify its directors, officer or agents under the circumstances involved in any particular case, an association always has the authority to purchase and maintain insurance protecting its directors, officers and agents from liability.[165]

CHAPTER IX

FINANCIAL STRUCTURE: ASSESSMENTS, FEES AND RESERVE FUNDS

The financial structure of most CID associations is not complicated. Yet many property owners living in CIDs do not understand the assessments levied against their properties, how the assessment funds are used, and the potential consequences resulting from a failure to pay an assessment. Directors and managers may not have a clear understanding of their duties with respect to the levying, enforcement and collection of assessments and the association's responsibilities for meeting the financial requirements of the development. Some large associations have budgets similar to those of small cities. As a consequence, there is much at stake in the proper fiscal management of an association. Chapter IX is intended to help directors, officers, members and managers understand these and related issues of equal importance.

ASSESSMENTS:

Nature Of Assessments:

In the context of common interest development associations, an assessment is a charge or fee imposed or levied against each privately-owned separate interest located within the development and their respective owners. The assessments are used to pay for the expenses incurred by the association in performing its duties in accordance with applicable law and the governing documents. The assessments are a personal obligation of the owner of each separate interest and, if appropriate notice is recorded in the public records, a lien against the separate interest which can be foreclosed in the same manner as a mortgage or deed of trust to enforce payment of the assessment.

Authority For Assessments:

Common interest development associations are authorized by regulation and statute to levy and collect assessments to pay for the expenses necessary for the operation, maintenance and management of the development and the association.[1] Section 1366(a) of the Civil Code states in relevant part that:

> "(a) Except as provided in this section, the association shall levy regular and special assessments sufficient to perform its obligations under the governing documents and this title."

As stated in Civil Code Section 1366(a), the association is not only empowered to levy assessments, it is required to levy assessments in amounts sufficient to meet its obligations as the managing association of the common interest development commensurate with its obligations under the Davis-Stirling Common Interest Development Act and the association's governing documents.

Commencement Of Assessments:

The inception of the association's authority to levy and collect the assessments is found in the California Department of Real Estate ("DRE") regulations which prescribe the contents of an association's governing documents.[2]

The regulations provide for governing document provisions which will typically state that assessments equal in amount will be levied against each separate interest. Generally, the assessments are determined by dividing the association's authorized budgeted expenses by the number of separate interests against which assessments are levied in the development. On the other hand, where one or more separate interests will derive as much as ten percent or more of the benefit of the services provided by the association, the regulations authorize assessments which may be determined according to a formula designed to spread the assessments in an equitable fashion against the separate interests in proportion to the benefit conferred on each.[3]

Section 2792.16 of Title 10 California Code of Regulations provides the developer with the initial authority for the establishment of an assessment strategy and procedure in the governing documents:

> "(a) Regular assessments to defray expenses attributable to the ownership, operation and furnishing of common interests by the Association shall ordinarily be levied against each owner according to the ratio of the number of subdivision interests owned by the owner assessed to the total number of interests subject to assessment.

"(b) In the case of a subdivision offering in which it is reasonable to anticipate that any owner will derive as much as 10% more than any other owner in the value of common services supplied by the Association, the assessment against each owner may be determined according to a formula or schedule under which the assessments against the various subdivision interests bear a relationship which is equitably proportionate to the value of the common services furnished to the respective interests."

The property owners' obligation to pay assessments first commences upon the date of the first conveyance of a separate interest in the development under the authority of a Public Report issued by the DRE for the development.[4]

Developer's Obligation To Pay Assessments:

In order to help ensure that the CID association is properly managed and funded during the period of time that the developer or subdivider owns separate interests in the development, the DRE regulations require that the developer be subject to the payment of assessments in the same manner as any other owner of a separate interest.[5] The developer is required to keep accurate records of all assessments paid by the developer and all expenditures paid for which the developer may claim a credit against assessments owed.[6]

Ordinarily, the DRE public report issued for the common interest development requires the developer to pay assessments on lots, units or other separate interests which the developer has not yet sold. Any agreement that might later be reached between the developer and the association exempting the developer from the payment of assessments is void and unenforceable.[7]

Limited Exemptions May Be Provided Under The Governing Documents:

If the association's governing documents so provide, the developer and any other owner of a separate interest may be allowed a limited exemption for a limited amount of time from assessments against separate interests which are vacant and do not yet have a completed residential dwelling or other structural improvement for human occupation.[8] The exemption applies only to that portion of an assessment which is directly attributable to the existence and use of the structural improvement, for example, roof replacement, exterior maintenance, walkway lighting, refuse disposal, cable television and domestic water expenses. In addition, the developer and other owners may be exempted by appropriate governing document provisions from that portion of assessments which are levied for the purposes of defraying expenses and reserves directly attributable to common facilities which are not complete at the time the assessments commence.[9]

The availability of association funds to defray the expenses of common area and facility maintenance during the early stages of the development is critical to the financial soundness of the association and the development. To ensure that adequate funds are available, the DRE regulations prohibit the final closing of escrow on the sale of any separate interest in the development until at least 80% of the separate interests have been sold or, alternatively, require the developer to furnish funds, a surety bond or some other security convertible to cash in an amount sufficient to pay all the expenses of common area maintenance, operation and services and reserves for a period of six months.[10] The funds or other security must be deposited by the developer in a neutral escrow account satisfactory to the Department of Real Estate. The funds or other security must remain available to pay assessments for which the developer is obligated until the escrow receives written notice from the developer that 80% of the interests in the development have been sold and escrow closed, and written notice from the association that the developer is not delinquent in the payment of assessments for which the developer is obligated.[11]

Increasing Assessments: Prerequisites To Valid Assessments And Assessment Liens:

If the association has complied with certain budget preparation and financial disclosure requirements, it may, without the approval of the association members, increase regular assessments up to 20 percent greater than the regular assessment for the preceding fiscal year and levy special assessments which do not in the aggregate exceed five percent of the budgeted gross expenses for the current fiscal year.[12]

However, before the association can increase regular assessments (increased over the amount of the regular assessment for the association's prior fiscal year), the association must either: (1) obtain the approval of its members, or (2) ensure that a pro forma operating budget has been prepared with respect to that fiscal year, and distributed to the association members, in accordance with certain prescribed criteria.[13]

The pro forma operating budget must be prepared and distributed not less than 45 days nor more than 60 days before the beginning of the association's fiscal year. The budget must contain (1) the association's estimated revenue and expenses on an accrual basis, (2) a summary of the association's reserves based on the most recent review or reserve study conducted pursuant to statute, (3) a statement as to whether the board of directors has determined or anticipates that one or more special assessments will be required to repair, replace, or restore, any major component or to provide adequate reserves therefor, and (4) a general statement addressing the procedures used to calculate and establish those reserves necessary to defray future repair, replacement, or additions to those major components the association is obligated to maintain.[14]

Instead of distributing the complete pro forma operating budget, the board of directors may elect to distribute a summary of the budget to all members, together with written notice that the complete pro forma operating budget is available at the association's business office and that copies thereof will be provided on request at the expense of the association.[15] This notice must be in 10-point boldface type on the front page of the budget summary.[16] If any member requests that a copy of the pro forma operating budget be mailed to him or her, the association must deliver it by first-class mail, within five days of the request.[17]

Limitations On Assessments And Increases In Assessments:

Section 1366.1 of the Civil Code contains a general prohibition against excessive assessments which must be observed and followed in all circumstances:

"An association shall not impose or collect an assessment or fee that exceeds the amount necessary to defray the costs for which it is levied."

Regardless of whether the association has complied with the pro forma budget preparation and distribution requirements, it cannot, except for "emergency situations", impose a regular assessment that is more than 20 percent greater than the regular assessment for the association's preceding fiscal year, without the approval of the property owners. Nor can the association levy special assessments which in the aggregate exceed five percent of the association's budgeted gross expenses for the current fiscal year, without the approval of the property owners.[18]

The "emergency situations" for which the association may increase assessments without being subject to the limitations described above are defined as: (1) an extraordinary expense required by a court order, (2) an extraordinary expense necessary to repair or maintain the development or any part of it for which the association is responsible where a threat to personal safety on the property is discovered, (3) an extraordinary expense necessary to repair or maintain the development or any part of it for which the association is responsible that could not have been reasonably foreseen by the board of directors in preparing and distributing the required pro forma operating budget, and (4) an extraordinary expense in making the first payment of the earthquake insurance surcharge pursuant to Section 5003 of the California Insurance Code.[19]

Notice Of Increased Assessments:

If the association does increase the regular or special assessments of the association, it must provide notice to the members by first-class mail not less than 30 days nor more than 60 days prior to the increased assessment becoming due.[20]

Assessments Are Both A Personal Debt Of The Owner And A Lien Against The Separate Interest:

Any regular or special assessment imposed under an association's governing documents, together with late charges, the reasonable costs of collection, and interest becomes a debt of the owner at the time the assessments and other sums are levied.[21]

The assessment debt is only a personal obligation of the property owner until and unless the association records in the public records a notice of delinquent assessment.[22] Section 1367(b) of the Civil Code establishes the association's authority to enforce regular and special assessments through the mechanism of a lien against the separate interest against which the assessments are levied:

> "(b) The amount of the assessment, plus any costs of collection, late charges, and interest assessed in accordance with Section 1366, shall be a lien on the owner's interest in the common interest development from and after the time the association causes to be recorded with the county recorder of the county in which the separate interest is located, a notice of delinquent assessment, ..."

A "lien" can generally be defined as a mechanism for securing the payment of a debt. The lien establishes the creditor's right to enforce payment of the debt by recourse against property, usually by foreclosure of the lien, subsequent sale of the property, and application of the sale proceeds to the payment of the debt. In the case of CID associations, Section 1367(b) of the

Civil Code establishes the associations' lien rights against the separate interest of the delinquent property owner.

In most circumstances, a secured creditor (whose right to collect a debt is secured by a lien) must first foreclose the lien against the property securing the debt and sell the property, before the creditor can pursue legal action directly against the debtor. This is commonly referred to as the "one action rule".

Associations are not hampered by the "one action rule", however, in seeking to enforce an owner's obligation to pay assessments. The practical effects of the Civil Code's treatment of an assessment debt as both a personal obligation of the owner and a lien are that the association, unlike most other creditors whose debts are secured by a lien against property, may enforce the assessment directly against the owner[23] and/or foreclose the association's assessment lien.

Property owners cannot escape the obligation to pay assessments by abandoning their property, through nonuse of the common areas and facilities, or through a claim that the association has breached its obligations under the governing documents.[24] Nor can a property owner successfully argue that he or she has no obligation to pay assessments because his or her association membership rights have been suspended.[25] Instead, the obligation to pay assessments under a recorded declaration of covenants, conditions and restrictions is an independent covenant that "runs with the land", continuing in effect even where the owner of the assessed land vacates the premises.[26]

The rationale of the courts has been that members of associations who, despite nonuse of the common areas or a breach by the association of its obligations, continue to own property in the development, also continue to enjoy the benefits of the association's ongoing schedule of management, operation, maintenance and repairs of the association's common areas, facilities and amenities. Among the benefits discussed by the courts is the enhancement of the value and attractiveness of the member's property through the association's management and operation of the common areas and facilities.

As discussed fully in this Chapter, associations have several effective alternative methods through which they can enforce the property owners' obligations to pay assessments, including lawsuits against the delinquent owner, the recording of assessment liens, and the enforcement of the liens through foreclosure. An association cannot, however, deny association membership to the purchaser of a separate interest based on the fact the seller is delinquent in the payment of assessments levied against the separate interest.[27]

Nature Of Assessment Lien:

Once an assessment lien has been properly created by the association's recordation of a notice of delinquent assessment in the Office of the County Recorder, it constitutes an encumbrance against the owner's interest in the common interest development, including the owner's separate interest (whether a condominium unit, community apartment interest, or separately-owned parcel of real property) and all interests which may be appurtenant to the separate interest.[28]

Because an assessment, by statute, becomes delinquent no earlier than 15 days after its due date,[29] the 15th day after the assessment is due is the earliest date the association can record its notice of delinquent assessment (unless the CC&Rs or other applicable association document specify a later date in which case the association should rely on such later date).

The notice of delinquent assessment lien must be recorded in the County Recorder's Office in the county where the delinquent owner's separate interest is located.[30]

Associations are not liable for slander of title or other claims asserted by property owners based on an association's recording of an assessment lien. The association's action in recording a lien is absolutely privileged.[31]

Required Contents Of Notice Of Delinquent Assessment:

The notice of delinquent assessment lien must contain the following information:[32] (1) the total amount of the outstanding assessment obligations and other delinquent sums; (2) a description of the owner's separate interest (a correct legal description should be used, not a street address or other common designation); (3) the names of the record title owner(s) of the separate interest; (4) the name and address of the trustee authorized by the association, if any, to enforce the lien by nonjudicial foreclosure sale; (5) the signature of the association's president or other person authorized by the association through its declaration of covenants, conditions and restrictions or by board resolution; and (6) a notary public's acknowledgement of the association officer's signature so the lien will be accepted for recording.

Priority Of Assessment Liens:

A proper notice of delinquent assessment lien takes priority over all other liens recorded subsequent to it, except where the declaration of covenants, conditions and restrictions may subordinate the notice of delinquent assessment lien to another lien or encumbrance.[33]

Duration Of Lien:

Once recorded, a valid assessment lien continues to exist indefinitely, although action to enforce the lien should be filed within any applicable period of limitations, for example, the four-year statute of limitations applicable to written contracts[34] or some shorter period which may be specified in the association's declaration of CC&Rs and/or other governing documents.[35]

If the delinquent amounts are paid, the association must ordinarily prepare and record in the County Recorder's Office a release of lien stating the delinquencies have been cured. Such releases are necessary to clear from the public records the encumbrance on the owner's title created by the recordation of the assessment lien.

Enforcement Of Assessment Obligation In General:

A CID association's assessment lien may be enforced through either or both judicial or nonjudicial foreclosure processes.[36] And, unlike most other secured debts, even though an assessment lien has been recorded, the association is exempt from application of the "one-action" rule which means the association may still sue the property owner directly for a personal money judgment instead of resorting to foreclosure of the lien against the property.[37] The association may also choose to pursue delinquent assessments through Small Claims Court or through the efforts of a reputable debt collection agency.

Nonjudicial Foreclosure:

It is only because the nonjudicial foreclosure remedy is expressly conferred by statute on CID associations that associations have the power to exercise this remedy. Although no cases have yet been published with respect to nonjudicial foreclosure of assessment liens, because such liens are to be foreclosed nonjudicially in the same manner as deeds of trust and mortgages,[38] the cases dealing with trust deeds provide adequate guidance on the subject.

Generally speaking, strict compliance with the statutory foreclosure and sale procedures must be adhered to by the association in order to avoid later challenges to the validity of the foreclosure and resulting sale.

The nonjudicial foreclosure remedy may be exercised by the trustee named in the notice of delinquent assessment, or a later substituted trustee, in the same manner as deed of trust or mortgage.[39] The statutes governing the foreclosure of trust deeds and assessment liens are extremely detailed, intricate and exacting. Ordinarily, the association should engage the services of a qualified professional to handle the foreclosure process. The process is initiated by recording a notice of delinquent assessment lien naming a trustee authorized to foreclose the lien no earlier than 15 days after the assessment becomes due.[40]

The trustee will then ordinarily obtain a trustee's sale guarantee to acquire the information necessary to determine whether other senior liens, including property tax liens, exist against the property in an aggregate amount exceeding the value of the property and the association's lien amount. If, after such determination, foreclosure is warranted, the trustee will prepare and record a notice of default in the public records in the County Recorder's Office and mail copies of the notice to the property owner(s) and all persons who may have recorded a request for copies of notices of default.

Within one month following recordation of the notice of default, the trustee must send, by registered or certified mail, a copy of the recorded notice of default to certain prescribed persons with a recorded interest in the subject property.

Once at least three months have elapsed since the notice of default was recorded, and the default has not been cured, the trustee must prepare a notice of trustee's sale which must contain certain required information including the name of the owner, the legal description of the property, the street address or other common designation of the property, a statement of the total amount of the unpaid balance of the debt as of the date of the notice, and the date and time of the sale.

At least 20 days before the date of the sale, the trustee must post a copy of the notice of sale in one public place in the city in which the property is to be sold and in a conspicuous place on the property to be sold. During this same 20-day period, the trustee must publish the notice of sale, once per week, in a newspaper of general circulation in the city, judicial district or county in which the property is located.

At least 14 days prior to the date of the sale, the trustee must record the notice of sale in the County Recorder's Office. At the sale, the trustee may require payment of amounts bid for the property by one of following methods: cash, a cashier's check, a check drawn by a state or federal credit union, savings and loan association, or bank, or a cash equivalent that has been designated in the notice of sale as acceptable to the trustee.

The trustee may accept a "credit bid" only from the association, as the creditor under the assessment lien, and only up to an amount not exceeding the total amount due the association (including trustee's fees and sale expenses). The trustee must sell the property to the highest bidder and complete the sale by an announcement, the fall of hammer or some other customary manner. If full payment of the winning bid has not been deposited prior to the sale, the trustee must demand payment of the highest bid in full. After final payment of the highest bid is received, the trustee may execute, acknowledge and deliver to the successful bidder a trustee's deed to the property.

At any time until five business days prior to the date of the sale, the property owner or holders of liens junior to the association's lien may "reinstate" the obligation by paying the amount stated in the recorded notice of default plus reasonable costs and expenses and trustee's and attorney's fees.[41]

The right of reinstatement may be exercised unilaterally by the property owner or holders of junior liens up until five business days before the date of the sale specified in the notice of sale. Reinstatement is possible even after that time but before the actual sale if the association is willing to accept such an offer because the notice of sale may be vacated at any time by the parties' agreement.

Unlike some judicial foreclosure sales, the property owner has no right to redeem the property by paying the debt once the time for reinstatement has passed.[42]

Judicial Foreclosure:

As mentioned earlier, an association's notice of delinquent assessment may be enforced through either or both judicial or nonjudicial foreclosure processes.[43]

If the association chooses to enforce the lien through judicial foreclosure, an appropriate lawsuit seeking a court decree of foreclosure may be filed in the Municipal Court if the debt owed does not exceed $25,000.[44] In all cases where the debt exceeds $25,000, the lawsuit must be filed in Superior Court.

The chief object of the judicial foreclosure lawsuit is a final judgment directing the County Sheriff or other levying officer to sell the property at a public sale. The proceeds of the sale are to be used to pay for the costs and expenses of the sale, the satisfaction of debts secured by senior liens with priority over the association's lien, the satisfaction of the debt owed to the association, including interest, late charges and attorney's fees. If there are any excess proceeds, they are delivered to the property owner.

The judicial foreclosure lawsuit is initiated by the association's attorney preparing and filing with the appropriate court a complaint to foreclose the notice of delinquent assessment lien. The summons and complaint must then be served on all defendants.

Because the foreclosure of a junior lien has no effect on valid senior liens, the holders of senior liens need not be named as defendants in the lawsuit. However, in order to extinguish junior liens and terminate the junior lienholders' redemption and reinstatement rights, the holders of junior liens must be named as defendants in the lawsuit and served with the summons and complaint. If a junior lienholder is omitted from the lawsuit, it does not affect the validity of the lawsuit or the foreclosure sale, but: (1) the property sold at the foreclosure sale is sold subject to the junior liens and the junior lienholders retain the powers to reinstate and/or redeem the property by paying off the debt owed under the notice of delinquent assessment lien; and (2) the purchaser then generally has two choices: (i) he can acknowledge the junior lien(s) and pay them off, or (ii) he can act as if he has purchased the senior lien (the notice of delinquent assessment lien), rather than the property, at the sale. The purchaser may then elect to file a separate foreclosure action to clear off the junior lien(s) and insist that the junior lienholder either pay off the senior lien (the notice of delinquent assessment lien) or lose the right to redeem the property.

Before initiating a judicial foreclosure lawsuit, it is important for the association to purchase a litigation guarantee from a reputable title insurance company. The litigation guarantee serves a function similar to the trustee's sale guarantee used in the nonjudicial foreclosure process. The guarantee discloses the names and addresses of all senior and junior lienholders of record, and it generally insures the association against loss resulting from the omission of the names of junior lienholders of record.

At the time the lawsuit is filed with the Court, or promptly afterwards, the attorney should prepare and record in the public records a "Lis Pendens" or "Notice of Pending Action" which has the effect of imparting constructive notice to all subsequent purchasers or encumbrancers that the property is the subject of a pending foreclosure lawsuit. This should effectively prevent debtors from transferring the property to others in hopes of avoiding the debt.

The expediency of the judicial foreclosure lawsuit is governed largely by the mandatory procedural rules governing all lawsuits, as well as the extent to which the defendants resist and defend the lawsuit. In some cases, a default judgment may be obtained relatively quickly where the debtor fails to respond to the lawsuit. And in some cases where the defendants do respond, a judgment by summary judgment motion may be obtained where the evidence is clear that the assessments were lawfully levied and that the debt is owed.

If the final court judgment ordering sale of the property after foreclosure determines that a "deficiency judgment" may be ordered against the defendant, the property must be sold subject to the right of redemption.[45] Redemption is the right of the property owner to reacquire title to the property by paying the amount of the judgment under which the lien was foreclosed, in addition to certain costs and fees incurred in connection with the sale. A "deficiency" occurs when the sale proceeds are less than the amount of the judgment. A deficiency judgment, that is the right to a money judgment against the debtor for the difference between the sales proceeds and the judgment, may be available to an association under certain circumstances.

Depending on the facts and circumstances of each case, sometimes an association may choose to waive or give up its right to a deficiency judgment in order that the property may be sold without being subject to redemption rights. If that is the course of action chosen, the association may, in its complaint to foreclose the notice of delinquent assessment lien, expressly waive any rights to a deficiency judgment which waiver should, as in the case of a trust deed, preclude any redemption rights allowing the foreclosure sale purchaser to purchase the property free of redemption rights.

Real property sold subject to the right of redemption may be redeemed only by the judgment debtor or the judgment debtor's successor in interest.[46] If the sale is subject to the right of redemption, the right of redemption expires either three months after the date of the sale if the sale proceeds are sufficient to satisfy the secured indebtedness, including interest, the costs of the action and costs of the sale,[47] or one year after the date of the sale if the sale proceeds are insufficient to satisfy the amount of secured indebtedness, the costs of the action and costs of the sale.[48]

The redemption amount consists of the following sums: (i) the purchase price at the foreclosure sale (as opposed to the fair market value of the property)[49]; (ii) any assessments or taxes and reasonable amounts for fire insurance, maintenance, upkeep, and repair of improvements on the property[50]; (iii) amounts paid by the sale purchaser on a prior obligation secured by the property to the extent payment was necessary to protect the purchaser's interest[51]; (iv) interest on the foregoing amounts from the time such amounts were paid until the date on which the redemption price is deposited with the levying officer[52]; (v) the amount of any liens the foreclosure sale purchaser has on the property which are subordinate to the lien under which the property was sold, plus interest.[53]

Prior to July, 1983, if the judgment debtor redeemed the property he was restored to the estate he owned prior to the foreclosure sale and if the redemption price paid did not completely satisfy the amount of the foreclosure judgment lien, the lien reattached to the property for the amount of the lien unpaid.[54] This rule, however, was discontinued with the enactment of Code of Civil Procedure Sections 729.060, 729.080 and 701.630 in 1982 (effective July, 1983) and the foreclosure judgment lien is extinguished by the sale and does not reattach to the property, whether or not paid in full by the redemption.

Depending on whether or not a deficiency judgment is available or has been waived or is prohibited, the sale may or may not be held subject to the judgment debtor's right of redemption. If a deficiency judgment is waived or is prohibited, the property must be sold without any rights of redemption pursuant to Code of Civil Procedure Section 716.020.[55] If a deficiency judgment is not waived or prohibited, the property must be sold subject to the right of redemption pursuant to Code of Civil Procedure Sections 729.010 through 729.090.[56]

When property is sold subject to the right of redemption, the levying officer must execute and deliver to the purchaser a certificate of sale and record a duplicate of the certificate of sale in the office of the county recorder.[57] The certificate of sale must contain: (1) the price paid for each distinct lot or parcel of property sold, (2) the total price paid, and (3) a statement that the property is subject to the right of redemption and indicating the redemption period.[58]

If the property is sold subject to the right of redemption, promptly after the sale the levying officer must serve a notice of the right of redemption on the judgment debtor either personally or by mail.[59] From the time of the sale until a redemption or until the redemption period expires, the purchaser is entitled: (1) to receive, from any person in possession of the property, the rents and profits from the property or the value of the use and occupation of the property,[60] and to enter the property during reasonable hours to repair and maintain the premises and to a court order restraining waste on the property.[61]

If the redemption price is not deposited by the judgment debtor before the expiration of the redemption period, the levying officer must promptly execute and deliver to the purchaser a deed of sale.[62]

When the property sold at a foreclosure sale is not sold subject to the right of redemption, and the highest bid does not exceed $5,000, the successful purchaser, other than the association as the judgment creditor, must pay the sale price in cash, or by certified check or cashier's check.[63]

The association, as the judgment creditor, may make a "credit bid" to purchase the property and acquire title to the property in exchange for all or part of the amount of the judgment. A credit bid is made by giving the levying officer a written receipt crediting all or part of the amount required to satisfy the judgment, except that the levying officer's remaining unsatisfied costs and the amount of preferred labor claims, exempt proceeds and any other claim that is required by statute to be satisfied, must be paid in cash or by certified check or cashier's check.[64]

If the highest bid for the property exceeds $5,000, the successful bidder may treat the sale as a credit transaction and deposit with the levying officer at least $5,000 or ten percent of the amount bid, whichever is greater, and within 10 days after the sale pay the balance due plus costs and interest accruing between the date of sale and the date of full payment.[65]

When the purchaser pays the full amount due, the levying officer must execute and deliver a deed to the purchaser and record a duplicate of the deed in the office of the county recorder.[66]

Unless the sale was improper because of irregular proceedings or any other reason, the sale is absolute and cannot be set aside for any reason.[67]

If the purchaser at the foreclosure sale is the judgment creditor, the judgment debtor may commence, within 90 days after the date of sale, an action to set aside the sale.[68]

Competing Liens And Encumbrances:

An association's notice of delinquent assessment lien takes effect on the date that it is recorded in the records of the County Recorder.[69] The assessment lien takes priority over all other liens recorded subsequent to it, except where the declaration of covenants, conditions and restrictions may subordinate the notice of delinquent assessment lien to another lien or encumbrance.[70]

When associations seek to enforce a delinquent assessment debt, they frequently find themselves in competition with other liens which have been recorded against the member's property. Before proceeding with lien enforcement and incurring any substantial costs in doing so, the association needs to determine the priority of its assessment lien. If the value of the property does not equal or exceed the amount of the association's lien plus the amounts of all senior liens, it may not be in the association's best economic interests to seek lien enforcement at that time.

Generally speaking, liens and encumbrances take priority in the order they are recorded, i.e., the "first in time wins." There are several important exceptions to this general rule, for example, real property tax liens, which take priority over all other liens (see below) regardless of the time at which they are created.

The following paragraphs contain a brief summary of the general priority of liens against real property which associations should understand and take into account when examining any lien enforcement circumstances.

Liens for real property taxes have priority over all other earlier recorded liens.[71] By operation of law, all real property tax liens and all public improvement assessment liens have priority over all other liens on the real property (including assessment liens), regardless of the time of their creation.[72] Similarly, local district special assessments are accorded the same priority as real property tax liens.[73]

All other liens generally take priority in the order of the time of their creation (as between lien holders without actual notice of another lien on the property, this is generally the date of recordation in the public land records).[74]

Internal Revenue Service ("IRS") liens for delinquent income taxes are created as of the date the income tax is assessed, but the lien is not valid against other persons with an interest in the taxpayer's real property until a notice of the lien is recorded in the public land records.[75]

State and county personal property taxes may become a lien on the real property upon which the personal property is located if the tax collector records a certificate of delinquency of unsecured property taxes in the public land records, but such lien does not have priority over any other lien which attached prior to the date the tax collector's certificate was recorded.[76]

Effect Of Foreclosure Of Senior Liens:

The foreclosure of a lien against real property generally results in the extinguishment of all other liens which are junior or subordinate to the lien being foreclosed.[77] Once a lien is foreclosed or extinguished, if the judgment debtor redeems the property within the redemption period, the liens do not reattach to the property and the property may not be applied to satisfy the judgment under which the lien was created.[78]

For example, the author once ran across a case in which the association foreclosed its assessment lien in the amount of several thousands of dollars. The property was sold subject to the right of redemption. The association and its attorney attended the foreclosure sale where, for reasons not apparent to the author, the association's attorney credit bid the amount of $1.00 for the purchase of the property. Several days later, the judgment debtor-property owner redeemed the property for $2.00. Under the governing law, the debtor was able to reacquire title to his property and extinguish the association's lien. A very strange result. For these reasons, associations need to approach foreclosure sales with a complete understanding of the applicable laws.

Subordination By Declaration:

The association's declaration of CC&Rs will ordinarily make the association's assessment liens junior to "purchase money" deeds of trust whether or not the assessment lien is recorded prior to the deed of trust. This process is called "subordination" and subordination language is typically found in most declarations. Subordination of the assessment liens to "purchase money" or "first" trust deeds and mortgages is necessary in order to induce real estate lenders to loan money to buyers to purchase their property in the first instance. Foreclosure of the purchase money deed of trust will then extinguish the subordinated assessment lien.[79]

Foreclosure of any other lien, for example, a mechanic's lien, which is senior (recorded earlier) to the association's assessment lien will likewise extinguish the assessment lien.

Although the new owner who purchases a separate interest at a foreclosure sale is not responsible for assessments accruing prior to the transfer of title, the new owner continues to be liable for the payment of assessments which are levied and accrue following the transfer of title pursuant to the foreclosure.[80]

Because CID association's are exempted from the "one action rule" as discussed earlier, if the association's delinquent assessment lien is extinguished by the foreclosure of a senior lien, the association may still pursue legal action or other collection efforts against the property owner directly.

If the real property subject to the foreclosed assessment lien is ultimately sold pursuant to the judgment of foreclosure, the sale extinguishes the assessment lien, any subordinate liens and any "state tax liens" which may have existed against the property. In other words, the purchaser takes title free of all such liens.[81] "State tax liens" should not be confused with real property tax liens, which have priority over all liens.[82]

Effect Of Property Owner's Bankruptcy On assessment Obligations:

The federal courts have exclusive jurisdiction of bankruptcy cases and most aspects of bankruptcy are governed by federal law, commonly known as the Bankruptcy Code and found in Title 11 United States Code ("U.S.C.") Sections 101 - 1330. Bankruptcy is designed to provide persons and entities with a mechanism of debt relief and/or "breathing room" within which to reorganize and restructure debt without interference by the debtor's creditors.

Generally speaking, debts arising prior to the time the debtor files a bankruptcy petition and which are listed by the debtor on schedules filed with the bankruptcy court are dischargeable. Debts that arise after the bankruptcy case is filed or which the debtor fails to list on the schedules filed with the bankruptcy court are generally nondischargeable.[83]

When a debt is discharged in bankruptcy, the debtor is no longer personally liable for payment of that debt or obligation.

Probably, the two most important aspects of bankruptcy with which the association should be concerned are: (1) not violating the "automatic stay" of bankruptcy (discussed below), and (2) protecting the association's interests to the maximum practicable extent possible under the Bankruptcy Code, in other words, protecting the association's right to enforce and collect assessments.

Automatic Stay Of Bankruptcy Court:

When a bankruptcy debtor files a bankruptcy petition, an automatic stay (or injunction order) is immediately issued by operation of law. The automatic stay precludes virtually any and all further creditor action to collect or enforce an obligation or debt that arose before the filing of the bankruptcy petition.[84] The scope of the automatic stay is extremely broad and applies to prohibit all types of creditor collection activities, including the commencement of lawsuits against the debtor, the continuation of any pending lawsuit or proceeding against the debtor, the commencement or continuation of arbitration, actions to enforce liens against the debtors' property, attachment, including but not limited to the enforcement of attachment or judgment liens against property of the bankruptcy estate, service of process, seeking the setoff of mutual debts, and all nonjudicial collection actions such as writing letters and making telephone calls to the debtor with respect to collection of the debt.

The prosecution of action against the debtor on claims and obligations that arise after the bankruptcy case is filed are not stayed. However, even if an action is not stayed, the creditor must ordinarily first obtain permission from the Bankruptcy Court to pursue collection of the debt from assets of the bankruptcy estate.

Although some property owners may argue that where the obligation to pay assessments is provided in a recorded declaration of covenants the obligation preceded the bankruptcy case and collection or enforcement of any assessment is therefore barred by the automatic stay, the California Civil Code is contrary. Civil Code Section 1367(a) provides that: "A regular or special assessment and any late charges, reasonable costs of collection, and interest, as assessed in accordance with Section 1366, shall be a debt of the owner of the separate interest at the time the assessment or other sums are levied." For bankruptcy purposes, the time when the debt or claim arises is a matter of state law. Under Civil Code Section 1367(a), the assessment becomes a debt at the time it is levied and assessments levied after the filing of the bankruptcy petition are not subject to the automatic stay. However, associations need to be aware that some

Bankruptcy Courts have held that post-petition assessments are pre-petition debts.[85]

The bankruptcy automatic stay generally does not prevent action against third party debtors, in other words, debtors who owe an obligation to the creditor but who have not filed for bankruptcy protection. As an example, if two (unmarried) persons own property on which the assessments are delinquent and only one of the persons files a bankruptcy petition, the association would be free to pursue the other owner personally through collection letters, Small Claims action or Municipal or Superior Court lawsuits.

The automatic stay applies to all creditors whether or not they have actual or constructive notice of the stay.[86] Ordinarily, if a property owner files a bankruptcy petition, he or she will list the assessment as a debt and the association will receive notice of the bankruptcy from the Bankruptcy Court or the debtor's bankruptcy attorney. However, even if no such notice is received, the automatic stay applies to all creditors, including the association.

Violations of the bankruptcy automatic stay expose the creditor to possible sanctions including but not limited to monetary fines levied by the Bankruptcy Court, particularly if the violation was a knowing violation where the creditor had notice of the bankruptcy petition. In addition, a violation of the stay may prejudice the association's other rights and remedies it may have in the Bankruptcy Court.

Generally speaking, acts in violation of the stay are void and of no legal force or effect.[87] Any judgment, lien enforcement, foreclosure proceeding or sale or other collection is void if it was done in violation of the Bankruptcy Court's automatic stay.

Recording Assessment Lien:

Section 362(b)(3) of the Bankruptcy Code[88] provides that the filing of the debtor's bankruptcy petition does not operate to stay acts to "perfect an interest in real property". A lien or lien rights in real property constitute an interest in real property and legal practitioners routinely rely on this statutory provision to advise their contractor clients they may proceed with the recording of mechanic's liens against bankruptcy debtors in order to perfect their mechanic's lien rights. This practice has been approved by the courts and held not to violate the automatic stay.[89] However, one California Bankruptcy Court has indicated that relief from the automatic stay must be obtained in order for a CID association to attach its lien if the property is part of the bankruptcy estate.[90]

Association's Remedies In Bankruptcy:

Upon first receiving notice of a property owner's bankruptcy filing, the association should refrain from any further collection activities and/or proceedings, including but not limited to lawsuits, foreclosures, collection letters and telephone calls to or with respect to the bankruptcy debtor.

The association should then examine its records to determine whether the association's claim is secured or unsecured. If an assessment lien has been recorded prior to the property owner's bankruptcy filing, the association's claim is secured. Otherwise, the association's claim is unsecured.

If no delinquent assessment lien has been recorded, the association should prepare and record a lien for post-petition assessments, that is, those assessments which have or will accrue after the property owner's bankruptcy petition has been filed. However, depending on the Bankruptcy District, relief from the automatic stay may first be necessary before recording and attaching an assessment lien.[91]

A claim secured by an association's proper assessment lien which has been timely recorded, will ordinarily provide much greater protection of the association's interests than an unsecured claim for payment of assessments. However, the bankruptcy trustee has certain "lien avoidance powers" which he or she may exercise under the Bankruptcy Code to avoid liens thereby rendering the claim unsecured.

Unsecured claims are frequently not paid or not paid in full in bankruptcy because the bankruptcy estate often does not contain sufficient assets free and clear of liens with which to pay the unsecured claims. If the bankruptcy debtor receives a final discharge from the Bankruptcy Court, he or she is then relieved of all personal liability for assessments which accrued prior to the bankruptcy petition being filed.

Generally, the association should always complete and file with the Bankruptcy Court a "Proof of Claim". The bankruptcy debtor's attorney or the bankruptcy trustee ordinarily mails a Proof of Claim form to all creditors listed by the debtor in the bankruptcy petition together with the notice of bankruptcy proceedings. If the association does not receive this form, it should be able to obtain one from its attorney or a stationery and office supply store which carries legal forms. The Proof of Claim should be completed properly to show whether the assessment debt is secured (an assessment lien has been recorded) or unsecured. If the assessment debt is secured by a lien, the association should attach a copy of the recorded assessment lien to the Proof of Claim.

If a Proof of Claim is not completed and filed in a timely manner,[92] the association will probably lose all rights it may have had for payment of the assessments owed by the bankrupt property owner. Failing to timely file a Proof of Claim renders the debt uncollectible and unenforceable in all but the rarest of circumstances.[93]

In appropriate circumstances, for example where the size of the assessment debt and the property owner's equity in the property justify the expense of doing so, the association may wish to consider filing a motion for relief from the automatic stay in the Bankruptcy Court. If the motion is granted, the association may be permitted to proceed with enforcement of its lien, including foreclosure.

A creditor may file and prosecute a complaint to avoid dischargeability of the debt owed to the creditor on various prescribed grounds.[94] Of all the grounds provided for in the Bankruptcy Code, those most potentially applicable to the association's position as a creditor are: (1) the debtor obtained an extension of credit or financing through false pretenses, false representation or actual fraud; (2) debts the debtor did not list or schedule in a way that would provide the association with the opportunity to file a Proof of Claim, but the creditor cannot have actual knowledge of the bankruptcy case in time to permit the creditor to file a Proof of Claim or objection to discharge; (3) claims for fraud or defalcation while the debtor was acting in a fiduciary capacity; (4) claims involving embezzlement or larceny by the debtor; and (5) a claim that could have been scheduled in a prior bankruptcy case if the debtor waived discharge or was denied a discharge.

Effect Of Bankruptcy:

The primary goal of most debtors in filing bankruptcy petitions is to discharge their debts. For others, "breathing room" to reorganize a business or restructure debt load is the primary goal. When a bankruptcy petition is filed, everything owned by the debtor becomes part of the bankruptcy estate (except for certain exempt property as provided by statute). If the debtor obtains a discharge in bankruptcy, the creditor cannot assert the claim any further against the debtor.[95]

If discharge of a debt or debts is denied or the bankruptcy case is dismissed by the Bankruptcy Court (this sometimes happens when the debtor fails to complete a Chapter 13 plan or has attempted to defraud the Court or creditors in a Chapter 7, 11, or 13 case), the debtor remains personally liable for the debts.

Are Common Interest Development Assessments "Post-petition" Or "Pre-petition" Debts Of The Property Owner ?

The basic rule of dischargeability of debts in bankruptcy is that prepetition debts, those debts that arise prior to the bankruptcy debtor filing a bankruptcy petition, are dischargeable in bankruptcy. Those debts that arise after the filing of the bankruptcy petition are not dischargeable, the debtor remains personally liable for such post-petition debts.

The central issue with respect to assessments then becomes whether assessments are pre-petition debts or post-petition debts. The courts have adopted three different positions.

One line of cases holds that the property owner's personal liability for assessments is nondischargeable in bankruptcy because the obligation arises out of a recorded declaration of covenants, conditions and restrictions, and constitutes a "real covenant", running with the land, and is a post-petition debt because the debtor owns the land post-petition.[96]

The second line of cases holds that debtor's personal liability for assessments is dischargeable because the obligation arises out of a prepetition "executory" (not yet fully performed) contract. These cases view the declaration of covenants, conditions and restrictions and the covenant to pay assessments as a "contract" entered into by the debtor prior to the bankruptcy petition being filed.[97] It is this line of cases which one California Federal District Court has followed,[98] however, the 9th Circuit Court of Appeals has not yet addressed the issue.

The third line of cases holds that a bankruptcy debtor may be discharged from his personal liability for assessments despite retaining post-petition ownership of his separate interest, if the debtor relinquishes possession or other incidents of ownership in clear and unequivocal terms.[99]

Specific Bankruptcy Code Provisions Now Address Common Interest Development Assessments:

In 1994, the Bankruptcy Code was amended by Congress with the addition of 11 U.S.C. Section 523(a)(16) which provides broad protection for bankrupt property owners in common interest developments.[100]

Under Section 523(a)(16), all discharged debtors, except those who continue to physically occupy a dwelling unit in the development or those who rent the dwelling unit to another person and receive rent payments, are relieved from and have no personal liability for assessments levied after the bankruptcy petition has been filed.

However, Section 523(a)(16) does not prohibit an association from enforcing an assessment lien for post-petition assessments.[101] However, before enforcing the lien through foreclosure against the property of an owner who has received a discharge in bankruptcy, the association should seek the advice of an attorney experienced in such matters. Ordinarily, permission from the Bankruptcy Court must be obtained or the association risks violating the automatic stay and the permanent injunction against collection efforts issued at the close of a case in which the debtor receives a discharge.

BUDGETS AND OTHER DOCUMENTS:

As discussed in the earlier part of this Chapter on Assessments, CID associations are required to prepare and distribute to the members on a regular basis a pro forma operating budget and other financial documents.

Pro Forma Operating Budget:

The pro forma operating budget must be prepared and distributed annually, not less than 45 days nor more than 60 days before the beginning of the association's fiscal year. The budget must contain (1) the association's estimated revenue and expenses on an accrual basis, (2) a summary of the association's reserves based on the most recent review or reserve study conducted pursuant to statute, (3) a statement as to whether the board of directors has determined or anticipates that one or more special assessments will be required to repair, replace, or restore, any major component or to provide adequate reserves therefor, and (4) a general statement addressing the procedures used to calculate and establish those reserves necessary to defray future repair, replacement, or additions to those major components the association is obligated to maintain.[102]

Instead of distributing the complete pro forma operating budget, the board of directors may elect to distribute a summary of the budget to all members with a written notice that the complete budget is available at the association's business office and that copies will be provided on request at the expense of the association.[103] This notice must be in 10-point boldface type on the front page of the budget summary.[104] If any member requests that a copy of the pro forma operating budget be mailed to him or her, the association must deliver it by first-class mail, within five days of the request.[105]

Review of Financial Statement:

For each fiscal year in which the association's gross income exceeds $75,000, the association must cause a review of its financial statements to be prepared in accordance with generally accepted accounting principles by a California licensed certified public accountant or public accountant. A copy of the review must be distributed to the association members within 120 days after the close of each fiscal year of the association for which a review is required.[106]

Assessment Lien Enforcement Policies:

Associations must annually distribute to their members, during the 60-day period immediately preceding the beginning of the association's fiscal year, a statement describing the association's policies and practices in enforcing lien rights or other legal remedies for the default in payment of assessments.[107]

Summary Of Insurance Policies:

The association must distribute to its members a summary of the association's general liability insurance policy, a summary of the association's directors and officers errors and omissions liability insurance policy, and a summary of the association's earthquake and flood insurance policy, if one has been issued.[108]

If the information required to be summarized and disclosed for each policy appears on the insurance policy declaration page, the association may distribute copies of those pages to the members.[109]

In the event any of the insurance policies are canceled and not immediately renewed, the association must, as soon as reasonably practical, notify its members, by first-class mail, of that fact. If the association renews any of the policies or a new policy is issued to replace a policy and there is no lapse in coverage, the association must notify its members of that fact in the next available mailing to all members.[110]

Summary Of Alternative Dispute Resolution Procedures:

Associations must annually distribute a summary of the Civil Code Section 1354 alternative dispute resolution process, either at the time the pro forma budget is distributed or at the time the association mails or delivers a newsletter or magazine to all of its members. The summary must include the following mandatory language: "Failure by any member of the association to comply with the prefiling requirements of Section 1354 of the Civil Code may result in the loss of your rights to sue the association or another member of the association regarding enforcement of the governing documents."[111]

Notice Of Members' Rights To Obtain Minutes Of Meetings:

Associations must notify their members in writing, at the time the required pro forma budget is distributed, or at the time of any general mailing to the entire membership, of their right to have copies of the minutes of meetings of the board of directors, and how and where those minutes may be obtained.[112]

Copies Of Governing Documents Upon Request By A Property Owner:

Owners of property located in common interest developments who contemplate selling their property, must provide prospective purchasers with certain documents related to the development and the association.[113] In order to assist the owner in complying with that requirement, the Civil Code requires that upon written request of a property owner, the association must, within 10 days of the mailing or delivery of the request, provide the owner with copies of: (1) the association's governing documents, (2) if there is a restriction in the governing documents limiting the occupancy, residency, or use of a separate interest on the basis of age in a manner different from that provided in Civil Code Section 51.3, a statement that the restriction is only enforceable to the extent permitted by Civil Code Section 51.3 and a statement specifying the applicable provisions of Section 51.3, (3) the most recently distributed pro forma operating budget, financial statement review, statement of lien enforcement policies, and summary of insurance policies, and (4) a written statement from an authorized association representative as to the amount of the association's current regular and special assessments and fees, as well as any assessments levied upon the owner's interest in the common interest development which are unpaid on the date of the statement. The statement must also include true information on late charges, interest, and costs of collection which, as of the date of the statement, are or may be made a lien upon the owner's interest.[114]

The association may charge a fee for providing the requested documents to the owner, but the fee cannot exceed the reasonable costs of preparing and reproducing the requested documents.[115]

OPERATING FUNDS AND RESERVES:

Nature of Reserves:

Reserves are those monies or funds which the association has identified and set aside for the future repair, replacement or addition to the "major components" of the development for which the association is responsible.[116] Reserves and reserve funds must be distinguished from the association's operating funds which are used for the routine management, maintenance and operation of the development.

The term "major components" is not defined by the Civil Code. The term probably refers to all the significant items of real and personal property which make up all or part of the common areas, facilities, and services which the association is obligated to maintain and provide under the Davis-Stirling Common Interest Development Act and its governing documents.

Each association is responsible for identifying the "major components" for which it is responsible and for which adequate reserves must be accumulated.[117] Association directors may be held individually liable for breach of their fiduciaries for the failure to establish and maintain adequate reserve funds sufficient to satisfy the property maintenance, repair, replacement and restoration obligations the association bears under its governing documents.[118]

Reserves are ordinarily accumulated over time through the allocation of part of the regular assessments and the levy of special assessments for the purposes of repairing, replacing or adding to the major components of the development as they wear out or become obsolete with use and time. The association should regularly evaluate the projected financial requirements which are necessary to repair or replace the major items of property owned and maintained by the association.

Many associations have declarations of CC&Rs which include general provisions describing the methods by which reserves should be calculated. In addition to such provisions which may be found in the declaration, the

Civil Code contains several important and mandatory requirements which must be met with respect to the establishment of adequate reserve funds.

The calculation of adequate reserves generally requires the association to identify each major component for which it is responsible and estimate the current replacement cost, useful life, and remaining life of each major component.[119] The regular analysis of reserve requirements and establishment of adequate reserve funds is critical to the life of the association and its members. Without timely and sufficient reserve analyses, an association may unexpectedly find itself facing tremendous financial responsibility for the repair or replacement of a major component and no or inadequate funds with which to meet its obligations.

Use Of Reserve Funds:

Other than some temporary borrowing of reserves to meet short-term cash-flow requirements (see discussion below),[120] the association cannot use reserve funds for any purposes other than the repair, restoration, replacement, or maintenance of the major components of the development for which the association is obligated.[121]

Mandatory Reserve Studies:

At least once every three years, the association's board of directors must cause a study of the association's reserve requirements and reserve funds to be performed if the current replacement value of the major components for which the association is obligated is equal to or greater than one-half of the gross budget of the association for any fiscal year.[122] The association's board of directors must review the reserve study at least annually and consider and implement any necessary adjustments to the board's analysis of the reserve account requirements as a result of the review.[123]

The required reserve study must, at a minimum, include: (1) identification of the major components which the association is obligated to repair, replace, restore, or maintain which, as of the date of the study, have a remaining useful life of less than 30 years, (2) identification of the probable remaining useful life of the identified components as of the date of the study, (3) an estimate of the cost of repair, replacement, restoration, or maintenance of the identified components during and at the end of their useful life, and (4) an estimate of the total annual contribution necessary to defray the cost to repair, replace, restore, or maintain the identified components during and at the end of their useful life, after subtracting total reserve funds as of the date of the study.[124]

Periodic Reviews Of Reserve Accounts:

If the association's governing documents do not require more stringent or frequent reviews, the board of directors must review, on at least a quarterly basis: (1) a current reconciliation of the association's reserve accounts,[125] (2) the current year's actual reserve revenues and expenses compared to the current year's budget,[126] and (3) an income and expense statement for the association's operating and reserve accounts.[127]

In addition, the board of directors must also review the latest account statements prepared by the financial institutions where the association keeps its operating and reserve accounts.[128]

Withdrawal Of Funds From Reserve Account:

The association must ensure that the signatures of at least two persons, who must be members of the association's board of directors, or one officer who is not a member of the board of directors and a member of the board of directors, are required for the withdrawal of money from the association's reserve accounts.[129]

Borrowing From Reserve Funds Generally:

As mentioned earlier, the association cannot expend funds designated as reserve funds for any purpose other than the repair, restoration, replacement, or maintenance of, or litigation involving the repair, restoration, replacement, or maintenance of, the major components for which the association is responsible.[130]

The board may, however, authorize a temporary transfer of money from a reserve fund to the association's general operating fund to meet short-term cash-flow requirements or other expenses. Before authorizing any such transfer, the board must make a written finding, recorded in the board's minutes, explaining the reasons that the transfer is needed, and describing when and how the money will be repaid to the reserve fund.[131]

The transferred reserve funds must be restored to the reserve fund within one year of the date of the initial transfer, except that the board may, upon making a finding supported by documentation that a temporary delay would be in the best interests of the development, temporarily delay the restoration. In delaying restoration of the reserve funds, the board must exercise prudent fiscal management and must, if necessary, levy a special assessment to recover the full amount of the expended funds within the time limits required.[132] Any such special assessment which may be necessary is subject to the limitations on the amount of increased assessments discussed earlier in this Chapter as imposed by Civil Code Section 1366. The board may, in its discretion, extend the date the payment on the special assessment is due, but any extension does not prevent the association from pursuing any legal remedy to enforce the collection of an unpaid special assessment.[133]

Borrowing Reserve Funds To Pay For Litigation:

When the decision is made to use reserve funds or to temporarily transfer money from the reserve fund to pay for litigation, the association must notify its members of the association of that decision and of the availability of an accounting of those expenses in the next available mailing to all members.[134] Unless the governing documents impose more stringent standards, the association must account for the expenses related to the litigation on at least a quarterly basis. The accounting shall be made available for inspection by members of the association at the association's office.[135]

Periodic Review Of Operating Funds And Accounts:

If the association's governing documents do not require more frequent reviews, the board of directors must review, on at least a quarterly basis: (1) a current reconciliation of the association's operating accounts,[136] and (2) an income and expense statement for the association's operating accounts.[137]

The association's board of directors must also review the latest account statements prepared by the financial institutions where the association keeps its operating accounts.[138]

The reviews of the association's operating and reserve funds and accounts as required by statute are only minimum standards the association and its board of directors must satisfy. Where the circumstances indicate the need, prudent associations and boards will review the matters more frequently. Regular and special assessments are typically the only sources of association revenue for the operation and management of the development and the establishment of adequate reserves to repair and replace the development's major components. Prudent and responsible management and use of the funds are essential to continued operation of the association and the community and the lives of the association members.

CHAPTER NOTES

INTRODUCTION

1. Citizens for Covenant Compliance v. Anderson (1995) 12 Cal. App. 4th 345, 47 Cal. Rptr. 2d 898, 906 P.2d 1314.

2. Citizens for Covenant Compliance v. Anderson (1995) 12 Cal. App. 4th 345, 47 Cal. Rptr. 2d 898, 906 P.2d 1314.

CHAPTER I: COMMON INTEREST DEVELOPMENTS - GENERAL OVERVIEW

1. Duffey v. Superior Court (Coast Homeowners Association (1992) 3 Cal. App. 4th 425, 4 Cal. Rptr. 2d 334. Even more recently, the California Supreme Court, in Citizens for Covenant Compliance v. Anderson (1995) 12 Cal. App. 4th 345, 47 Cal. Rptr. 2d 898, 906 P.2d 1314, offered the following comments with respect to the significance of associations, community living and land use restrictions:

'The Andersons want to plant and harvest grapes, operate a winery, and keep llamas on their property in Woodside. Some neighbors object, and claim such activities are prohibited by covenants, conditions and restrictions (CC&Rs) that limit the Andersons' property, and theirs, to residential use. The Andersons counter, thus far successfully, that the CC&Rs are not enforceable because they are not mentioned in any deed to their property. The dispute is now before us.

"Its resolution requires us to penetrate a legal thicket entangled by the ancient doctrines of covenants that run with the land and equitable servitudes. The task is not easy. 'The law of easements, real covenants, and equitable servitudes is the most complex and archaic body of American property law remaining in the twentieth century.' . . . 'The law in this area is an unspeakable quagmire. The intrepid soul who ventures into this formidable wilderness never emerges unscarred. Some, the smarter ones, quickly turn back to take up something easier like the income taxation of trusts and estates. Others, having lost their way, plunge on and after weeks of effort emerge not far from where they began, clearly the worse for wear. On looking back they see the trail they thought they broke obscured with foul smelling waters and noxious weeds. Few willingly take up the challenge again.'

"It is, however, necessary to take up the challenge. In vino veritas. Although the relevant doctrines go back centuries, they are more vital than ever today as California becomes increasingly crowded and people live in closer proximity to one another. Planned communities have developed to regulate the relationships between neighbors so all may enjoy the reasonable use of their property. Mutual restrictions on the use of property that are binding upon, and enforceable by, all units in a development are becoming ever more common and desirable. We recently confronted the question of what restrictions may reasonably be imposed in a condominium setting. (Nahrstedt v. Lakeside Village Condominium Association ...) This case addresses an earlier step in the process, considering how a general plan of restrictions is created in the first place.

"The CC&Rs of this case were recorded before any of the properties they purport to govern were sold, thus giving all buyers constructive notice of their existence. They state they are to bind and benefit each parcel of property as part of a planned community. Nevertheless, the Court of Appeal held they are not enforceable because they were not also mentioned in a deed or other document when the property was sold. We disagree, and adopt the following rule: If a declaration establishing a common plan for the ownership of property in a subdivision and containing restrictions upon the use of the property as part of the common plan, is recorded before the execution of the contract of sale, describes the property it is to govern, and states that it is to bind all purchasers and their successors, subsequent purchasers who have constructive notice of the recorded declaration are deemed to intend and agree to be bound by, and to accept the benefits of, the common plan; the restrictions, therefore, are not unenforceable merely because they are not additionally cited in a deed or other document at the time of the sale."

2. Civil Code Section 1363(a): "A common interest development shall be managed by an association which may be incorporated or unincorporated. The association may be referred to as a "community association". Unless otherwise noted, all statutory references in this book are to California statutes.

3. A covenant in a recorded declaration of covenants, conditions and restrictions making membership in a homeowners association mandatory for all owners of lots located in the development covered by the declaration is a valid, enforceable real covenant running with the land or enforceable as an equitable servitude. Anthony v. Brea Glenbrook Club (1976) 58 Cal. App. 3d 506, 130 Cal. Rptr. 32.

4. Civil Code Sections 1350 - 1374.

5. Civil Code Section 1351(b).

6. Business & Professions Code Section 11010.

7. Business & Professions Code Section 11001, Title 10 California Code of Regulations Sections 2790 - 2799.1.

8. Civil Code Section 1351(a).

9. Civil Code Section 1354(a).

10. Business and Professions Code Section 11018.5: "... the commissioner shall issue a public report if the commissioner finds the following with respect to any such subdivision or interest: . . . (c) After transfer of title to the first lot, apartment, or condominium in the subdivision to any purchaser, the provisions of the declaration of restrictions, articles of incorporation, bylaws, management contracts (and the provisions of any and all other documents establishing, in whole or in part, the plan for use, enjoyment, maintenance, and preservation of the subdivision) as last submitted to the commissioner prior to issuance of the final public report, shall be binding upon the purchaser and occupant of every other lot, apartment, or condominium in the subdivision, including, except with regard to a limited-equity housing cooperative or a time-share project, purchasers acquiring title by foreclosure, whether judicial or nonjudicial, or by deed in lieu thereof under any mortgage or deed of trust, whether or not the mortgage or deed of trust was recorded prior to recordation of the covenants, conditions and restrictions applicable to such first lot, apartment or condominium.

11. Business and Professions Code Section 11018.7, Title 10 California Code of Regulations Section 2800.

12. Civil Code Section 1351(k).

13. Civil Code Section 1351(f).

14. Civil Code Section 1351(b), (f), (l)(2).

15. Civil Code Section 1351(l)(2).

16. Civil Code Section 1364(a).

17. Civil Code Section 1351(d), Bakanauskas v. Urdan (1988) 206 Cal. App. 3d 621, 253 Cal. Rptr. 764, Adler v. Elphick (1986) 184 Cal. App. 3d 642, 229 Cal. Rptr. 254.

18. Civil Code Section 1351(m), Shelter Creek Development Corporation v. City of Oxnard (1983) 34 Cal. 3d 733, 195 Cal. Rptr. 361, 669 P.2d 948, Strauss v. Summerhays (1984) 157 Cal. App. 3d 806, 204 Cal. Rptr. 227.

19. Civil Code Section 1351(b).

20. Civil Code Section 1351(i).

21. Civil Code Section 1358.

22. Civil Code Section 1351(i) (1).

23. Civil Code Section 1351(l)

24. Business & Professions Code Sections 11001, 11018.5, 10 California Code of Regulations Sections 2792.9, 2792.10, 2792.11.

25. Civil Code Section 1366(a).

CHAPTER II: MANAGEMENT, PRESERVATION AND MAINTENANCE

1. As discussed more fully in Chapter III, the declaration of any particular association may be titled differently. For example, some declarations may be titled "Declaration of Restrictions", or "Declaration of Covenants, Conditions and Restrictions", or "Declaration of Protective Covenants". But regardless of the title, the declarations all serve the same general purpose. For purposes of uniformity and convenience, the declaration will be referred to in this book as the "declaration of covenants, conditions and restrictions", or the "declaration of CC&Rs."

2. Cohen v. Kite Hill Community Association (1983) 142 Cal. App. 3d 642, 191 Cal. Rptr. 209.

3. Duffey v. Superior Court (Coast Homeowners Association) (1992) 3 Cal. App. 4th 425, 4 Cal. Rptr. 2d 334, Posey v. Leavitt (1991) 229 Cal. App. 3d 1236, 280 Cal. Rptr. 568, Cohen v. Kite Hill Community Association (1983) 142 Cal. App. 3d 642, 191 Cal. Rptr. 209, Raven's Cove Townhomes, Inc. v. Knuppe Dev. Co. (1981) 114 Cal. App. 3d 783, 171 Cal. Rptr. 334.

4. Civil Code Section 1354(a), Nahrstedt v. Lakeside Village Condominium Association, Inc. (1994) 8 Cal. 4th 361, 33 Cal. Rptr. 2d 63, 878 P.2d 1275.

CHAPTER III: LAND USE CONTROL AND PROPERTY REGULATION

1. Most states, including California, have "reception" statutes which explicitly adopt the common law of England as the governing law of the state. In the case of California, Civil Code Section 22.2 provides: "The common law of England, so far as it is not repugnant to or inconsistent with the Constitution of the United States, or the Constitution or laws of this State, is the rule of decision in all the courts of this State."

2. For a period of time in English legal history, two different court systems existed: the law courts which strictly applied the existing laws and principles of jurisprudence to reach a decision, and the courts of equity which applied equitable principles to reach a just decision when the existing laws would dictate a different result.

3. Nahrstedt v. Lakeside Village Condominium Association, Inc. (1994) 8 Cal. 4th 361, 375, 33 Cal. Rptr. 2d 63, 878 P.2d 1275, Riley v. Bear Creek Planning Committee (1976) 17 Cal. 3d 500, 507, 131 Cal. Rptr. 381, 551 P.2d 1213.

4. Tulk v. Moxhay 2 Phil. 774, 41 Eng. Rep. 1143 (1848 Ch.).

5. In Tulk v. Moxhay, 2 Phil. 774, 778, 41 Eng. Rep. 1143, 1144 (1848 Ch.), the English Chancery Court stated in part that: "for if an equity is attached to the property by the owner, no one purchasing with notice of that equity can stand in a different situation from the party from whom he purchases."

6. Civil Code Section 1353.

7. Civil Code Sections 18, 19, 1217.

8. Civil Code Sections 1213 - 1215.

9. Civil Code Section 1352.

10. Nahrstedt v. Lakeside Village Condominium Association, Inc. (1994) 8 Cal. 4th 361, 33 Cal. Rptr. 2d 63, 878 P.2d 1275.

11. Nahrstedt v. Lakeside Village Condominium Association, Inc. (1994) 8 Cal. 4th 361, 33 Cal. Rptr. 2d 63, 878 P.2d 1275.

12. Nahrstedt v. Lakeside Village Condominium Association, Inc. (1994) 8 Cal. 4th 361, 33 Cal. Rptr. 2d 63, 878 P.2d 1275.

13. (1994) 8 Cal. 4th 361, 33 Cal. Rptr. 2d 63, 878 P.2d 1275.

14. Bernardo Villas Management Corp. v. Black (1987) 190 Cal. App. 3d 153, 235 Cal. Rptr. 509, Portola Hills Community Association v. James (1992) 4 Cal. App. 4th 289, 5 Cal. Rptr. 2d 580, both opinions were explicitly disapproved by the Supreme Court in Nahrstedt to the extent they differed from the holding of Nahrstedt.

15. Nahrstedt v. Lakeside Village Condominium Association, Inc. (1994) 8 Cal. 4th 361, 386, 33 Cal. Rptr. 2d 63, 878 P.2d 1275.

16. Nahrstedt v. Lakeside Village Condominium Association, Inc. (1994) 8 Cal. 4th 361, 33 Cal. Rptr. 2d 63, 878 P.2d 1275.

17. Duffey v. Superior Court (Coast Homeowners Association) (1992) 3 Cal. App. 4th 425, 4 Cal. Rptr. 2d 334.

18. Duffey v. Superior Court (Coast Homeowners Association (1992) 3 Cal. App. 4th 425, 4 Cal. Rptr. 2d 334: "[I]f there is a good faith dispute concerning the interpretation of the CC&Rs, a homeowner association need not vigorously advocate any particular interpretation- individual owners can do that if they want to under section 1354 [of the Civil Code]. ... If those owners want to press their own interpretations, section 1354 allows them to jump into the fray directly. Otherwise, they are free to stay on the sidelines. . . . Given this 'no-win' position [where disputing homeowners hold different interpretations of the CC&Rs], it is enough for the association to seek a [judicial] determination of the controversy joining only the arguably offending property owners."

19. Beehan v. Lido Isle Community Association (1977) 70 Cal. App. 3d 858, 137 Cal. Rptr. 528, Katz v. Chevron Corporation (1994) 22 Cal. App. 4th 1352, 27 Cal. Rptr. 2d 681.

20. Shelley v. Kraemer (1948) 334 U.S. 1, 68 S.Ct. 836, 92 L.Ed. 1161, Nahrstedt v. Lakeside Village Condominium Association, Inc. (1994) 8 Cal. 4th 361, 33 Cal. Rptr. 2d 63, 878 P.2d 1275.

21. Whether because the statute itself expressly states that it will operate prospectively only, or because the courts have interpreted the statute to be prospective only. The courts ordinarily will construe statutes to operate prospectively only, unless the legislature makes it clear that retroactive effect is intended. Krause v. Rarity (1930) 210 Cal. 644, 293 P. 62, Saso v. Furtado (1951) 104 Cal. App. 2d 759, 232 P.2d 583.

22. Although Section 714.5 does not explicitly mention "mobilehomes" or "manufactured homes", it was enacted as part of Statutes 1987, Chapter 1339, which included amendments and additions to the then existing Health & Safety Code provisions relating to "mobilehomes" and "manufactured homes."

23. Civil Code Section 1376 reads in full as follows:

Any covenant, condition, or restriction contained in any deed, contract, security instrument, or other instrument affecting the transfer or sale of, or any interest in, a common interest development that effectively prohibits or restricts the installation or use of a video or television antenna, including a satellite dish, or that effectively prohibits or restricts the attachment of that antenna to a structure within that development where the antenna is not visible from any street or common area, except as otherwise prohibited or restricted by law, is void and unenforceable as to its application to the installation or use of a video or television antenna that has a diameter or diagonal measurement of 36 inches or less.

"(b) This section shall not apply to any covenant, condition, or restriction, as described in subdivision (a), that imposes reasonable restrictions on the installation or use of a video or television antenna, including a satellite dish, that has a diameter or diagonal measurement of 36 inches or less. For purposes of this section, 'reasonable restrictions' means those restrictions that do not significantly increase the cost of the video or satellite antenna system, including all related equipment, or significantly decrease its efficiency or performance and include all of the following:

"(1) Requirements for application and notice to the association prior to the installation.

"(2) Requirement of the owner of a separate interest, as defined in Section 1351, to obtain the approval of the association for the installation of a video or television antenna that has a diameter or diagonal measurement of 36 inches or less on a separate interest owned by another.

"(3) Provision for the maintenance, repair, or replacement of roofs or other building components.

"(4) Requirements for installers of a video or television antenna to indemnify or reimburse the association or its members for loss or damage caused by the installation, maintenance, or use of a video or television antenna that has a diameter or diagonal measurement of 36 inches or less.

"(c) Whenever approval is required for the installation or use of a video or television antenna, including a satellite dish, the application for approval shall be processed by the appropriate approving entity for the common interest development in the same manner as an application for approval of an architectural modification to the property, and the issuance of a decision on the application shall not be willfully delayed.

"(d) In any action to enforce compliance with this section, the prevailing party shall be awarded reasonable attorney's fees."

24. Health and Safety Code Sections 1500 - 1567.8.

25. Health and Safety Code Sections 1569 - 1569.87.

26. Health and Safety Code Sections 1570 - 1596.5.

27. Health and Safety Code Sections 1596.70 - 1596.894.

28. Health and Safety Code Sections 1597.30 - 1597.621.

29. Health and Safety Code Section 1502(a).

30. Health and Safety Code Section 1502(a)(l).

31. Health and Safety Code Section 1502(a)(2).

32. Health and Safety Code Section 1502(a)(6).

33. Broadmoor San Clemente Homeowners Association v. Nelson (1994) 25 Cal. App. 4th 1, 30 Cal. Rptr. 2d 316.

34. The 1993 amendment of California Government Code Section 12955 added subdivision (1) which reads as follows: "It shall be unlawful: (1) To discriminate through public or private land use practices, decisions and authorizations because of race, color, religion, sex, familial status, marital status, disability, national origin, or ancestry. Discrimination includes, but is not limited to, restrictive covenants, zoning laws, denials of use permits, and other actions authorized under the Planning and Zoning Law (Title 7 (commencing with Section 65000)), that make housing opportunities unavailable."

35. Broadmoor San Clemente Homeowners Association v. Nelson (1994) 25 Cal. App. 4th 1, 30 Cal. Rptr. 2d 316.

36. In Broadmoor San Clemente Homeowners Association v. Nelson (1994) 25 Cal. App. 4th 1, 30 Cal. Rptr. 2d 316, the court agreed with a prior decision in Barrett v. Lipscomb (1987) 194 Cal. App. 3d 1524, 240 Cal. Rptr. 336 that Health and Safety Code Sections 1566.5

and 1569.87 clearly apply only to restrictions adopted on or after January 1, 1979. But the court went on to hold that the 1993 amendments of California Government Code Sections 12955 and 12955.6, part of the California Fair Employment and Housing Act, invalidated and repealed those portions of Sections Health and Safety Code Sections 1566.5 and 1569.87 exempting pre-1979 covenants and restrictions from operation of the statutes

37. Health and Safety Code Section 1596.78.

38. Health and Safety Code Section 1596.78(a).

39. Health and Safety Code Section 1596.78(b).

40. In Broadmoor San Clemente Homeowners Association v. Nelson (1994) 25 Cal. App. 4th 1, 30 Cal. Rptr. 2d 316, (involving Health and Safety Code Sections 1566.5 and 1569.87, statutes similar to Section 1597.40) the appellate court suggested that such arguments might be available and requested counsel for the association to brief the issues, but the association failed to do so. The court then held that the association had waived any such constitutional issues.

41. Government Code Sections 12900 - 12996.

42. Civil Code Sections 51 - 53.

43. Title 42 United States Code Sections 3601 - 3631.

44. Civil Code Section 51.

45. O'Connor v. Village Green Owners Association (1983) 38 Cal. 3d 790, 191 Cal. Rptr. 320, 662 P.2d 427. Similarly, another court has held that a privately owned, nonprofit country club which operates a restaurant, bar and recreational facilities, is a "business establishment" within the meaning of the "Unruh Civil Rights Act". Warfield v. Peninsula Golf and Country Club (1989) 214 Cal. App. 3d 646, 262 Cal. Rptr. 890.

46. Civil Code Section 51.3(d).

47. Laguna Royale Owners Association v. Darger (1981) 119 Cal. App. 3d 670, 174 Cal. Rptr. 136.

48. Title 10 California Code of Regulations Section 2792.25(a): "Except as provided in subdivision (c) [applicable to limited equity housing cooperatives only], any provision which purports to restrict or abridge whether directly or indirectly, the right of an owner to sell or lease his subdivision interest must include uniform, objective standards for invoking a restriction upon sale or lease, none of which shall be based upon the race, color, religion, sex, marital status, national origin or ancestry of the vendee or lessee."

49. City of Oceanside v. McKenna (1989) 215 Cal. App. 3d 1420, 264 Cal. Rptr. 275. In this case the court upheld a restriction which completely banned the leasing of separate interests by the owners. Part of the court's reasoning was based on the declaration of covenants, conditions and restrictions which stated in part that: "In order to achieve a stabilized community of owner-occupied dwelling units, to avoid artificial inflation of prices caused by resales by speculators and to prevent scarcity caused by vacant homes awaiting resale by speculators . . . [e]ach Owner shall use and occupy the . . . dwelling as such Owner's principal place of residence . . . [t]he Owner of each Dwelling on the property shall not lease or rent the Dwelling at any time for any reason."

50. Laguna Royale Owners Association v. Darger (1981) 119 Cal. App. 3d 670, 174 Cal. Rptr. 136.

51. Civil Code Section 1358 provides in part that in a community apartment project, condominium project, planned development and stock cooperative, "any conveyance, judicial sale, or other voluntary or involuntary transfer of the owner's entire estate also includes the owner's membership interest in the association."

Corporations Code Section 7320 states that:

"Subject to Section 7613 [Section 7613 authorizes members' use of proxies for voting purposes]:

"(a) Unless the articles or bylaws otherwise provide:

"(1) No member may transfer a membership or any right arising therefrom; and

"(2) subject to the provisions of subdivision (b), all rights as a member of the corporation cease upon the member's death or dissolution.

"(b) The articles or bylaws may provide for, or may authorize the board to provide for, the transfer of memberships, or of memberships within any class or classes, with or without restriction or limitation, including transfer upon the death, dissolution, merger, or reorganization of a member.

"(c) Where transfer rights have been provided, no restriction of them shall be binding with respect to memberships issued prior to the adoption of the restriction, unless the holders of such memberships voted in favor of the restriction."

52. Liebler v. Point Loma Tennis Club Community Corporation (1995) 40 Cal. App. 4th 1600, 47 Cal. Rptr. 2d 783. In this case the Court of Appeal addressed circumstances in which the association's recorded declaration did not contain any provisions prohibiting nonresident owners from using the common area facilities, but did manifest an intent that each separately owned lot or unit would have only one set of users of the facilities and amenities. The association then adopted an association rule which provided that the "recreational facilities shall be used only by residents of [the association] and their guests. The right to use the facilities is appurtenant to the individual condominium unit and can not be separated from it (CC&R Section 8). Nonresident owners, whose units are rented or available for rent, do not have the use of the recreational facilities."

In affirming the validity and reasonableness of the adopted rule, the Liebler Court commented on the value common interest development facilities add to the separately-owned properties even if the owners cannot use the facilities:

> "The added burden from use by nonresident owners in addition to tenants and owner-residents could potentially greatly increase the number of individuals competing for [tennis] court space, and this decrease in availability lessens the attractiveness of a tennis-oriented facility." . . . Maintaining a low density by excluding the public, and here, in long-standing restrictions, nonresident owners as well, confers a benefit on the residents for which many will pay a higher price. Thus [the plaintiff] himself has benefited from the restriction, since he is presumably thereby able to negotiate from his tenants a higher rent than he otherwise would have been able to obtain for the premises."

53. MaJor v. Miraverde Homeowners Association. Inc. (1992) 7 Cal. App. 4th 618, 9 Cal. Rptr. 2d 237. In this case the condominium owners were husband and wife. The owners purchased a condominium unit within the development and resided there for a few years. Subsequently, the owners moved out of the condominium, but continued to hold record title to the condominium unit. The wife's mother subsequently moved into the condominium unit. Pursuant to the association's declaration of CC&Rs all record title owners of condominium units were "members" of the association. Under the CC&Rs and association rules, the elderly mother was considered the "authorized" member. The association rules further provided that "non-resident" homeowners are not entitled to use of the facilities of the development, except as guests of an authorized member. The mother residing in the unit was eighty-two years old, senile, did not play tennis and was physically disabled to the extent she could not personally "sign-up" her children, the owners, as guests at the association guard building in order for the owners to play tennis. When the owners were informed they could not use the tennis court or any other facility, they filed a lawsuit.

In reaching its ruling, the Miraverde Court reasoned that the CC&Rs conferred membership on all record owners of condominium units, neither the association board of directors nor the association rules could override the CC&Rs to effectively strip membership rights, including the right to use and enjoy recreational facilities, from non-resident members. The Miraverde Court, however, expressly refrained from addressing the issue whether "under the CC&Rs, a delegation to a tenant or contract owner of the owner's right to enjoy common facilities would have the effect of terminating (or suspending) the owner's personal rights to use those facilities." This issue has now been decided in the Liebler case.

54. Order of Railroad Telegraphers v. Railway Express Agency (1944) 321 U.S. 342, 64 S.Ct. 582, 88 L.Ed. 788, Cutujian v. Benedict Hills Estates Association (1996) 41 Cal. App. 4th 1379, 48 Cal. Rptr. 2d 166.

55. Code of Civil Procedure Section 337, Cutujian v. Benedict Hills Estates Association (1996) 41 Cal. App. 4th 1379, 48 Cal. Rptr. 2d 166.

56. Cutujian v. Benedict Hills Estates Association (1996) 41 Cal. App. 4th 1379, 48 Cal. Rptr. 2d 166.

57. Code of Civil Procedure Section 337, Cutujian v. Benedict Hills Estates Association (1996) 41 Cal. App. 4th 1379, 48 Cal. Rptr. 2d 166.

58. White v. Dorfman (1981) 116 Cal. App. 3d 892, 192 Cal. Rptr. 326.

59. Seligman v. Tucker, 6 Cal. App. 3d 691, 86 Cal. Rptr. 187 (1970).

60. Mock v. Shulman (1964) 226 Cal. App. 2d 263, 38 Cal. Rptr. 39. In this case, a property owner asserted that the association was estopped from enforcing a six-foot hedge limitation because it allowed the owner to plant a row of cypress trees. The court held that the association was not estopped from enforcing the six-foot hedge limitation because when planted close together, cypress trees intertwine, form a hedge and can be trimmed to the six-foot height.

61. Harrison v. Frye (1957) 148 Cal. App. 2d 626, 307 P.2d 76 (1957). In this case, the court held that the defendant was entitled to prove that the plaintiff had waived enforcement of a restriction requiring the use of "high quality" materials by failing to enforce the restriction against other owners over a period of years.

62. Rice v. Heggy (1958) 158 Cal. App. 2d 89, 322 P.2d 53 (1958). In this particular case, the court held that simply because various setback restrictions had not been enforced over a period of time, this did not mean that a restriction against building multi-family structures had been waived.

63. Robertson v. Nichols (1949) 92 Cal. App. 2d 201, 206 P.2d 898. In this case the court held that even though owners of some lots had violated a single-family use restriction along Wilshire Boulevard in Los Angeles, the restriction was still enforceable against other owners in the same development. The court reasoned that although enforcement of the restriction may be inequitable and impracticable along Wilshire Boulevard, the size and location of the rest of the development was such that the original purpose of the restriction could still be satisfied in other areas of the development.

64. Wolff v. Fallon (1955) 44 Cal. 2d 695, 284 P.2d 802. In this case, the court held that a residential use restriction was no longer enforceable because the street the property faced had changed in character, after the time it was purchased, to a main street used by numerous commercial vehicles. Similarly, in Downs v. Kroeger (1927) 200 Cal. 743, 254 P.1101 (1927), the court held that a restriction limiting use of the land to residential purposes could not be enforced because the character of the surrounding neighborhood had changed dramatically to commercial uses after the defendant purchased the property.

65. Rice v. Heggy (1958) 158 Cal. App. 2d 89, 322 P.2d 53. In this case, both vehicular and pedestrian traffic in the area of the property burdened by the restriction had increased significantly. But, the court held that the change in circumstances did not frustrate or defeat the purpose of the restriction limiting the use of the property for single-family, residential purposes.

66. Welsch v. Goswick (1982) 130 Cal. App. 3d 398, 181 Cal. Rptr. 703. In this case, the court held that social, economic and legal conditions had changed to the extent that a single-family, residential use restriction should be interpreted so as to permit the operation of a residential health care facility for six or fewer persons.

67. Harrison v. Frye (1957) 148 Cal. App. 2d 626, 306 P.2d 76. In this case the plaintiff was seeking to enforce building restrictions against the defendants. The defendants alleged that the plaintiff had violated the same building restrictions and should therefore not be heard to complain about the defendants' violations, nor be awarded an injunction prohibiting the defendants' violations. The court held that the defendants were permitted to introduce evidence showing that the plaintiff had violated the same restrictions.

68. Northridge Hospital Foundation v. Pic 'N' Save No. 9, Inc. (1986) 187 Cal. App. 3d 1088, 232 Cal. Rptr. 329, Property Controllers, Inc. v. Shewfelt (1966) 245 Cal. App. 2d 755, 54 Cal. Rptr. 218.

69. Mackinder v. OSCA Dev. Co. (1984) 151 Cal. App. Sd 728, 198 Cal. Rptr. 864.

70. Cohen v. Kite Hill Community Association (1983) 142 Cal. App. 3d 642, 191 Cal. Rptr. 209, Laguna Royale Owners Association v. Darger (1981) 119 Cal. App. 3d 670, 174 Cal. Rptr. 136.

71. Strong v. Hancock (1927) 201 Cal. 530, 258 P.60, Mullally v. Ojai Hotel Company (1968) 266 Cal. App. 2d 9, 71 Cal. Rptr. 882, Rice v. Heggy (1958) 158 Cal. App. 2d 89, 322 P.2d 53, Wilkman v. Banks (1954) 124 Cal. App. 2d 451, 269 P.2d 33, Hotz v. Rich (1992) 4 Cal. App. 4th 1048, 6 Cal. Rptr. 2d 219 [federal agency administrative ruling] .

72. Hotz v. Rich (1992) 4 Cal. App. 4th 1048, 6 Cal. Rptr. 2d 219.

73. Ticor Title Insurance Co. v. Rancho Santa Fe Association (1986) 177 Cal. App. 3d 726, 223 Cal. Rptr. 175, Lushing v. The Riviera Estates Association (1961) 196 Cal. App. 2d 687, 16 Cal. Rptr. 763.

74. Title 10 California Code of Regulations Section 2792.28(a).

75. Ticor Title Insurance Co. v. Rancho Santa Fe Association (1986) 177 Cal. App. 3d 726, 223 Cal. Rptr. 175. In this case the court held that the association's denial of permission for an owner to build a tennis court was invalid because the association had no authority to require a 50-feet lot line setback when the declaration of CC&Rs specified a 20-feet setback.

Lushing v. The Riviera Estates Association (1961) 196 Cal. App. 2d 687, 16 Cal. Rptr. 763. In this case the association's recorded declaration of CC&Rs defined "building site" to be a lot or parcel of land, or portion thereof, with a frontage of not less than 100 feet. The declaration did not include any specifications with respect to minimum lot area or depth of the lot in order to qualify as a building site. The association refused to review and pass on the property owners' submission of building plans because it considered the owners' lot did not meet the requirements of a building site. In declaring the owners' lot was a "building site" within the meaning of the declaration, the court stated that:

> "Here, the restrictions, themselves, give the definition of a building site. [The association] cannot add to that definition a requirement with respect to square foot area or the depth of the site."

76. Civil Code Section 1354(a), Nahrstedt v. Lakeside Village Condominium Association, Inc. (1994) 8 Cal. 4th 361, 33 Cal. Rptr. 2d 63, 878 P.2d 1275.

77. Nahrstedt v. Lakeside Village Condominium Association, Inc. (1994) 8 Cal. 4th 361, 33 Cal. Rptr. 2d 63, 878 P.2d 1275. The California Supreme Court quoted a Florida court of appeal with approval: "In Hidden Harbour Estates v. Basso, the Florida court distinguished two categories of use restrictions: use restrictions set forth in the declaration or master deed of the condominium project itself, and rules promulgated by the governing board of the condominium association or the board's interpretation of a rule. The latter category of use restrictions, the court said, should be subject to a 'reasonableness' test, so as to 'somewhat fetter the discretion of the board of directors.' Such a standard, the court explained, best assures that governing boards will 'enact rules and make decisions that are reasonably related to the promotion of the health, happiness and peace of mind' of the project owners, considered collectively. By contrast, restrictions contained in the declaration or master deed of the condominium complex, the Florida court concluded, should not be evaluated under a 'reasonableness' standard. Rather, such use restrictions are 'clothed with a very strong presumption of validity' and should be upheld even if they exhibit some degree of unreasonableness. Nonenforcement would be proper only if such restrictions were arbitrary or in violation of public policy or some fundamental constitutional right."

78. Palos Verdes Homes Association v. Rodman (1986) 182 Cal. App. 3d 324, 227 Cal. Rptr. 81.

79. Ironwood Owners Association IX v. Solomon (1986) 178 Cal. App. 3d 766, 224 Cal. Rptr. 18.

80. Hannula v. Hacienda Homes, Inc. (1949) 34 Cal. 2d 442, 211 P.2d 302, Cohen v. Kite Hill Community Association (1983) 142 Cal. App. 3d 642, 191 Cal. Rptr. 209, Bramwell v. Kuhle (1960) 183 Cal. App. 2d 767, 6 Cal. Rptr. 839.

81. Ironwood Owners Association IX v. Solomon (1986) 178 Cal. App. 3d 766, 224 Cal. Rptr. 18, Laguna Royale Owners Association v. Darger (1981) 119 Cal. App. 3d 670, 174 Cal. Rptr. 136.

82. Clark v. Rancho Santa Fe Association (1989) 216 Cal. App. 3d 606, 265 Cal. Rptr. 41.

83. 7 Cal. App. 4th 618, 9 Cal. Rptr. 2d 237.

84. MaJor v. Miraverde Homeowners Association Inc. (1992) 7 Cal. App. 4th 618, 9 Cal. Rptr. 2d 237 (fn. 1): "... Here we do not address the issue whether the member's right and easement to the common areas is extinguished upon delegation to a third party." (fn. 2) : We note, for example, the Rasmussens were not seeking to both use the tennis court themselves and have a tenant or other delegatee use the court. Consequently the Rasmussens' unit was placing no greater burden on the Association's facilities than it did when the Rasmussens occupied that unit and no greater burden than if they still did. As mentioned earlier ..., we need not reach the question whether, under the CC&Rs, a delegation to a tenant or contract owner of the owner's right to enjoy common facilities would have the effect of terminating (or suspending) the owner's personal rights to use those facilities. We leave this question to the trial court for resolution in the first instance should new facts be developed on remand."

85. Liebler v. Point Loma Tennis Club Community Corporation (1995) 40 Cal. App. 4th 1600, 47 Cal. Rptr. 2d 783.

CHAPTER IV: ENFORCING THE DECLARATION OF COVENANTS, CONDITIONS AND RESTRICTIONS AND OTHER GOVERNING DOCUMENTS

1. Civil Code Section 1354(a): "... Unless the declaration states otherwise, these servitudes may be enforced by any owner of a separate interest or by the association, or by both. ...."

Franklin v. Marie Antoinette Condominium Owners Association, Inc. (1993) 19 Cal. App. 4th 824, 23 Cal. Rptr. 2d 744: A condominium owner may enforce the declaration of CC&Rs under the law of equitable servitudes without having to sue the association for breach of contract.

2. Alderson v. Cutting (1912) 163 Cal. 503, 126 P. 157, Posey v. Leavitt (1991) 229 Cal. App. 3d 1236, 280 Cal. Rptr. 568, Knox v. Streatfield (1978) 79 Cal. App. 3d 565, 145 Cal. Rptr. 39.

3. Posey v. Leavitt (1991) 229 Cal. App. 3d 1236, 280 Cal. Rptr. 568.

4. Civil Code Sections 1363(a),(c), 1363.5.

5. Civil Code Section 1363(c).

6. Corporations Code Section 7341.

7. Corporations Code Section 7341(f).

8. Corporations Code Section 7341(b): "but a court may also find other procedures to be fair and reasonable when the full circumstances of the suspension, termination, or expulsion are considered." De Mille v. American Federation of Radio Artists (1947) 31 Cal. 2d 139, 187 P.2d 769, Westbrook v. Social Center Hall Association of Stockton (1957) 148 Cal. App. 2d 815, 307 P.2d 640, Williams v. Inglewood Board of Realtors (1963) 219 Cal. App. 2d 479, 33 Cal. Rptr. 289, Annandale Golf Club v. Smith (1930) 110 Cal. App. 765 Super., 289 p. 806, Anthony v. Brea Glenbrook Club (1976) 58 Cal. App. 3d 506, 130 Cal. Rptr. 32 (dicta).

9. Id.

10. California Riviera Homeowners Association v. Superior Court (1995) 37 Cal. App. 4th 1599, 44 Cal. Rptr. 2d 595, rev. denied November 16, 1995 and Reporter of Decisions ordered not to publish this opinion in the Official Reports, 1995 Cal. Lexis 6973.

11. California Riviera Homeowners Association v. Superior Court (1995) 37 Cal. App. 4th 1599, 44 Cal. Rptr. 2d 595, rev. denied November 16, 1995 and Reporter of Decisions ordered not to publish this opinion in the Official Reports, 1995 Cal. Lexis 6973.

12. California Riviera Homeowners Association v. Superior Court (1995) 37 Cal. App. 4th 1599, 44 Cal. Rptr. 2d 595, rev. denied November 16, 1995 and Reporter of Decisions ordered not to publish this opinion in the Official Reports, 1995 Cal. Lexis 6973.

13. Civil Code Section 1363(i).

14. Liebler v. Point Loma Tennis Club Community Corporation (1995) 40 Cal. App. 4th 1600, 47 Cal. Rptr. 2d 783.

15. Nahrstedt v. Lakeside Village Condominium Association, Inc. (1994) 8 Cal. 4th 361, 33 Cal. Rptr. 2d 63, 878 P.2d 1275.

16. Nahrstedt v. Lakeside Village Condominium Association, Inc. (1994) 8 Cal. 4th 361, 33 Cal. Rptr. 2d 63, 878 P.2d 1275. In this case, the California Supreme Court stated: "The power to regulate pertains to a 'wide spectrum of activities,' such as the volume of playing music, hours of social gatherings, use of patio furniture and barbecues, and rental of units." (fn. 6).

In Liebler v. Point Loma Tennis Club Community Corporation (1995) 40 Cal. App. 4th 1600, 47 Cal. Rptr. 2d 783, the association imposed monetary fines against an owner for his flagrant disregard of the association's authority and continued use of the common area facilities even after he was instructed not to do so and his use privileges card was revoked. The owner asserted that the association had no legal authority to fine him because there was no such authority granted to the association in the recorded declaration of covenants. The Liebler Court flatly rejected the owner's argument and held that where the recorded declaration authorizes the association to adopt rules in connection with the operation and maintenance of the development, the association may, by rules consistent with applicable law and the declaration, provide for the imposition of monetary fines. In reaching its conclusion, the court cited the Nahrstedt decision and stated that:

> "[The plaintiff] last contends that, absent an express provision in the . . . CC&Rs authorizing such, the Board lacks the authority to subject him to fines. CC&R article 3.2.9 states the corporation may 'establish and publish such rules and regulations as the Board may deem reasonable in connection with the use, occupancy and maintenance of all of the Property ...' [The association's] rule 5.2 provides in part that 'enforcement shall be carried out in a fair and timely manner by means of fines . . . and other legal action as appropriate.' Section VI of the [association's] rules is a schedule of fines, providing that for 'Misuse of the common area' the fine will be $50. [The plaintiff] received copies of the [association's] rules when he purchased his condominium unit. For the reasons which follow, we reject [the plaintiff's] assertion these provisions cannot support the imposition of fines upon him."
>
> ".....our supreme Court in Nahrstedt ... stated that one of the characteristics of condominium ownership is 'mandatory membership in an owners association, which, through an elected board of directors, is empowered to enforce any use restrictions contained in the project's declaration or master deed and to enact new rules governing the use and occupancy of property within the project.' . . . While cautioning against abuses of such regulatory power ..., the Nahrstedt court . . . went on to observe: 'Generally, courts will uphold decisions made by the governing board of an owners association so long as they represent good faith efforts to further the purposes of the common interest development, are consistent with the development's governing documents, and comply with public policy. . . . Civil Code Section 1363 . . . provides in pertinent part that 'if an association adopts or has adopted a policy imposing any monetary penalty, including any fee, on any association member for a violation of the governing documents or rules or rules of the association . . . the board of directors shall adopt and distribute to each member . . . a schedule of the monetary penalties that may be assessed for those violations. . . ' "
>
> "Because the [association's] governing documents establishing the right to fine offending association members comply with the cited code section, and because the authorization for the challenged rules is itself contained in the recorded . . . CC&Rs, [the plaintiff] is incorrect in asserting such fines are

unauthorized. The trial court correctly found [the association] had the power to impose fines upon [the plaintiff] for his violations of [the association's] rules, although the court did not address the question of the means by which such fines might be collected. . . . We also need not here reach the question of the means by which such fines may be collected, as there is at present no actual case or controversy concerning this matter."

17. During the 1993 legislative session, the legislature considered the enactment of Assembly Bill 1793 which addressed community association monetary penalties. The bill, if enacted, would have required a 15-days noticed hearing prior to imposition of monetary penalties. Assembly Bill 1793 was not enacted.

18. Title 10 California Code of Regulations Section 2792.26(c): "A monetary penalty imposed by the Association as a disciplinary measure for failure of a member to comply with the governing instruments or as a means of reimbursing the Association for costs incurred by the Association in the repair of damage to common areas and facilities for which the member was allegedly responsible or in bringing the member and his subdivision interest into compliance with the governing instruments may not be characterized nor treated in the governing instruments as an assessment which may become a lien against the member's subdivision interest enforceable by a sale of the interest in accordance with the provisions of Sections 2924, 2924(b) and 2924(c) of the Civil Code.

19. Civil Code Section 1363(g).

20. Code of Civil Procedure Section 525: "An injunction is a writ or order requiring a person to refrain from a particular act. It may be granted by the court in which the action is brought, or by a judge thereof; and when granted by a judge, it may be enforced as an order of the court.

21. Code of Civil Procedure Section 527(d) (1).

22. Code of Civil Procedure Section 527(a).

23. Code of Civil Procedure Section 1060: "Any person interested under a written instrument excluding a will or a trust, or under a contract, or who desires a declaration of his or her rights or duties with respect to another, or in respect to, in, over or upon property, . . . may, in cases of actual controversy relating to the legal rights and duties of the respective parties, bring an original action or cross-complaint in the superior court or in the municipal or justice court ... for a declaration of his or her rights and duties in the premises, including a determination of any question of construction or validity arising under the instrument or contract. ..."

24. Code of Civil Procedure Section 383. Duffey v. Superior Court (1992) 3 Cal. App. 4th 425, 4 Cal. Rptr. 2d 334: "... we conclude section [383] authorizes homeowners associations to file declaratory relief actions such as this one where there is a need for an authoritative interpretation of governing documents."

25. Civil Code Section 1354(f).

26. Code of Civil Procedure Section 86(a)(7),(8).

27. Ironwood Owners Association IX v. Solomon (1986) 178 Cal. App. 3d 766, 224 Cal. Rptr. 18, Cohen v. Kite Hill Community Association (1983) 142 Cal. App. 3d 642, 191 Cal. Rptr. 209, Laguna Royale Owners Association v. Darger (1981) 119 Cal. App. 3d 670, 174 Cal. Rptr. 136.

28. (1986) 178 Cal. App. 3d 766, 224 Cal. Rptr. 18.

29. Civil Code Section 1354(b).

30. Civil Code Section 1354(b).

31. Civil Code Section 1354(b).

32. Code of Civil Procedure Section 116.340(a)(2).

33. Code of Civil Procedure Sections 116.340, 415.20(b).

34. Code of Civil Procedure Sections 116.340, 415.20(a).

35. Code of Civil Procedure Sections 116.340(a), (3), 116.340(c), 415.20.

36. Civil Code Section 1354(b).

37. Civil Code Section 1354(b).

38. Civil Code Section 1354(b).

39. Civil Code Section 1354(b).

40. Civil Code Section 1354(h).

41. Civil Code Section 1354(b).

42. Civil Code Section 1354(c).

CHAPTER V: COMMON AREAS AND COMMUNITY AMENITIES AND FACILITIES

1. Civil Code Section 1358 provides in part that in a community apartment project, condominium project, planned development and stock cooperative, "any conveyance, judicial sale, or other voluntary or involuntary transfer of the owner's entire estate also includes the owner's membership interest in the association."

Corporations Code Section 7320 states that:

"Subject to Section 7613 [Section 7613 authorizes members' use of proxies for voting purposes]:

"(a) Unless the articles or bylaws otherwise provide:

"(1) No member may transfer a membership or any right arising therefrom; and

"(2) Subject to the provisions of subdivision (b), all rights as a member of the corporation cease upon the member's death or dissolution.

"(b) The articles or bylaws may provide for, or may authorize the board to provide for, the transfer of memberships, or of memberships within any class or classes, with or without restriction or limitation, including transfer upon the death, dissolution, merger, or reorganization of a member.

"(c) Where transfer rights have been provided, no restriction of them shall be binding with respect to memberships issued prior to the adoption of the restriction, unless the holders of such memberships voted in favor of the restriction."

2. Liebler v. Point Loma Tennis Club Community Corporation (1995) 40 Cal. App. 4th 1600, 47 Cal. Rptr. 2d 783. In this case the Court of Appeal addressed circumstances in which the association's recorded declaration did not contain any provisions prohibiting nonresident owners from using the common area facilities, but did manifest an intent that each separately owned lot or unit would have only one set of users of the facilities and amenities. The association then adopted an association rule which provided that the "recreational facilities shall be used only by residents of [the association] and their guests. The right to use the facilities is appurtenant to the individual condominium unit and can not be separated from it (CC&R Section 8). Nonresident owners, whose units are rented or available for rent, do not have the use of the recreational facilities."

In affirming the validity and reasonableness of the adopted rule, the Liebler Court commented on the value common interest development facilities add to the separately-owned properties even if the owners cannot use the facilities:

> "The added burden from use by nonresident owners in addition to tenants and owner-residents could potentially greatly increase the number of individuals competing for [tennis] court space, and this decrease in availability lessens the attractiveness of a tennis-oriented facility." . . . Maintaining a low density by excluding the public, and here, in long-standing restrictions, nonresident owners as well, confers a benefit on the residents for which many will pay a higher price. Thus [the plaintiff] himself has benefited from the restriction,

since he is presumably thereby able to negotiate from his tenants a higher rent than he otherwise would have been able to obtain for the premises."

3. MaJor v. Miraverde Homeowners Association, Inc. (1992) 7 Cal. App. 4th 618, 9 Cal. Rptr. 2d 237

4. In Laguna Publishing Company v. Golden Rain Foundation of Laguna Hills (1982) 131 Cal. App. 3d 816, 182 Cal. Rptr. 813, the court addressed access to a CID in which a private association owned and maintained the streets and sidewalks. The Laguna court stated the general rule as follows:

> "In other words, Golden Rain, in the proper exercise of its private property rights, may certainly choose to exclude all give-away, unsolicited newspapers from Leisure World, but once its chooses to admit one, where that decision is not made in concert with the residents, then the discriminatory exclusion of another such newspaper represents an abridgement of the free speech, free press rights of the excluded newspaper secured under our state Constitution..."

****

> "Based upon the foregoing, keeping in view the greater status of the rights of free speech and free press existing under the California Constitution . . . and keeping in mind also that discriminatory proscription of free speech on private property may even be questionable under the federal Constitution . . . we hold that Golden Rain, acting with implicit sanction of the state's police power behind it, impermissibly discriminated against the free speech and free press rights of plaintiff, guaranteed to it under the state Constitution, by excluding it from Leisure World after it, Golden Rain, without authority from the residents of Leisure World, had chosen to permit the unsolicited delivery of the Leisure World News to the residents of Leisure World. As a consequence, for so long as Golden Rain permits the unsolicited delivery of the Leisure World News to the residents of Leisure World, then it cannot permissibly discriminate against plaintiff's opportunity to communicate with the residents of Leisure World by excluding unsolicited delivery of its newspaper to these same residents ..."

****

> "In short, for purposes of avoiding discrimination against the state constitutional guarantees of free speech and free press, the right of any and all to enter this private, gated community to exercise this state constitutional right must be exactly measured by the right accorded to one, both as to the nature of the activity of that one as well as to the conditions of his admission. Under such a rule, the owners of this private property still remain required only to act fairly and without discrimination toward others in the exercise of their state constitutional rights of free speech and free press which rights Golden Rain itself has chosen to accord exclusively to the Leisure World News while acting wholly beyond the knowledge and complicity of any resident of Leisure World."

Part of the Laguna Publishing Court's rationale was premised on its characterization of "Leisure World" as a "mini-government" or "company town", based on a consideration of the characteristics of a typical town or city including the fact that although the development was private community with access restricted by a secured gate, vendors, contractors and guests of property owners were routinely permitted access, and the existence of commercial areas and retail stores.

5. Vehicle Code Sections 22658.2, 22853.

6. Vehicle Code Section 22658.2(c).

7. Government Code Section 61621.8.

8. Citizens Against Gated Enclaves v. Whitley Heights Civic Association (1994) 23 Cal. App. 4th 812, 28 Cal. Rptr. 2d 451.

9. Civil Code Section 1364.

10. Del Mar Beach Club Owners Association v. Imperial Contracting Company (1981) 123 Cal. App. 3d 898, 176 Cal. Rptr. 886, Kriegler v. Eichler Homes (1969) 269 Cal. App. 2d 224, 74 Cal. Rptr. 749.

11. Share v. Casiano Bel-Air Homeowners Association (1989) 215 Cal. App. 3d 515, 263 Cal. Rptr. 753.

12. Corporations Code Section 7231, Frances T. v. Village Green Owners Association (1986) 42 Cal. 3d 490, 229 Cal. Rptr. 456, 723 p.2d 573, Raven's Cove Townhomes, Inc. v. Knuppe Development Company, Inc. (1981) 114 Cal. App. 3d 783, 171 Cal. Rptr. 334, Smith v. Superior Court (Bonita Park Homeowners Association) (1990) 217 Cal. App. 3d 950, 266 Cal. Rptr. 253. In Raven's Cove Townhomes, the court stated: "We note that the duty of undivided loyalty . . . applies when the board of directors of the Association considers maintenance and repair contracts, the operating budget, creation of reserve and operating accounts, etc. Thus, a developer and his agents and employees who also serve as directors of an association, like the instant one, may not make decisions for the Association that benefit their own interests at the expense of the association and its members. ... We think that here, the failure of the initial Association directors to exercise supervision which permits mismanagement or nonmanagement is an independent ground for the breach of fiduciary duty by the Developer during the initial period of the Association, when the Developer and its employees controlled the Association."

13. Corporations Code Section 7231, Raven's Cove Townhomes. Inc. (1981) 114 Cal. App. 3d 783, 171 Cal. Rptr. 334.

14. For example, in Smith v. Superior Court (Bonita Park Homeowners Association) (1990) 217 Cal. App. 3d 950, 266 Cal. Rptr. 253, the court held that the association's lawsuit against the developer seeking damages for latent construction defects was barred because it was not filed within 10 years after valid notices of completion had been recorded by the developer.

15. Code of Civil Procedure Section 340(3).

16. Code of Civil Procedure Section 338(b).

17. Code of Civil Procedure Section 337.

18. Code of Civil Procedure Section 339.

19. Code of Civil Procedure Section 359, Smith v. Superior Court (Bonita Park Homeowners Association) (1990) 217 Cal. App. 3d 950, 954, 266 Cal. Rptr. 253.

20. Kirby v. Albert D. Seeno Construction Company (1992) 11 Cal. App. 4th 1059, 14 Cal. Rptr. 2d 604, CAMSI IV v. Hunter Technology Corp. (1991) 230 Cal. App. 3d 1525, 282 Cal. Rptr. 80. The Kirby case involved the homeowners' claims that the defendant builder had falsely represented the home was constructed on a cut lot with no more than 2 feet of fill, when it was actually constructed on 8 to 16 feet of improperly compacted fill which eventually resulted in major foundation movement.

21. Kirby v. Albert D. Seeno Construction Company (1992) 11 Cal. App. 4th 1059, 14 Cal. Rptr. 2d 604, Leaf v. City of San Mateo (1980) 104 Cal. App. 3d 398, 163 Cal. Rptr. 711.

22. San Leandro Canning Co., Inc. v. Perillo (1931) 211 Cal. 482, 487, 295 P.2d 1126, Admiralty Fund v. Peerless Insurance Co. (1983) 143 Cal. App. 3d 379, 191 Cal. Rptr. 753, Smith v. Superior Court (1990) 217 Cal. App. 3d 950, 266 Cal. Rptr. 253 (dicta).

23. Code of Civil Procedure Sections 337.1, 337.15.

24. Code of Civil Procedure Section 337.1(e). Section 337.1 reads in full as follows:

"(a) Except as otherwise provided in this section, no action shall be brought to recover damages from any person performing or furnishing the design, specifications, surveying, planning, supervision or observation of construction or construction of an improvement to real property more than four years after the substantial completion of such improvement for any of the following:

"(1) Any patent deficiency in the design, specifications, surveying, planning, supervision or observation of construction or construction of an improvement to, or survey of, real property;

"(2) Injury to property, real or personal, arising out of any such patent deficiency; or

"(3) Injury to the person or for wrongful death arising out of any such patent deficiency.

"(b) If, by reason of such patent deficiency, an injury to property or the person or an injury causing wrongful death occurs during the fourth year after such substantial completion, an action in tort to recover damages for such an injury or wrongful death may be brought within one year after the date on which such injury occurred, irrespective of the date of death, but in no event may such an action be brought more than five years after the substantial completion of construction of such improvement.

"(c) Nothing in this section shall be construed as extending the period prescribed by the laws of this state for the bringing of any action.

"(d) The limitation prescribed by this section shall not be asserted by way of defense by any person in actual possession or the control, as owner, tenant or otherwise, of such an improvement at the time any deficiency in such an improvement constitutes the proximate cause of the injury or death for which it is proposed to bring an action."

"(e) As used in this section, 'patent deficiency' means a deficiency which is apparent by reasonable inspection.

"(f) Subdivisions (a) and (b) shall not apply to any owneroccupied single-unit residence."

25. Preston v. Goldman (1986) 42 Cal. 3d 108, 227 Cal. Rptr. 817, 720 P.2d 476, Geertz v. Ausonio (1992) 4 Cal. App. 4th 1363, 6 Cal. Rptr. 2d 318, Wagner v. State of California (1978) 86 Cal. App. 3d 922, 150 Cal. Rptr. 489.

26. Winston Square Homeowner's Association v. Centex West, Inc. (1989) 213 Cal. App. 3d 282, 261 Cal. Rptr. 605, Geertz v. Ausonio (1992) 4 Cal. App. 4th 1363, 6 Cal. Rptr. 2d 318, Renown, Inc. v. Hensel Phelps Construction Co. (1984) 154 Cal. App. 3d 413, 201 Cal. Rptr. 242.

27. Code of Civil Procedure Section 337.15(b). Section 337.15 reads in full as follows:

"(a) No action may be brought to recover damages from any person, or the surety of a person, who develops real property or performs or furnishes the design, specifications, surveying, planning, supervision, testing, or observation of construction or construction of an improvement to real property more than 10 years after the substantial completion of the development or improvement for any of the following:

"(1) Any latent deficiency in the design, specifications, surveying, planning, supervision, or observation of construction or construction of an improvement to, or survey of, real property;

"(2) Injury to property, real or personal, arising out of any such latent deficiency.

"(b) As used in this section, 'latent deficiency' means a deficiency which is not apparent by reasonable inspection.

"(c) As used in this section, 'action' includes an action for indemnity brought against a person arising out of that person's performance or furnishing of services or materials referred to in this section, except that a cross-complaint for indemnity may be filed pursuant to subdivision (b) of Section 428.10 in an action which has been brought within the time period set forth in subdivision (a) of this section.

"(d) Nothing in this section shall be construed as extending the period prescribed by the laws of this state for bringing any action .

"(e) The limitation prescribed by this section shall not be asserted by way of defense by any person in actual possession or the control, as owner, tenant or otherwise, of such an improvement, at the time any deficiency in the improvement constitutes the proximate cause for which it is proposed to bring an action.

"(f) This section shall not apply to actions based on willful misconduct or fraudulent concealment.

"(g) The 10-year period specified in subdivision (a) shall commence upon substantial completion of the improvement, but not later than the date of one of the following, whichever first occurs:

"(1) The date of final inspection by the applicable public agency .

"(2) The date of recordation of a valid notice of completion .

"(3) The date of use or occupation of the improvement.

"(4) One year after termination or cessation of work on the improvement .

"The date of substantial completion shall relate specifically to the performance or furnishing design, specifications, surveying, planning, supervision, testing, observation of construction or construction services by each profession or trade rendering services to the improvement."

28. Preston v. Goldman (1986) 42 Cal. 3d 108, 227 Cal. Rptr. 817, 720 P.2d 476, Geertz v. Ausonio (1992) 4 Cal. App. 4th 1363, 6 Cal. Rptr. 2d 318

29. Code of Civil Procedure Section 337.1

30. Code of Civil Procedure Section 337.15

31. Code of Civil Procedure Section 337.15(f)

32. Code of Civil Procedure Section 337.15(g)

33. Schwetz v. Minnerly (1990) 220 Cal. App. 3d 296, 269 Cal. Rptr. 417

34. Smith v. Superior Court (Bonita Park Homeowners Association) (1990) 217 Cal. App. 3d 950, 266 Cal. Rptr. 253. In this case the trial court ruled that the association's lawsuit against the developer seeking damages for latent construction defects was barred by the statute of repose stated in section 337.15 of the Code of Civil Procedure because it was not filed within 10 years after valid notices of completion had been recorded by the developer. The association subsequently filed a lawsuit against its board of directors and former board members for breach of fiduciary duties for the failure to investigate the common area defects and pursue appropriate legal action against the developer. The court held that this lawsuit was barred by the three-year statute of limitations applicable to breach of fiduciary duty lawsuits against corporate directors.

35. Regents of University of California v. Hartford Accident I Indemnity Co. (1978) 21 Cal. 3d 624, 641, 147 Cal. Rptr. 486, 581 P.2d 197, Winston Square Homeowner's Association v. Centex West, Inc. (1989) 213 Cal. App. 3d 282, 261 Cal. Rptr. 605. To illustrate the effects of both statutes, in Winston Square the court stated: "Even if the drainage problems could be characterized as a latent deficiency, the evidence establishes the trial court's alternative ground for barring recovery was correct; Winston Square discovered or should have discovered the problem and did not file suit within three years. Sections 337.15 and 338 provide a 'two-step limitation' for latent deficiencies. ... '[A]ctions founded upon a latent defect in the development of real property must be filed within three or four years of discovery, depending on whether the action rests on breach of warranty or negligence, but in any case within ten years of the date of substantial completion of the improvement."

36. Civil Code Section 1368.4. Section 1368.4 reads in full as follows:

"(a) Not later than 30 days prior to the filing of any civil action by the association against the declarant or other developer of a common interest development for alleged damage to the common areas, alleged damage to the separate interests that the association is obligated to maintain or repair, or alleged damage to the separate interests that arises out of, or is integrally related to, damage to the common areas or separate interests that the association is obligated to maintain or repair, the board of directors of the association shall [sic] a provide written notice to each member of the association who appears on the records of the association when the notice is provided. This notice shall specify all of the following:

"(1) That a meeting will take place to discuss problems that may lead to the filing of a civil action.

"(2) The options, including civil actions, that are available to address the problems.

"(3) The time and place of this meeting.

"(b) Notwithstanding subdivision (a), if the association has reason to believe that the applicable statute of limitations will expire before the association files the civil action, the association may give the notice, as described above, within 30 days after the filing of the action."

37. Civil Code Section 1368.4.

38. Civil Code Section 1375.

39. Civil Code Section 1375(a),(b).

40. Civil Code Section 1375(b) (2).

41. Civil Code Section 1375(b) (3) (A).

42. Civil Code Section 1375(b) (3) (B).

43. Civil Code Section 1375(b) (3) (B).

44. Civil Code Section 1375(g)(2). If the association's governing documents provide a different procedure for calling special meetings of the members, the notice must inform the members of that procedure.

45. Civil Code Section 1375(g)(2). If the association's governing documents provide a different procedure for calling special meetings of the members, the notice must inform the members of that procedure.

46. Code of Civil Procedure Section 411.35.

47. Code of Civil Procedure Section 411.35(g).

48. Code of Civil Procedure Section 411.36.

49. Code of Civil Procedure Section 411.36.

50. Code of Civil Procedure Section 411.36(g).

51. Code of Civil Procedure Section 411.36(i).

52. Kovich v. Paseo Del Mar Homeowners' Association (1996) 41 Cal. App. 4th 863, 48 Cal. Rptr. 26 758.

CHAPTER VI: ASSOCIATION STRUCTURE AND GOVERNANCE: GOVERNING DOCUMENTS, LAWS AND REGULATIONS

1. Findley v. Garrett (1952) 109 Cal. App. 2d 166, Scott v. Los Angeles Mountain Park Co. (1928) 92 Cal. App. 258, 267 P. 914.

2. Corporations Code Section 7210, Communist Party of the United States v. 522 Valencia, Inc. (1995) 35 Cal. App. 4th 980, 41 Cal. Rptr. 2d 618, Kennerson v. Burbank Amusement Co. (1953) 120 Cal. App. 2d 157.

3. Corporations Code Section 7213(b) provides in relevant part:

"Except as otherwise provided by the articles or bylaws, officers shall be chosen by the board and serve at the pleasure of the board, subject to the rights, if any, of an officer under any contract of employment."

4. As noted in Chapter 1, all references to statutes in this book are to California statutes, unless the reference otherwise specifically states that it is a citation of a federal statute or the statute of another state

5. Under a legal doctrine called "res judicata" persons who are members of an association which is given statutory authority to sue on behalf of itself and its members may be bound by a judgment entered against the association, even though the association members did not participate in the lawsuit. Rynsburger v. Dairymen's Fertilizer Coop., Inc. (1968) 266 Cal. App. 2d 269, 72 Cal. Rptr. 102

6. California Rules of Court, Rule 976: "(a) All opinions of the Supreme Court shall be published in the Official Reports. (b) No opinion of a Court of Appeal or an appellate department of the superior court may be published in the Official Reports unless the opinion: (1) establishes a new rule of law, applies an existing rule to a set of facts significantly different from those stated in published opinions, or modifies, or criticizes with reasons given, an existing rule; (2) resolves or creates an apparent conflict in the law; (3) involves a legal issue of continuing public interest; or (4) makes a significant contribution to legal literature by reviewing either the development of a common law rule or the legislative or judicial history of a provision of a constitution, statute, or other written law."

7. California Rules of Court, Rule 976(c)(2): "An opinion certified for publication shall not be published, and an opinion not so certified shall be published, on an order of the Supreme Court to that effect". Monterey Club Management Association v. Morgan (1991) 91 Daily Journal DAR 10392, 1991 Cal. Lexis 3891, in which the California Supreme Court ordered that the Reporter of Decisions is directed not to publish in the Official Appellate Reports the opinion in Monterey Club Management Association v. Morgan (1991) 230 Cal. App. 36 1465, 281 Cal. Rptr. 880.

8. California Rules of Court, Rule 977: "(a) An opinion that is not ordered published shall not be cited or relied on by a court or a party in any other action or proceeding except as provided in subdivision (b) . (b) Such an opinion may be cited or relied on: (1) when the opinion is relevant under the doctrines of law of the case, res judicata, or collateral estoppel; or (2) when the opinion is relevant to a criminal or disciplinary action or proceeding because it states reasons for a decision affecting the same defendant or respondent in another such action or proceeding."

9. Title 10 California Code of Regulations Sections 2790 - 2800.

10. Title 2 California Code of Regulations Sections 7285, et seq.

11. Civil Code Sections 1350 - 1374.

12. Department of Real Estate Legislative Analysis Report- June 10, 1985. As stated in this report, the Department of Real Estate supported the enactment of the Davis-Stirling Common Interest Development Act "because it believes that understanding and administration of the law of common-interest subdivisions would be enhanced by its provisions."

13. Civil Code Section 1352.

14. Civil Code Section 1351(b).

15. Civil Code Section 1363(a).

16. Corporations Code Section 9910: "As used in Sections 9910 to 9927 of this part: (a) 'New . . . mutual benefit ... corporation law' means Part 1 (commencing with Section 5002) . . . [and] Part 3 (commencing with Section 7110) . . . of Division 2 of Title 1 of the Corporations Code enacted by the California Legislature during the 1977-1978 Regular Session and, except as required by Section 9912, operative January 1, 1980."

Corporations Code Section 9911(b): "The new mutual benefit corporation law applies to all corporations which are incorporated on or after January 1, 1980, under Part 3 of this division or which are expressly governed by Part 3 pursuant to a particular provision of this division or Division 3 (commencing with Section 12000) or other specific statutory provision."

Corporations Code Section 9912(a): "Each corporation which is subject (pursuant to the terms of the prior nonprofit law or some other specific statutory provision) to the prior nonprofit law shall, on and after January 1, 1980, be subject to the new public benefit corporation law, the new mutual benefit corporation law, or the new religious corporation law based on the following:

"(1) Any corporation of a type designated by statute as being subject to the new public benefit corporation law, the new mutual benefit corporation law, or the new religious corporation law, shall be subject to such law.

"(5) Any corporation which does not come within paragraphs 1 , 2 [religious corporation], 3 [public benefit corporation] or 4 [public benefit corporation] of this subdivision and which permits distribution of assets to its members upon dissolution shall be subject to the new mutual benefit corporation law.

"(6) Any corporation not otherwise described in this subdivision shall be subject to the new mutual benefit corporation law."

17. 1977-78 Regular Session, Assembly Bill 2180.

18. Corporations Code Sections 21301 - 21310.

19. Civil Code Section 1363(a),(c).

20. Civil Code Section 1363(c), Code of Civil Procedure Sections 369.5, 383.

21. Corporations Code Section 7140(a)-(l).

22. Corporations Code Section 7140.

23. In O'Connor v. Village Green Owners Association (1983) 38 Cal. 3d 790, 191 Cal. Rptr. 320, 662 P.2d 427, the California Supreme Court has held that an association which engages in typical business transactions such as hiring property managers, procuring insurance, maintaining common areas and collecting assessments, is a "business establishment" within the meaning of the "Unruh Civil Rights Act" and therefore subject to its prohibitions of discriminatory policies and practices.

24. California Rules of Court, Rule 976: "(a) All opinions of the Supreme Court shall be published in the Official Reports. (b) No opinion of a Court of Appeal or an appellate department of the superior court may be published in the Official Reports unless the opinion: (1) establishes a new rule of law, applies an existing rule to a set of facts significantly different from those stated in published opinions, or modifies, or criticizes with reasons given, an existing rule; (2) resolves or creates an apparent conflict in the law; (3) involves a legal issue of continuing public interest; or (4) makes a significant contribution to legal literature by reviewing either the development of a common law rule or the legislative or judicial history of a provision of a constitution, statute, or other written law."

25. Many older court opinions addressed land use restrictions found in deeds or declarations applicable to real estate, but which did not involve a CID or association. Nevertheless, an opinion deciding whether a restriction against using land for commercial purposes is valid and enforceable will, if otherwise applicable, still govern similar questions in the context of CIDs and associations.

26. Title 10 California Code of Regulations Sections 2790 - 2800.

27. Business and Professions Code Section 11018.7, Title 10 California Code of Regulations Section 2800.

28. Title 10 California Code of Regulations Section 2792.8(a)(1).

29. Title 10 California Code of Regulations Section 2792.8(a)(4), (5), (6).

30. Title 10 California Code of Regulations Section 2792.8(a)(8).

31. Title 10 California Code of Regulations Section 2792.8(a)(10).

32. Title 10 California Code of Regulations Section. 2792.8(a)(11).

33. Title 10 California Code of Regulations Section. 2792.8(a)(23).

34. Title 10 California Code of Regulations Section 2792.17.

35. Title 10 California Code of Regulations Section 2792.18.

36. Title 10 California Code of Regulations Section 2792.19.

37. Title 10 California Code of Regulations Section 2792.20.

38. Title 10 California Code of Regulations Section 2792.21.

39. Title 10 California Code of Regulations Section 2792.22.

40. Corporations Code Section 7120: "(a) One or more persons may form a corporation under this part by executing and filing articles of incorporation. . . . (c) The corporate existence begins upon the filing of the articles and continues perpetually, unless otherwise expressly provided by law or in the articles."

41. Corporations Code Section 7133.

42. Corporations Code Section 7130.

43. Civil Code Section 1363.5(a).

44. Corporations Code Section 7131.

45. Corporations Code Section 7132(c)(1).

46. Corporations Code Section 7132(c)(2).

47. Corporations Code Section 7132(c)(3).

48. Corporations Code Section 7132(c)(5).

49. Corporations Code Section 7151(c) provides in part that: "The bylaws may contain any provision, not in conflict with law or the articles, for the management of the activities and for the conduct of the affairs of the corporation."

50. Corporations Code Section 7151(a).

51. Corporations Code Section 7150(a). However, with a few exceptions, under Corporations Code Section 7150(c), the articles of incorporation or the bylaws may restrict or eliminate the power of the board of directors to adopt, amend or repeal any or all bylaws.

52. Corporations Code Section 7150(b).

53. Corporations Code Section 7151(d).

54. Corporations Code Section 7151(e).

55. Corporations Code Section 8320 reads in part that: "(a) Each corporation shall keep: (2) Minutes of the proceedings of its members, board and committees of the board ... (c) Minutes shall be kept in written form. Other books and records shall be kept either in written form or in any other form capable of being converted into written form."

56. Civil Code Section 1363(d) states. "Meetings of the membership of the association shall be conducted in accordance with a recognized system of parliamentary procedure or such parliamentary procedures as the association may adopt." The Department of Real Estate Regulations, at Title 10 California Code of Regulations Section 2792.17(b), contains a similar requirement.

57. Civil Code Sections 18, 19, 1217, 1354(a).

58. Civil Code Section 1366(a) reads in part as follows: ". . . However, annual increases in regular assessments for any fiscal year, as authorized by subdivision (b), shall not be imposed unless the board has complied with subdivision (a) of Section 1365 with respect to that fiscal year, or has obtained the approval of owners, . . ."

59. Title 10 California Code of Regulations Section 2800(o), Business and Professions Code Section 11018.7.

60. Title 10 California Code of Regulations Section 2792.24(a), Civil Code Sections 1355, 1356, 1357.

61. Business and Professions Code Sections 11018, et seq., Title 10 California Code of Regulations Section 2792.8.

62. Title 10 California Code of Regulations Section 2792.24(a).

63. Title 10 California Code of Regulations Section 2792.24(a).

64. Civil Code Section 1355(a).

65. Civil Code Section 1355(b).

66. Civil Code Section 1356.

67. Civil Code Section 1356 reads in full as follows:

"(a) If in order to amend a declaration, the declaration requires owners having more than 50 percent of the votes in the association, in a single class voting structure, or owners having more than 50 percent of the votes in more than one class in a voting structure with more than one class, to vote in favor of the amendment, the association, or any owner of a separate interest, may petition the superior court of the county in which the common interest development is located for an order reducing the percentage of the affirmative votes necessary for such an amendment. The petition shall describe the effort that has been made to solicit approval of the association members in the manner provided in the declaration, the number of affirmative and negative votes actually received, the number or percentage of affirmative votes required to effect the amendment in accordance with the existing declaration, and other matters the petitioner considers relevant to the court's determination. The petition shall also contain, as exhibits thereto, copies of all of the following:

"(1) The governing documents.

"(2) A complete text of the amendment.

"(3) Copies of any notice and solicitation materials utilized in the solicitation of owner approvals.

"(4) A short explanation of the reason for the amendment.

"(5) Any other documentation relevant to the court's determination.

"(b) Upon filing the petition, the court shall set the matter for hearing and issue an ex parte order setting forth the manner in which notice shall be given.

"(c) The court may, but shall not be required to, grant the petition if it finds all of the following:

"(1) The petitioner has given not less that 15 days written notice of the court hearing to all members of the association, to any mortgagee of a mortgage or beneficiary of a deed of trust who is entitled to notice under the terms of the declaration, and to the city, county, or city and county in which the common interest development is located that is entitled to notice under the terms of the declaration.

"(2) Balloting on the proposed amendment was conducted in accordance with all applicable provisions of the governing documents.

"(3) A reasonably diligent effort was made to permit all eligible members to vote on the proposed amendment.

"(4) Owners having more than 50 percent of the votes, in a single class voting structure, voted in favor of the amendment. In a voting structure with more than one class, where the declaration requires a majority of more than one class to vote in favor of the amendment, owners having more than 50 percent of the votes of each class required by the declaration to vote in favor of the amendment voted in favor of the amendment.

"(5) The amendment is reasonable.

"(6) Granting the petition is not improper for any reason stated in subdivision (e).

"(d) If the court makes the findings required by subdivision (c) , any order issued pursuant to this section may confirm the amendment as being validly approved on the basis of the affirmative votes actually received during the balloting period or the order may dispense with any requirement relating to quorums or to the number or percentage of votes needed for approval of the amendment that would otherwise exist under the governing documents.

"(e) Subdivisions (a) to (d), inclusive, notwithstanding, the court shall not be empowered by this section to approve any amendment to the declaration that:

"(1) Would change provisions in the declaration requiring the approval of owners having more than 50 percent of the votes in more than one class to vote in favor of an amendment, unless owners having more than 50 percent of the votes in each affected class approved the amendment.

"(2) Would eliminate any special rights, preferences, or privileges designated in the declaration as belonging to the declarant, without the consent of the declarant.

"(3) Would impair the security interest of a mortgagee of a mortgage or the beneficiary of a deed of trust without the approval of the percentage of the mortgagees and beneficiaries specified in the declaration, if the declaration requires the approval of a specified percentage of the mortgagees and beneficiaries.

"(f) An amendment is not effective pursuant to this section until the court order and amendment have been recorded in every county in which a portion of the common interest development is located. The amendment may be acknowledged by, and the court order and amendment may be recorded by, any person designated in the declaration or by the association for that purpose, or if no one is designated for that purpose, by the president of the association. Upon recordation of the amendment and court order, the declaration, as amended in accordance with this section, shall have the same force and effect as if the amendment were adopted in compliance with every requirement imposed by the governing documents.

"(g) Within a reasonable time after the amendment is recorded the association shall mail a copy of the amendment to each member of the association, together with a statement that the amendment has been recorded."

68. Civil Code Section 1356(d).

69. Corporations Code Sections 7812.

70. Corporations Code Section 7812 reads in part as follows:

"(a) Except as provided in this section or Section 7813, amendments may be adopted if approved by the board and approved by the members (Section 5034) and approved by such other person or persons, if any, as required by the articles. The approval by the members or other person or persons may be before or after the approval of the board.

"(b) Notwithstanding subdivision (a), the following amendments may be adopted by approval of the board alone:

"(1) An amendment extending the corporate existence or making the corporate existence perpetual, if the corporation was organized prior to August 14, 1929.

"(2) An amendment deleting the names and addresses of the first directors or the name and address of the initial agent.

"(3) Any amendment, at a time the corporation has no members; provided, however, that if the articles require approval by any person for an amendment, an amendment may not be adopted without such approval.

"(4) An amendment adopted pursuant to Section 9913."

71. Corporations Code Section 7813 requires that:

"An amendment must also be approved by the members (Section 5034) of a class, whether or not such class is entitled to vote thereon by the provisions of the articles or bylaws, if the amendment would:

"(a) Materially and adversely affect the rights, privileges, preferences, restrictions or conditions of that class as to voting, dissolution, redemption or transfer in a manner different than such action affects another class;

"(b) Materially and adversely affect such class as to voting, dissolution, redemption or transfer by changing the rights, privileges, preferences, restrictions or conditions of another class;

"(c) Increase or decrease the number of memberships authorized for such class;

"(d) Increase the number of memberships authorized for another class;

"(e) Effect an exchange, reclassification or cancellation of all or part of the memberships of such class; or

"(f) Authorize a new class of memberships."

72. Corporations Code Section 7150(a),(c). Corporations Code Section 7150(c) provides:

"The articles or bylaws may restrict or eliminate the power of the board to adopt, amend or repeal any or all bylaws, subject to subdivision (e) of Section 7151."

73. Corporations Code Section 7150(a) reads in full as follows:

"Except as provided in subdivision (c) and Sections 7151, 7220, 7224, 7512, 7613, and 7615, bylaws may be adopted, amended or repealed by the board unless the action would:

"(1) Materially and adversely affect the rights of members as to voting, dissolution, redemption, or transfer;

"(2) Increase or decrease the number of memberships authorized in total or for any class;

"(3) Effect and exchange, reclassification or cancellation of all or part of the memberships; or

"(4) Authorize a new class of membership."

74. Corporations Code Section 7150(b) reads as follows:

"Bylaws may be adopted, amended or repealed by approval of the members (Section 5034); provided, however, that such adoption, amendment or repeal also requires approval by the members of a class if such action would:

"(1) Materially and adversely affect the rights, privileges, preferences, restrictions or conditions of that class as to voting, dissolution, redemption, or transfer in a manner different than such action affects another class;

"(2) Materially and adversely affect such class as to voting, dissolution, redemption, or transfer by changing the rights, privileges, preferences, restrictions or conditions of another class;

"(3) Increase or decrease the number of memberships authorized for such class;

"(4) Increase the number of memberships authorized for another class;

"(5) Effect an exchange, reclassification or cancellation of all or part of the memberships of such class; or

"(6) Authorize a new class of memberships."

75. Corporations Code Section 5034.

76. Corporations Code Section 5033.

77. Corporations Code Section 7151(e) provides:

"The bylaws may require, for any or all corporate actions (except as provided in paragraphs (1) and (2) of subdivision (a) of Section 7222, subdivision (c) of Section 7615, and Section 8610) the vote of a larger proportion of, or all of, the members or the members of any class, unit, or grouping of members or the vote of a larger proportion of, or all of, the directors, than is otherwise required by this part. Such a provision in the bylaws requiring such greater vote shall not be altered, amended or repealed except by such greater vote, unless otherwise provided in the bylaws."

78. Corporations Code Section 7515(a),(c),(d). Corporations Code Section 7515 reads in full as follows:

"(a) If for any reason it is impractical or unduly difficult for any corporation to call or conduct a meeting of its members, delegates or directors, or otherwise obtain their consent, in the manner prescribed by its articles or bylaws, or this part, then the superior court of the proper county, upon petition of a director, officer, delegate or member, may order that such a meeting be called or that a written ballot or other form of obtaining the vote of members, delegates or directors be authorized, in such a manner as the court finds fair and equitable under the circumstances.

"(b) The court shall, in an order issued pursuant to this section, provide for a method of notice reasonably designed to give actual notice to all parties who would be entitled to notice of a meeting held pursuant to the articles, bylaws and this part, whether or not the method results in actual notice to every such person, or conforms to the notice requirements that would otherwise apply. In a proceeding under this section the court may determine who the members or directors are.

"(c) The order issued pursuant to this section may dispense with any requirement relating to the holding of and voting at meetings or obtaining of votes, including any requirement as to quorums or as to the number or percentage of votes needed for approval, that would otherwise be imposed by the articles, bylaws, or this part.

"(d) Wherever practical any order issued pursuant to this section shall limit the subject matter of the meetings or other forms of consent authorized to items, including amendments to the articles or bylaws, the resolution of which will or may enable the corporation to continue managing its affairs without further resort to this section; provided, however, that an order under this section may also authorize the obtaining of whatever votes and approvals are necessary for the dissolution, merger, sale of assets or reorganization of the corporation.

"(e) Any meeting or other method of obtaining the vote of members, delegates or directors conducted pursuant to an order issued under this section, and which complies with all the provisions of such order, is for all purposes a valid meeting or vote, as the case may be, and shall have the same force and effect as if it complied with every requirement imposed by the articles, bylaws, and this part."

79. Corporations Code Section 7515(a).

80. Corporations Code Section 7515(c).

81. Section 8724 of the Corporations Code prohibits the termination or dissolution of an association without the approval of 100 percent of the members by providing that:

"Without the approval of 100 percent of the members, any contrary provision in this part or the articles or bylaws notwithstanding, so long as there is any lot, parcel, area, apartment or unit for which an owners association . . . is obligated to provide management, maintenance, preservation or control:

"(a) The owners association or any person acting on its behalf shall not:

(1) Transfer all or substantially all of its assets; or

(2) File a certificate of dissolution [voluntary dissolution]; and

"(b) No court shall enter an order declaring the owners association duly wound up and dissolved."

CHAPTER VII: THE ASSOCIATION MEMBERS

1. Title 10 California Code of Regulations Section 2792.8(a) (1).

2. Corporations Code Section 5056.

3. Corporations Code Section 5057.

4. Corporations Code Sections 7310, 7315.

5. Anthony v. Brea Glenbrook Club (1976) 58 Cal. App. 3d 506, 130 Cal. Rptr. 32.

6. California Civil Code Section 2985 defines "real property sales contracts" as follows: "A real property sales contract is an agreement wherein one party agrees to convey title to real property to another party upon the satisfaction of specified conditions set forth in the contract and which does not require conveyance of title within one year from the date of formation of the contract."

For example, the buyer under a real property sales contract is the owner of the real property for all purposes. Stromerson v. Averill (1943) 133 P.2d 617, Elliott v. McCombs (1941) 17 Cal. 2d 23, 109 P.2d 329, Roemer v. Pappas (1988) 203 Cal. App. 3d 201, 249 Cal. Rptr. 743, Kosloff v. Castle (1981) 115 Cal. App. 3d 369, 171 Cal. Rptr. 308, County of Los Angeles v. Butcher (1957) 155 Cal. App. 2d 744, 318 P.2d 838, Sherman v. Quinn (1947) 179 P.2d 24.

7. Corporations Code Section 7312: "No person may hold more than one membership, and no fractional memberships may be held, provided, however, that: (d) In the case of membership in an owners association, . . . the articles or bylaws may permit a person who owns an interest, or who has a right of exclusive occupancy, in more than one lot, parcel, area, apartment or unit to hold a separate membership in the owners association for each such lot, parcel, area, apartment or unit."

8. Corporations Code Section 7312(a).

9. Corporations Code Section 5058.

10. Corporations Code Section 7313.

11. Corporations Code Section 7313(b).

12. Corporations Code Section 5058.

13. Corporations Code Section 7220(d).

14. Title 10 California Code of Regulations Section 2792.19(c)(1).

15. Corporations Code Sections 7513 - 7515.

16. Corporations Code Section 7615(a)

17. Title 10 California Code of Regulations Sections 2792.19, 2800, Business and Professions Code Section 11018.7.

18. Corporations Code Section 7615(a) reads in part that: "If the articles or bylaws authorize cumulative voting, but not otherwise, every member entitled to vote at any election of directors may cumulate the member's votes and give one candidate a number of votes equal to the number of directors to be elected multiplied by the number of votes to which the member is entitled, or distribute the member's votes on the same principle among as many candidates as the member thinks fit. . ."

19. Corporations Code Section 7221.

20. Corporations Code Section 7222(a).

21. Corporations Code Section 7223.

22. Corporations Code Section 7222(d): "Except as provided in this section and Sections 7221 [board's declaration that the office of a director is vacant based on "cause"] and 7223, a director may not be removed prior to the expiration of such director's term of office."

23. Corporations Code Sections 7222(a)(1), 5033.

24. Corporations Code Sections 7222(a)(2), 5034.

25. Corporations Code Section 7151(e): "The bylaws may require, for any or all corporate actions (except as provided in paragraphs (1) and (2) of subdivision (a) of Section 7222 ...) the vote of a larger proportion of, or all of, the members or the members of any class, unit, or grouping of members . . . than is otherwise required by this part. . ."

26. Corporations Code Section 7222(b)(1).

27. Corporations Code Section 7222(b)(2).

28. Corporations Code Section 7223.

29. Corporations Code Section 7223(b).

30. Corporations Code Section 5036.

31. Under Corporations Code Section 5036, "authorized number" means 5% of the voting power or, where the total number of votes entitled to be cast for a director is more than 1,000 but less than 5,000, 2 1/2% of the voting power but not less than 50, or where the total number of votes entitled to be cast for a director is 5,000 or more, 1/20 of 1% of the voting power but not less than 125.

32. Civil Code Sections 1355, 1355.5, 1356, 1357, Corporations Code Sections 7150(b), 7812, 7813, 7813.5, Title 10 California Code of Regulations Section 2792.24.

33. Civil Code Section 1366(a) reads:

"Except as provided in this section, the association shall levy regular and special assessments sufficient to perform its obligations under the governing documents and this title. However, annual increases in regular assessments for any fiscal year, as authorized by subdivision (b), shall not be imposed unless the board has complied with subdivision (a) of Section 1365 with respect to that fiscal year, or has obtained the approval of owners, constituting a quorum, casting a majority of the votes at a meeting or election of the association conducted in accordance with Chapter 5 (commencing with Section 7510) of part 3 of Division 2 of Title 1 of the Corporations Code and Section 7613 of the Corporations Code. For the purposes of this section, 'quorum' means more than 50 percent of the owners of an association."

34. Civil Code Section 1365(a).

35. Civil Code Section 1365(a).

36. Civil Code Section 1365(a).

37. Civil Code Section 1366(b).

38. Civil Code Section 1366(b).

39. Civil Code Section 1363.05(b).

40. Section 1363.05 of the Civil Code reads in full as follows:

> "Section 1363.05. (a) This section shall be known and may be cited as the Common Interest Development Open Meeting Act.
>
> "(b) Any member of the association may attend meetings of the board of directors of the association, except when the board adjourns to executive session to consider litigation, matters relating to the formation of contracts with third parties, member discipline, or personnel matters. The board of directors of the association shall meet in executive session, if requested by a member who may be subject to a fine, penalty, or other form of discipline, and the member shall be entitled to attend the executive session.
>
> "(c) Any matter discussed in executive session shall be generally noted in the minutes of the board of directors.
>
> "(d) The minutes, minutes proposed for adoption that are marked to indicate draft status, or a summary of the minutes, of any meeting of the board of directors of an association, other than an executive session, shall be available to members within 30 days of the meeting.
>
> "The minutes, proposed minutes, or summary minutes shall be distributed to any member of the association upon request and upon reimbursement of the association's costs for making that distribution.
>
> "(e) Members of the association shall be notified in writing at the time that the pro forma budget required in Section 1365 is distributed, or at the time of any general mailing to the entire membership of the association, of their right to have copies of the minutes of meetings of the board of directors, and how and where those minutes may be obtained.
>
> "(f) As used in this section, 'meeting' includes any congregation of a majority of the members of the board at the same time and place to hear, discuss, or deliberate upon any item of business scheduled to be heard by the board, except those matters that may be discussed in executive session.
>
> "(g) Unless the time and place of meeting is fixed by the bylaws, or unless the bylaws provide for a longer period of notice, members shall be given notice of the time and place of a meeting as defined in subdivision (f), except for an emergency meeting, at least four days prior to the meeting. Notice may

be given by posting the notice in a prominent place or places within the common area, by mail or delivery of the notice to each unit in the development, or by newsletter or similar means of communication.

"(h) An emergency meeting of the board may be called by the president of the association, or by any two members of the governing body other than the president, if there are circumstances that could not have been reasonably foreseen which require immediate attention and possible action by the board, and which of necessity make it impracticable to provide notice as required by this section."

41. Civil Code Section 1363.05(h).

42. Civil Code Section 1363(f), Corporations Code Sections 8330-8338.

43. Civil Code Section 1363(f), Corporations Code Section 8330(a)(1).

44. Civil Code Section 1363(f), Corporations Code Section 8330(a)(2).

45. Civil Code Section 1363(f), Corporations Code Section 8333.

46. Civil Code Section 1363(f), Corporations Code Section 8333.

47. Civil Code Sections 1363(f), 1363.05(c), (d) , (e), Corporations Code Section 8333. Under Civil Code Section 1363.05(d) the minutes of board meetings, minutes proposed for adoption and marked as draft status, or a summary of the minutes, of any meeting of the board, other than an executive session, must be available to the members within 30 days of the meeting and must be distributed to any member upon request and upon reimbursement of the association's costs in making that distribution. Under Civil Code Section 1363.05(e) members of the association must be notified in writing at the time the pro forma budget required under Civil Code Section 1365 is distributed, or at the time of any general mailing to the entire membership of their right to have copies of the minutes of meetings of the board of directors and how and where copies of the minutes may be obtained.

48. Corporations Code Section 7160.

49. Civil Code Section 1368(a)(1), (b).

50. Civil Code Section 1368(a)(2), (b).

51. Civil Code Section 1368 (a)(3), (b).

52. Civil Code Section 1368 (a)(4), (b).

53. Under Section 6104(e) of the Internal Revenue Code and the Internal Revenue Service regulations implementing that statute, any person, including a member of the filing corporation is entitled to inspect and copy the form, together with its supporting schedules and attachments, with the exception of the schedule of contributors, if any exists for the corporation. The person's inspection and copying is limited in time to the regular business hours of the corporation. This right of inspection is held by "any individual" and exists for three years following the date each return is filed. The right of inspection may also be exercised by any person at the national or regional offices of the Internal Revenue Service.

54. Civil Code Section 1363.05(d).

55. Civil Code Section 1363.05(e).

56. Corporations Code Section 8311.

57. Corporations Code Section 8333, Civil Code Section 1363.05(d).

58. Corporations Code Section 7160.

59. Civil Code Section 1368(b).

60. Corporations Code Section 8333.

61. Goldstein v. Lees (1975) 46 Cal. App. 3d 614, 120 Cal. Rptr. 253: "Mooney v. Bartenders Union Local No. 284 contains the statement that 'It is provided by statute that all corporate records in this state shall be open to inspection upon the written demand of any shareholder ...' We do not take this to mean that a shareholder has the right to inspect corporate documents of every kind. Such a reading would contradict the language of section 3003. Rather, we take the sentence to mean that the categories of documents described in section 3003 comprise the formal records of the corporation and that the shareholder (assuming the other requisites of the statute are met) is entitled to inspect all of the formal records of the corporation."

62. Corporations Code Section 8330(b)(1).

63. Corporations Code Section 8330(c).

64. Corporations Code Section 8331.

65. Corporations Code Section 8331(h).

66. KQED, Inc. v. Hall (1982) 135 Cal. App. 3d 951, 185 Cal. Rptr. 630.

67. Corporations Code Section 8338(a).

68. Corporations Code Section 8338(b), (c), (d).

69. Corporations Code Section 5009

70. Corporations Code Section 5015

71. Corporations Code Section 5016

72. Civil Code Section 1363.05(b)

73. Title 10 C.C.R. § 2792.26 provides:

"(b) The governing instruments shall include provisions which authorize the governing body to impose monetary penalties, temporary suspensions of an owner's rights as a member of the Association or other appropriate discipline for failure to comply with the governing instruments provided that the procedures for notice and hearing, satisfying the minimum requirements of Section 7341 of the Corporations Code, are followed with respect to the accused member before a decision to impose discipline is reached."

74. Corporations Code Section 7341 reads in full as follows:

"(a) No member may be expelled or suspended, and no membership or memberships may be terminated or suspended, except according to procedures satisfying the requirements of this section. An expulsion, termination or suspension not in accord with this section shall be void and without effect .

"(b) Any expulsion, suspension, or termination must be done in good faith and in a fair and reasonable manner. Any procedure which conforms to the requirements of subdivision (c) is fair and reasonable, but a court may also find other procedures to be fair and reasonable when the full circumstances of the suspension, termination, or expulsion are considered.

"(c) A procedure is fair and reasonable when:

"(1) The provisions of the procedure have been set forth in the articles or bylaws, or copies of such provisions are sent annually to all the members as required by the articles or bylaws;

"(2) It provides the giving of 15 days' prior notice of the expulsion, suspension or termination and the reasons therefor; and

"(3) It provides an opportunity for the member to be heard, orally or in writing, not less than five days before the effective date of the expulsion, suspension or termination by a person or body authorized to decide that the proposed expulsion, termination or suspension not take place.

"(d) Any notice required under this section may be given by any method reasonably calculated to provide actual notice. Any notice given by mail must be given by first-class or registered mail sent to the last address of the members shown on the corporation's records.

"(e) Any action challenging an expulsion, suspension or termination of membership, including any claim alleging defective notice, must be commenced within one year after the date of the expulsion, suspension or termination. In the event such an action is successful the court may order any relief, including reinstatement, it finds equitable under the circumstances, but no vote of the members or of the board may be set aside solely because a person was at the time of the vote wrongfully excluded by virtue of the challenged expulsion, suspension or termination, unless the court finds further that the wrongful expulsion, suspension or termination was in bad faith and for the purpose, and with the effect, of wrongfully excluding the member from the vote or from the meeting at which the vote took place, so as to affect the outcome of the vote.

"(f) This section governs only the procedures for expulsion, suspension or termination and not the substantive grounds therefor. An expulsion, suspension or termination based upon substantive grounds which violate contractual or other rights of the member or are otherwise unlawful is not made valid by compliance with this section."

75. Corporations Code Section 7341(c)(1)-(3).

76. Corporations Code Section 7341(f).

77. Corporations Code Section 7341(f).

78. Corporations Code Section 7341(e).

79. Cason v. Glass Bottle Blowers Association (1951) 37 Cal. 2d 134, 231 P.2d 6, Hackethal v. California Medical Association (1982) 138 Cal. App. 3d 435, 187 Cal. Rptr. 811, Aluisi v. Fort Washington Golf & Country Club (1995) 36 Cal. App. 4th 799, 42 Cal. Rptr. 2d 761.

80. Beehan v. Lido Isle Community Association (1977) 70 Cal. App. 3d 858, 137 Cal. Rptr. 528, Katz v. Chevron Corporation (1994) 22 Cal. App. 4th 1352, 27 Cal. Rptr. 2d 681.

81. Pinsker v. Pacific Coast Society of Orthodontists (1974) 12 Cal. 3d 541, 116 Cal. Rptr. 245, 526 P.2d 253, Aluisi v. Fort Washington Golf & Country Club (1995) 36 Cal. App. 4th 799, 42 Cal. Rptr. 2d 761.

82. Cason v. Glass Bottle Blowers Association (1951) 37 Cal. 2d 134, 231 P.2d 6, Hackethal v. California Medical Association (1982) 138 Cal. App. 3d 435, 187 Cal. Rptr. 811, Aluisi v. Fort Washington Golf & Country Club (1995) 36 Cal. App. 4th 799, 42 Cal. Rptr. 2d 761

83. De Mille v. American Federation of Radio Artists, 31 Cal. 26 139, 187 P.26 769 (Cal. Supreme Court, en banc 1947), Westbrook v. Social Center Hall Association of Stockton (1957) 148 Cal. App. 2d 815, 307 P.2d 640, Williams v. Inglewood Board of Realtor (1963) 219 Cal. App. 2d 479, 33 Cal. Rptr. 289.

84. There are no published California court decisions addressing this question. The only California court decision even remotely related to the pertinent issue is found in Green Gables Home Owners Association v. Sunlite Homes, Inc. (1949) 202 P.2d 143.

This case was decided by the California Court of Appeal in 1949, but the opinion was not published in the official reports and it cannot be relied upon or cited as legal authority. In this case, a recorded declaration of covenants provided in part:

> . . the majority of the property owners within said subdivision may at any time while these restrictions or a substantial portion of them remain in force, form under the laws of the State of California a non-profit cooperative corporation without capital stock, but with one share thereof appurtenant to each of the lots in such subdivision. . . . In light of these definitions 'a share . . . appurtenant to each lot' takes on its proper significance. It entitles the owner of the lot to membership in the corporation and by acquiring a lot he thereby becomes a member. If he acquires several lots he does not become several members. That is an absurdity to which reason cannot yield."

85. Malibou Lake Mountain Club, Ltd. v. Robertson (1963) 219 Cal. App. 2d 181, 33 Cal. Rptr. 74. In this case, the court commented that: "The prosecution, in good faith, of a legal right for redress, even if unsuccessful, is not a ground for expulsion from an organization such as this."

86. Title 10 California Code of Regulations Section 2792.17(a).

87. Corporations Code Section 7510(b).

88. Corporations Code Section 7510(b).

89. Corporations Code Section 7510(a).

90. Civil Code Section 1363(d).

91. Corporations Code Section 7510(e).

92. Corporations Code Section 7511(c).

93. Corporations Code Section 7512(c).

94. Corporations Code Section 7512(c).

95. Although it may be possible to read Corporations Code Section 7511(a) conservatively to mean that if the notice is not mailed with first-class postage and registered or certified, it must be mailed not less than 20 days before the meeting, in light of the language of Section 601(a) of the Corporations Code, governing stock corporations, "a written notice of the [shareholders'] meeting shall be given not less than 10 (or, if sent by third-class mail, 30) nor more than 60 days before the date of the meeting ...", the better interpretation is that mailing the notice by first-class mail not less than 10 days before the date of the meeting complies with the statutory requirements.

96. Corporations Code Section 7511(a),(f).

97. Corporations Code Section 7222.

98. Corporations Code Section 7224.

99. Corporations Code Section 7233.

100. Corporations Code Section 7613(f)(1).

101. Corporations Code Section 7812.

102. Corporations Code Section 7911(a)(2).

103. Corporations Code Section 8012.

104. Corporations Code Section 8015.

105. Corporations Code Section 8610.

106. Corporations Code Section 7512. Section 7512(b) provides: "Where a bylaw authorizes a corporation to conduct a meeting with a quorum of less than one-third of the voting power, then the only matters that may be voted upon at any regular meeting actually attended, in person or by proxy, by less than one-third of the voting power are matters notice of the general nature of which was given, pursuant to the first sentence of subdivision (a) of Section 7511."

107. Title10 California Code of Regulations Section 2792.18(a), (b).

108. Title 10 California Code of Regulations Section 2792.18(b).

109. Corporations Code Section 7610.

110. Corporations Code Section 7312 reads in part as follows:

"No person may hold more than one membership, and no fractional memberships may be held, provided, however, that:
"(d) In the case of membership in an owners association, ... the articles or bylaws may permit a person who owns an interest, or who has a right of exclusive occupancy, in more than one lot, parcel, area, apartment, or unit to hold a separate membership in the owners association for each such lot, parcel, area, apartment, or unit."

111. Corporations Code Section 7312

112. Corporations Code Section 7612

113. King v. Oakmore Homes Association (1987) 195 Cal. App. 3d 779, 241 Cal. Rptr. 140. The King court held that if there are nonvoting co-owners, the voting owner's vote should count as one full vote so long as the nonvoting co-owner authorized such vote on his or her behalf; if the nonvoting co-owner has not so authorized such vote, the voting co-owner's vote does not reflect "joint action" of all owners and should not be considered a valid vote under the bylaw. The bylaw provision under consideration controlled over Corporations Code Section 704 (which contains language substantially identical to Section 7612). California Corporations Code Sections 704 and 7612, under the rule established in King appear, then, to be "default" rules that will control when an incorporated association's bylaws fail to address the issue of voting joint memberships or jointly owned shares. The King court stated that "[t]he key phrase of the bylaw is 'joint action,' and "... the bylaw should control questions of voting by cotenants because it constitutes 'written notice to the contrary' to the secretary."

114. Corporations Code Section 7615(a).

115. Corporations Code Section 7615(b).

116. Corporations Code Section 7615(b).

117. Corporations Code Section 7613(a).

118. Corporations Code Section 7613(f).

119. Fletcher Corporation Forms Annotated (4th ed. 1986 revised volume), Vol. 2, Sec. 1880.

120. Although there are no published California judicial decisions squarely addressing the issue, the Delaware courts have held that where multiple proxyholders are appointed in the proxy, they must act by majority, not individually. Callister v. Graham-Paige Corporation, 146 F. Supp. 399 (D. Del. 1956). In this case, the form of corporate proxy read in relevant part:

"The undersigned, the holder of record of shares of the Common Stock ... hereby appoints John J. Bergen, Irving Mitchell Felt and William M. Jennings, or a majority of such thereof as shall act, attorneys and proxies, with power of substitution, to vote said shares of stock for the election or removal of directors at any and all annual or special meetings of stockholders. . ."

In holding that the proxyholders appointed must act by majority action and not individually, the Callister Court stated:

"The giving of a proxy brings into play many of the principles of principal and agent and it has always been the law that in a private transaction (as distinguished from a public matter) an appointment of several agents shall be construed to be a loint appointment unless it clearly appears from the instrument that such appointment was to be joint and several. . . . The term majority' when referring to three named persons and applied to a course of action by a 'majority of such thereof as shall act' means, I think, such action by more than half of those entitled to act. The term 'majority' is the antonym of 'minority' and the counterpart of it. There is no more a 'majority' where only one is concerned than there is a 'minority' and the same person cannot be both."

121. Corporations Code Section 5010 reads as follows: "Whenever . . . members are disqualified from voting on any matter, their memberships shall not be counted for the determination of a quorum at any meeting to act upon, or the required vote to approve action upon, that matter under any other provision of . . . Part 3 (commencing with Section 7110) or the articles or bylaws."

122. Corporations Code Sections 7512(a), 7514(b).

123. Corporations Code Section 5069.

124. Corporations Code Sections 5069, 5079.

125. Corporations Code Section 5070.

126. Corporations Code Section 7514(a).

127. Corporations Code Section 7516 reads as follows:

"Any action required or permitted to be taken by the members may be taken without a meeting, if all members shall individually or collectively consent in writing to the action. The written consent or consents shall be filed with the minutes of the proceedings of the members. The action by written consent shall have the same force and effect as the unanimous vote of the members."

128. Corporations Code Section 7513(a) reads in part as follows:

"Subject to subdivision (e), and unless prohibited in the articles or bylaws, any action which may be taken at any regular or special meeting of members may be taken without a meeting if the corporation distributes a written ballot to every member entitled to vote on the matter."

129. Corporations Code Section 5080.

130. Corporations Code Section 7513(e).

131. Corporations Code Section 7613(b).

132. Corporations Code Section 7613(b).

133. Corporations Code Section 7613(c).

134. Corporations Code Section 7613(b).

135. Corporations Code Section 7613(d).

136. Corporations Code Section 7613(d).

137. Corporations Code Section 7613(d).

138. Corporations Code Section 7613(g).

139. Corporations Code Sections 7613(g), 7222.

140. Corporations Code Sections 7613(g), 7224.

141. Corporations Code Sections 7613(g), 7233.

142. Corporations Code Section 7613(f)(1).

143. Corporations Code Sections 7613(g), 7812.

144. Corporations Code Sections 7613(g), 7911(a)(2).

145. Corporations Code Sections 7613(g), 8012.

146. Corporations Code Sections 7613(g), 8015.

147. Corporations Code Sections 7613(g), 8610.

148. Although the corporation may be an "Owner" within the meaning of the association's governing documents, it is not legally possible for a corporation to be a member of itself.

In addition, if an analogy is drawn with the same question in the setting of a regular stock corporation which owns its own shares, the law prohibits that corporation from voting those shares. Lawrence v. I.N. Parlier Estate Co. (1940) 15 Cal. 2d 220, 100 P.2d 765, Brewster v. Hartley (1869) 37 Cal. 15. The rule was developed by the courts to prevent incumbent boards from abusing their position to perpetuate themselves in office.

149. Corporations Code Section 7614(a), (b).

150. Corporations Code Section 7614(a).

151. Corporations Code Section 7614(a).

152. Corporations Code Section 7614(c).

153. Corporations Code Section 7614(c).

154. Corporations Code Section 7611(a).

155. Corporations Code Section 7611(a).

156. Corporations Code Section 7611(a).

157. Corporations Code Section 7611(b).

158. Corporations Code Section 7611(b).

159. Corporations Code Section 7611(b).

160. Corporations Code Section 7611(b).

161. Corporations Code Section 7611(c).

162. Corporations Code Section 7611(c).

163. Corporations Code Section 7611(c).

164. Civil Code Section 1358 provides in part that in a community apartment project, condominium project, planned development and stock cooperative, "any conveyance, judicial sale, or other voluntary or involuntary transfer of the owner's entire estate also includes the owner's membership interest in the association."

Corporations Code Section 7320 states that:

"Subject to Section 7613 [Section 7613 authorizes members' use of proxies for voting purposes]:

"(a) Unless the articles or bylaws otherwise provide:

"(1) No member may transfer a membership or any right arising therefrom; and

"(2) Subject to the provisions of subdivision (b), all rights as a member of the corporation cease upon the member's death or dissolution.

"(b) The articles or bylaws may provide for, or may authorize the board to provide for, the transfer of memberships, or of memberships within any class or classes, with or without restriction or limitation, including transfer upon the death, dissolution, merger, or reorganization of a member.

"(c) Where transfer rights have been provided, no restriction of them shall be binding with respect to memberships issued prior to the adoption of the restriction, unless the holders of such memberships voted in favor of the restriction."

165. Liebler v. Point Loma Tennis Club Community Corporation (1995) 40 Cal. App. 4th 1600, 47 Cal. Rptr. 2d 783. In this case the Court of Appeal addressed circumstances in which the association's recorded declaration did not contain any provisions prohibiting nonresident owners from using the common area facilities, but did manifest an intent that each separately owned lot or unit would have only one set of users of the facilities and amenities. The association then adopted an association rule which provided that the "recreational facilities shall be used only by residents of [the association] and their guests. The right to use the facilities is appurtenant to the individual condominium unit and can not be separated from it (CC&R Section 8). Nonresident owners, whose units are rented or available for rent, do not have the use of the recreational facilities."

In affirming the validity and reasonableness of the adopted rule, the Liebler Court commented on the value common interest development facilities add to the separately-owned properties even if the owners cannot use the facilities:

> "The added burden from use by nonresident owners in addition to tenants and owner-residents could potentially greatly increase the number of individuals competing for [tennis] court space, and this decrease in availability lessens the attractiveness of a tennis-oriented facility." . . . Maintaining a low density by excluding the public, and here, in long-standing restrictions, nonresident owners as well, confers a benefit on the residents for which many will pay a higher price. Thus [the plaintiff] himself has benefited from the restriction,

since he is presumably thereby able to negotiate from his tenants a higher rent than he otherwise would have been able to obtain for the premises."

166. Major v. Miraverde Homeowners Association, Inc. (1992) 7 Cal. App. 4th 618, 9 Cal. Rptr. 2d 237. In this case the condominium owners were husband and wife. The owners purchased a condominium unit within the development and resided there for a few years. Subsequently, the owners moved out of the condominium, but continued to hold record title to the condominium unit. The wife's mother subsequently moved into the condominium unit. Pursuant to the association's declaration of CC&Rs all record title owners of condominium units were "members" of the association. Under the CC&Rs and association rules, the elderly mother was considered the "authorized" member. The association rules further provided that "non-resident" homeowners are not entitled to use of the facilities of the development, except as guests of an authorized member. The mother residing in the unit was eighty-two years old, senile, did not play tennis and was physically disabled to the extent she could not personally "sign-up" her children, the owners, as guests at the association guard building in order for the owners to play tennis. When the owners were informed they could not use the tennis court or any other facility, they filed a lawsuit.

In reaching its ruling, the Miraverde Court reasoned that the CC&Rs conferred membership on all record owners of condominium units, neither the association board of directors nor the association rules could override the CC&Rs to effectively strip membership rights, including the right to use and enjoy recreational facilities, from non-resident members. The Miraverde Court, however, expressly refrained from addressing the issue whether "under the CC&Rs, a delegation to a tenant or contract owner of the owner's right to enjoy common facilities would have the effect of terminating (or suspending) the owner's personal rights to use those facilities." This issue has now been decided in the Liebler case.

167. Ruoff v. Harbor Creek Community Association (1992) 10 Cal. App. 4th 1624, 13 Cal. Rptr. 2d 755, Davert v. Larson (1985) 163 Cal. App. 3d 407, 209 Cal. Rptr. 445

168. Civil Code Section 1365.9 reads in full as follows:

"(a) It is the intent of the Legislature to offer civil liability protection to owners of the separate interests in a common interest development that have common areas owned in tenancy-in-common if the association carries a certain level of prescribed insurance that covers a cause of action in tort.

"(b) Any cause of action in tort against any owner of a separate interest arising solely by reason of an ownership interest arising solely by reason of an ownership interest as a tenant in common in the common area of a common interest development shall be brought only against the association and not against the individual owners of the separate interest, as defined in subdivision (1) of Section 1351, if both of the insurance requirements in paragraphs (1) and (2) are met:

"(1) The association maintained and has in effect for this cause of action, one or more policies of insurance which include coverage for general liability of the association.

"(2) The coverage described in paragraph (1) is in the following minimum amounts:

"(A) At least two million dollars ($2,000,000) if the common interest development consists of 100 or fewer separate interests.

"(B) At least three million dollars ($3,000,000) if the common interest development consists of more than 100 separate interests ."

169. Civil Code Section 1365.9(b)(1)

CHAPTER VIII: DIRECTORS, OFFICERS AND MANAGEMENT

1. Corporations Code Section 5047 defines directors as follows:

"Except where otherwise expressly provided, 'directors' means natural persons, designated in the articles or bylaws or elected by the incorporators, and their successors and natural persons designated, elected or appointed by any other name or title to act as members of the governing body of the corporation."

Corporations Code Section 7510(b) requires that meetings of members be held in each year in which directors are to be elected for the purpose of conducting such election.

Corporations Code Section 7220(a) provides that directors shall be elected for such terms as fixed in the articles of incorporation or bylaws, but no longer than four years. If the term is not fixed in the articles or bylaws, then the term of office of directors is one year.

2. Findley v. Garrett (1952) 109 Cal. App. 2d 166, Scott v. Los Angeles Mountain Park Co. (1928) 92 Cal. App. 258, 267 P. 914.

3. Communist Party of the United States v. 522 Valencia, Inc. (1995) 35 Cal. App. 4th 980, 41 Cal. Rptr. 2d 618, Compton College, Etc. v. Compton Comm., Etc. (1982) 132 Cal. App. 3d 704, 183 Cal. Rptr. 341.

4. Title 10 California Code of Regulations Section 2792.8(a) provides in relevant part that:

"(a) Governing instruments for the ownership and management of . . . common-interest subdivisions . . . including the Covenants, Conditions and Restrictions (CC&Rs), Articles of Incorporation (Articles) and Bylaws shall ordinarily provide for, but need not be limited to, the following:

"(8) Creation of a governing body for the Association;

"(9) Procedures for the election and removal of governing body members and officers of the Association;

"(10) Enumeration of the powers and duties of the governing body and the officers and of the limitations upon the authority of the governing body to act without the prior approval of members representing a majority of the voting power of the Association."

5. Corporations Code Section 7312 provides in relevant part:

"No person may hold more than one membership, and no fractional memberships may be held, provided, however, that:

"(a) Two or more persons may have an indivisible interest in a single membership when authorized by, and in a manner or under the circumstances prescribed by, the articles or bylaws subject to Section 7612.

"(d) In the case of membership in an owners association . . . the articles or bylaws may permit a person who owns an interest, or who has a right of exclusive occupancy, in more than one lot, parcel, area, apartment, or unit to hold a separate membership in the owners association for each lot, parcel, area, apartment, or unit."

Corporations Code Section 7610 provides:

"Except as provided in a corporation's articles or bylaws or Section 7615 [cumulative voting], each member shall be entitled to one vote on each matter submitted to a vote of the members. Single memberships in which two or more persons have an indivisible interest shall be voted as provided in Section 7612."

Corporations Code Section 7612 then provides in relevant part that:

"If a membership stands of record in the names of two or more persons . . . unless the secretary of the corporation is given written notice to the contrary and is furnished with a copy of the instrument or order appointing them or creating the relationship wherein it is so provided, their acts with respect to voting shall have the following effect:

"(a) If only one votes, such act binds all; or

"(b) If more than one vote, the act of the majority so voting binds all."

6. Title 10 California Code of Regulations Section 2792.18.

7. Title 10 California Code of Regulations Section 2792.18(b).

8. Title 10 California Code of Regulations Section 2792.18(b)(2).

9. Title 10 California Code of Regulations Section 2792.17(a).

10. Title 10 California Code of Regulations Section 2792.17(a).

11. Corporations Code Section 7520.

12. Corporations Code Section 7520(a)-(d).

13. Corporations Code Section 7521.

14. Corporations Code Section 7522.

15. Corporations Code Section 7523.

16. Corporations Code Section 7524.

17. Corporations Code Sections 7524, 8330(a)(1), (2).

18. Corporations Code Section 7525(a).

19. Corporations Code Section 7525.

20. Corporations Code Section 7525.

21. Corporations Code Section 7526.

22. Corporations Code Section 7614(a).

23. Corporations Code Section 7614(a).

24. Corporations Code Section 7614(c).

25. Corporations Code Section 7614(c).

26. Corporations Code Section 7614(b).

27. Corporations Code Section 7614(c).

28. Corporations Code Section 7616(a).

29. Corporations Code Sections 7616(a), 5068.

30. Corporations Code Section 7616(c).

31. Corporations Code Section 7616(c).

32. Corporations Code Section 7527.

33. Corporations Code Section 7151(c)(3) reads in relevant part as follows:

"The bylaws may contain any provision, not in conflict with law or the articles, for the management of the activities and for the conduct of the affairs of the corporation, including but not limited to:

"(3) The qualifications, duties and compensation of directors; the time of their election; and the requirements of a quorum for directors' and committee meetings."

34. There is an express statutory limitation governing the issue with respect to nonprofit public benefit corporations, but there is no similar statute applicable to nonprofit mutual benefit corporations. Section 5227 of the California Corporations Code (applicable to public benefit corporations only) reads in full as follows:

> "(a) Any other provision of this part notwithstanding, not more than 49 percent of the persons serving on the board of any corporation may be interested persons.
> "(b) For the purpose of this section, 'interested persons' means either:
>
> "(1) Any person currently being compensated by the corporation for services rendered to it within the previous 12 months, whether as a full- or part-time employee, independent contractor, or otherwise, excluding any reasonable compensation paid to a director as director; or
>
> "(2) Any brother, sister, ancestor, descendant, spouse, brother-in-law, sister-in-law, son-in-law, daughter-in-law, mother-in-law, or father-in-law of any such person.
>
> "(c) The provisions of this section shall not affect the validity or enforceability of any transaction entered into by a corporation."

There is no comparable statute applicable to nonprofit mutual benefit corporations. There are no reported California judicial decisions applying similar limitations to nonprofit mutual benefit corporations .

35. Katz v. Chevron Corporation (1994) 22 Cal. App. 4th 1352, 27 Cal. Rptr. 2d 681, Beehan v. Lido Isle Community Association (1977) 70 Cal. App. 3d 858, 137 Cal. Rptr. 528, Findley v. Garrett (1952) 109 Cal. App. 2d 166, 240 P.2d 421.

36. Will v. Engebretson & Co. (1989) 213 Cal. App. 3d 1033, 261 Cal. Rptr. 868.

37. California Trial Lawyers' Association v. Superior Court (1986) 187 Cal. App. 3d 575, 231 Cal. Rptr. 725, Fry v. Pekarovich (1975) 46 Cal. App. 3d 165, 120 Cal. Rptr. 55, Williams v. Inglewood Board of Realtors (1963) 219 Cal. App. 2d 479, 33 Cal. Rptr. 289.

38. Aluisi v. Fort Washington Golf & Country Club (1995) 36 Cal. App. 4th 799, 42 Cal. Rptr. 2d 761.

39. Black's Law Dictionary (5th ed. 1979).

40. Remillard Brick Company v. Remillard-Dandini Company (1952) 109 Cal. App. 2d 405, 241 P.2d 66.

41. Title 10 California Code of Regulations Section 2792.21(a).

42. Section 1365.5 of the Civil Code reads in full as follows:

"(a) Unless the governing documents impose more stringent standards, the board of directors of the association shall do all of the following:

"(1) Review a current reconciliation of the associations operating accounts on at least a quarterly basis.

"(2) Review a current reconciliation of the association's reserve accounts on at least a quarterly basis.

"(3) Review, on at least a quarterly basis, the current year's actual reserve revenues and expenses compared to the current year's budget.

"(4) Review the latest account statements prepared by the financial institutions where the association has its operating and reserve accounts.

"(5) Review an income and expense statement for the association's operating and reserve accounts on at least a quarterly basis.

"(b) The signatures of at least two persons, who shall be members of the association's board of directors, or one officer who is not a member of the board of directors and a member of the board of directors, shall be required for the withdrawal of moneys from the association's reserve accounts.

"(c) (1) The board of directors shall not expend funds designated as reserve funds for any purpose other than the repair, restoration, replacement, or maintenance of, or litigation involving the repair, restoration, replacement, or maintenance of, major components which the association is obligated to repair, restore, replace, or maintain and for which the reserve fund was established.

"(2) However, the board may authorize the temporary transfer of money from a reserve fund to the association's general operating fund to meet short-term cash-flow requirements or other expenses, provided the board has made a written finding, recorded in the board's minutes, explaining the reasons the transfer is needed, and describing when and how the money will be repaid to the reserve fund. The transferred funds shall be restored to the reserve fund within one year of the date of the initial transfer, except that the board may, upon making a finding supported by documentation that a temporary delay would be in the best interests of the common interest development, temporarily delay the restoration. The board shall exercise prudent fiscal management in delaying restoration of these funds and in restoring the expended funds to the reserve account, and shall, if necessary, levy a special assessment to recover the full amount of the expended funds within the time limits required by this section. This special assessment is subject to the limitation imposed by Section 1366. The board may, at its discretion, extend the date the payment on the special assessment is due. Any extension shall not prevent the board from pursuing any legal remedy to enforce the collection of an unpaid special assessment."

"(d) When the decision is made to use reserve funds or to temporarily transfer money from the reserve fund to pay for litigation, the association shall notify the members of the association of that decision in the next available mailing to all members pursuant to Section 5016 of the Corporations Code, and of the availability of an accounting of those expenses. Unless the governing documents impose more stringent standards, the association shall make an accounting of expenses related to litigation on at least a quarterly basis. The accounting shall be made available for inspection by members of the association at the association's office.

"(e) At least once every three years the board of directors shall cause a study of the reserve account requirements of the common interest development to be conducted if the current replacement value of the major components which the association is obligated to repair, replace, restore, or maintain is equal to or greater than one-half of the gross budget of the association for any fiscal year. The board shall review this study annually and shall consider and implement necessary adjustments to the board's analysis of the reserve account requirements as a result of that review.

"The Study required by this subdivision shall at a minimum include:

"(1) Identification of the major components which the association is obligated to repair, replace, restore, or maintain which, as of the date of the study, have a remaining useful life of less than 30 years.

"(2) Identification of the probable remaining useful life of the components identified in paragraph (1) as of the date of the study.

"(3) An estimate of the cost of repair, replacement, restoration, or maintenance of the components identified in paragraph (1) during and at the end of their useful life.

"(4) An estimate of the total annual contribution necessary to defray the cost to repair, replace, restore, or maintain the components identified in paragraph (1) during and at the end of their useful life, after subtracting total reserve funds as of the date of the study.

"(f) As used in this section, 'reserve accounts' means moneys that the association's board of directors has identified for use to defray the future repair or replacement of, or additions to, those major components which the association is obligated to maintain.

"(g) As used in this section, 'reserve account requirements' means the estimated funds which the association's board of directors has determined are required to be available at a specified point in time to repair, replace, or restore those major components which the association is obligated to maintain.

"(h) This section does not apply to an association that does not have a 'common area' as defined in Section 1351."

43. Civil Code Section 1368.

44. Civil Code Sections 1363(b), 1365.

45. Civil Code Section 1365(a).

46. Civil Code Section 1365.5(f), (g).

47. Civil Code Section 1365.5(a)(1), (2), (3), (5).

48. Civil Code Section 1365.5(a)(4).

49. Civil Code Section 1365.5(b).

50. Civil Code Section 1365.5(c)(1).

51. Civil Code Section 1365.5(c)(2).

52. Civil Code Section 1365.5(d), Corporations Code Section 5016.

53. Frances T. v. Village Green Owners Association (1986) 42 Cal. 3d 490, 229 Cal. Rptr. 456, 723 P.2d 573.

54. Corporations Code Section 7231(a).

55. Remillard Brick Co. v. Remillard-Dandini Co. (1952) 109 Cal. App. 2d 405, 241 P.2d 66. In this case the court described the director's duty of loyalty in the following way: " . . . directors, while not strictly trustees, are fiduciaries, and bear a fiduciary relationship to the corporation, and to all the stockholders. They owe a duty to all stockholders, including the minority stockholders, and must administer their duties for the common benefit. The concept that a corporation is an entity cannot operate so as to lessen the duties owed to all of the stockholders. Directors owe a duty of highest good faith to the corporation and its stockholders."

56. Raven's Cove Townhomes, Inc. v. Knuppe Development Company, Inc. (1981) 114 Cal. App. 3d 783, 171 Cal. Rptr. 334. In this case, the court ruled that the directors' duty of undivided loyalty prevents them from making decisions for an association which will benefit their own interests at the expense of the association and its members.

57. Corporations Code Section 7212(a).

58. Corporations Code Section 7212(a). Section 7212(a) reads in part: "The board may, by resolution adopted by a majority of the number of directors then in office, provided that a quorum is present, create one or more committees, each consisting of two or more directors, to serve at the pleasure of the board. Appointments to such committees shall be by a majority vote of the directors then in office, unless the articles or bylaws require a majority of the number of directors authorized in the articles or bylaws. The bylaws may authorize one or more committees, each consisting of two or more directors, and may provide that a specified officer or officers who are also directors of the corporation shall be a member or members of such committee or committees. The board may appoint one or more directors as alternate members of any committee, who may replace any absent member at any meeting of the committee. . ."

59. Corporations Code Section 7212(a). The exceptions to committee authority are stated in Corporations Code Section 7212(a)(1)-(8) as follows: "Any such committee, to the extent provided in the resolution of the board or in the bylaws, shall have all the authority of the board, except with respect to:

"(1) The approval of any action for which this part also requires the approval of the members (Section 5034) or approval of a majority of all members (Section 5033).

"(2) The filling of vacancies on the board or in any committee which has the authority of the board.

"(3) The fixing of compensation of the directors for serving on the board or on any committee.

"(4) The amendment or repeal of bylaws or the adoption of new bylaws.

"(5) The amendment or repeal of any resolution of the board which by its express terms is not so amendable or repealable.

"(6) The appointment of committees of the board or the members thereof .

"(7) The expenditure of corporate funds to support a nominee for director after there are more people nominated for director than can be elected.

"(8) With respect to any assets held in charitable trust, the approval of any self-dealing transaction except as provided in paragraph (3) of subdivision (6) of Section 5233."

60. Corporations Code Section 7212(a)(l)-(8), (c)

61. Corporations Code Sections 7151(c) (4), 7212(b), (c) . Section 7212(b) and (c) limit the authority of advisory committees in the following way:

"(b) Subdivision (a) [the establishment and delegation of authority to executive or board committees] shall not apply to any committee which does not exercise the authority of the board."

"(c) Unless the bylaws otherwise provide, the board may delegate to any committee, appointed pursuant to paragraph (4) of subdivision (c) of Section 7151 or otherwise, powers as authorized by Section 7210, but may not delegate the powers set forth in paragraphs (1) through (8) of subdivision (a) of this section."

62. Communist Party of the United States v. 522 Valencia, Inc. (1995) 35 Cal. App. 4th 980, 41 Cal. Rptr. 2d 618, Compton College, Etc. v. Compton Comm., Etc. (1982) 132 Cal. App. 3d 704, 183 Cal. Rptr. 341, Smith v. California Thorn Cordage, Inc. (1933) 129 Cal. App. 93, 18 P.2d 393. In Smith v. California Thorn Cordage, the court held that an agreement purporting to give a "finance committee" (composed of persons including nondirectors, an "advisory" committee) complete charge of the corporation's finances and empowering the committee to raise funds was illegal because it usurped the director's powers.

63. Corporations Code Section 7211(a)(2).

64. Corporations Code Sections 7211(a)(2) and (a)(3) read as follows:

"(2) Regular meetings of the board may be held without notice if the time and place of the meeting are fixed by the bylaws or the board. Special meetings of the board shall be held upon four days' notice by first-class mail or 48 hours' notice delivered personally or by telephone, including a voice messaging system or other system or technology designed to record and communicate messages, telegraph, facsimile, electronic mail, or other electronic means. The articles or bylaws may not dispense with notice of a special meeting. A notice, or waiver of notice, need not specify the purpose of any regular or special meeting of the board.

"(3) Notice of a meeting need not be given to a director who signed a waiver of notice or a written consent to holding the meeting or an approval of the minutes thereof, whether before or after the meeting, or who attends the meeting without protesting, prior thereto or at its commencement, the lack of notice to that director. These waivers, consents and approvals shall be filed with the corporate records or made a part of the minutes of the meetings."

65. Corporations Code Section 7224(a). Section 7224(a) provides in relevant part:

> "Unless otherwise provided in the articles or bylaws and except for a vacancy created by the removal of a director, vacancies on the board may be filled by approval of the board (Section 5032) or, if the number of directors then in office is less than a quorum, by (1) the unanimous written consent of the directors then in office, (2) the affirmative vote of a majority of the directors then in office at a meeting held pursuant to notice or waivers of notice complying with Section 7211, or (3) a sole remaining director."

66. Corporations Code Section 7224(b) reserves this right for the members:

> "The members may elect a director at any time to fill any vacancy not filled by the directors."

67. Corporations Code Section 7224(a).

68. Corporations Code Section 7224(c).

69. Corporations Code Section 7221.

70. Corporations Code Section 7222(a).

71. Corporations Code Section 7223.

72. Chantiles v. Lake Forest II Master Homeowners Association (1995) 37 Cal. App. 4th 914, 45 Cal. Rptr. 2d 1 (concur. opinion), State v. Scott 247 P.2d 543 (1952 Wash.). In this case, the Washington Supreme Court explained: "The right of a director to examine corporate records at all is based upon the principle that he must be able to do this in order to perform his corporate duties. His corporate duties require him to preserve and protect the corporation and to do nothing which damage or destroy it. He stands in a fiduciary relation to the corporation, and is commanded by statute to discharge his duties in good faith."

73. Corporations Code Section 8334.

74. Havlicek v. Coast-To-Coast Analytical Services (1995) 39 Cal. App. 4th 1844, 46 Cal. Rptr. 2d 696 (deciding the issue in the context of a stock corporation and the statutes applicable to such corporations, the language of which is substantially the sane as that of the statutes applicable to nonprofit mutual benefit corporations.)

75. Havlicek v. Coast-To-Coast Analytical Services (1995) 39 Cal. App. 4th 1844, 46 Cal. Rptr. 2d 696, Chantiles v. Lake Forest II Master Homeowners Association (1995) 37 Cal. App. 4th 914, 45 Cal. Rptr. 2d 1, Hoiles v. Superior Court (1984) 157 Cal. App. 3d 1192, 204 Cal. Rptr. 111. In Havlicek v. Coast-To-Coast Analytical Services, the court was addressing the inspection rights of a director of a regular stock corporation, but cited with approval the decision in Chantiles v. Lake Forest II Master Homeowners Association, and stated in part that: "... the trial court may impose 'just and proper conditions' upon [the director's] otherwise 'absolute' inspection rights. We admit that the Legislature's choice of the word

'absolute,' in section 1602 does give us pause. But one hypothetical illustrates that 'absolute' cannot mean 'absolute'. A disgruntled director unambiguously announces his or her intention to violate his or her fiduciary duties to the corporation and the shareholders by using inspection rights to learn trade secrets, gain access to confidential customer lists, and compete with the corporation. In this situation, does the Legislature want the judiciary to come to the aid of the disgruntled director, enforce the 'absolute right' to inspect and help the director commit a tort against the corporation? No. 'The literal meaning of the words of a statute may be disregarded to avoid absurd results ...' Fn5: We also note the recent case of Chantiles v. Lake Forest II Master Homeowners Association. There, an analogous provision in section 8334, provided for an 'absolute right' of inspection for a homeowner's association director. Notwithstanding the use of the word 'absolute, ' a majority of the court were of the opinion that the right to privacy could, and there did, outweigh the 'absolute' right of inspection. . . . The 'absolute right' to inspect documents is the general rule in California. However, section 1602 must be read in pari materia with section 1603. The language of section 1603 subdivision (a) is expansive. It is not expressly limited to an inspection request by a shareholder. Being a remedial statute, it must be liberally construed. Where the corporation determines that an unfettered inspection will result in a tort against the corporation, it may decline the request for inspection. In this situation, 'directors can enforce their inspection rights by court action.'"

76. Chantiles v. Lake Forest II Master Homeowners Association (1995) 37 Cal. App. 4th 914, 45 Cal. Rptr. 2d 1.

77. (1995) 37 Cal. App. 4th 914, 45 Cal. Rptr. 2d 1.

78. The trial court also permitted the director's attorney to take notes during the attorney's inspection, but ordered that the notes could not include the names of the members casting votes.

In affirming the trial court, the Court of Appeal held:

> "We reject [the director's] assertion that there is no similar expectation of privacy in a written proxy ballot. A member has three choices in casting a proxy vote. ... In choosing any of those options, a member has an expectation of privacy. 'And, of course, the custodian of such private information may not waive the privacy rights of persons who are constitutionally guaranteed their protection.' . . . The trial court correctly concluded homeowners' association voting was a class of information in which members have a reasonable expectation of privacy."

****

> "We reject [the director's] assertion because section 8334 gives him an 'absolute right' to inspect, this right need not yield to any other right, not even a constitutional right. As Sproul & Rosenberry note, '[Section 8334's] broad and unqualified statement of a director's inspection rights can present difficult ethical and legal issues . . . [For] example, what if a director who ran for office on a platform critical of the present general manager's conduct and salary demands the right to inspect the general manager's personnel file and to disclose its contents to the members ...? The manager's constitutional right of privacy under California Constitution, article I, section 1 may preempt a director's general rights of inspection.'"

****

"We hold that homeowners' association members have a constitutional privacy right in their voting decisions, even when conducted by proxy ballot. A homeowners' association director's statutory right to inspect the records of the association must be balanced against this privacy right."

79. (a) The Washington Supreme Court in State v. Scott (1952) 247 P.2d 543, has addressed the issue of limitations on a director's inspection rights where the director does not seek to exercise inspection rights in the best interests of the corporation. In this case, a minority stockholder and director of two corporations, filed a lawsuit seeking to enforce her right to inspect and copy the corporations' books and records. The corporations produced substantial evidence showing the director had been in contact with, and had furnished internal corporate information to, competitors of the corporations. The corporations refused the director's request for inspection claiming that she "had a scheme to interfere with, harass and sabotage the business by contacting distributors and customers, and by making information regarding the business available to competitors."

In denying the director's inspection rights, and holding that the director's inspection rights disappear altogether when it is determined the director is proceeding pursuant to a hostile and improper purpose, the court stated that: "A stockholder may adapt a reasonable and proper course of action for the purpose of reviewing management policies and bringing about a change in management. Such cannot be attributed to hostility against the corporation or be considered as inimical to its best interests. . . . The evidence here shows, however, that [the director], whatever her initial motives may have been, did not limit herself to action of this character. Instead, she made direct contact with the distributors, customers and competitors of the corporations. . . . The evidence shows that her activities in these respects have been very detrimental to the best interests of the corporations. Nor can it be doubted that she was well aware of the damage she was doing to the corporations. Yet [the director] persisted in this course. The inference is therefore warranted, if not compelled, that appellant desired to produce those results. . . . [The director's] present motives in seeking to inspect the corporate books and records must be judged in the light of her past motives and acts, unless there is convincing evidence of a complete change of attitude on her part. The record does not contain such evidence."

In explaining its holding, the court stated: "The right of a director to examine corporate records at all is based upon the principle that he must be able to do this in order to perform his corporate duties. His corporate duties require him to preserve and protect the corporation and to do nothing which damage or destroy it. He stands in a fiduciary relation to the corporation, and is commanded by statute to discharge his duties in good faith. His duty is not to entertain hostile and improper motives concerning his corporation. If he does entertain such motives, his duty is to refrain from using his position as a means of carrying his motives into execution. Indeed, the duty of such a director is to resign forthwith. . . . Hence, when a director, driven by hostile and improper motives, seeks to examine corporate books and records, he cannot do so under a claim of duty. On the contrary, his purposes and action are completely inconsistent with such duty. The basis of the right which a director has to examine corporate records- the performance of corporate duties- is then wholly lacking, and thus the right itself no longer exists."

(b) In Hoiles v. Superior Court (1984) 157 Cal. App. 3d 1192, 204 Cal. Rptr. 111, a California case, the court cited with approval and quoted extensively from the Delaware case of Henshaw v. American Cement Corporation (1969) 252 A.2d 125. In Henshaw, a director filed suit against a corporation after the corporation denied him access to the corporate books and records. The director requested access to these documents "so that he may perform his duties as a director." The corporation denied his request, alleging that the director was in reality seeking information to aid another director against whom the corporation had filed an action for fraud seeking damages of $1,600,000.00. The director filed suit seeking a court order allowing him to inspect the documents.

The Henshaw court noted that a director has a right to inspect corporate records and that this right is correlative with his duty to protect and preserve the corporation. A director makes a prima facie case against the corporation when he shows that (1) he is a director, (2) he has demanded inspection, and (3) his demand has been refused. Once this prima facie case has been made, the burden shifts to the corporation to show why the director should not be permitted to exercise his rights, or that such exercise should be conditioned. The Henshaw court held that "[a]n examination of books and records to ascertain the condition of corporate affairs and the propriety of certain actions is a proper purpose even though the one who seeks inspection may be hostile to management. [The plaintiff] showed a purpose germane to his position as a director and that entitles him to an examination of the books and records. His purpose is not improper because of the possibility that he may abuse his position as a director and make information available to persons hostile to the corporation or otherwise not entitled to it. If [the plaintiff] does violate his fiduciary duty in this regard, then the corporation has its remedy in the courts."

The Henshaw court then concluded that: "[The plaintiff], as a director, probably has a duty as well as a right to be fully informed as to the . . . matters in litigation. And as for disclosure, I emphasize that inspection is here given to Henshaw as a director, with all that implies. He has, as his counsel states, a fiduciary duty to the corporation and its stockholders with respect to such information that he receives as a director. If he violates that duty, the law provides a remedy."

(c) In Melup v. Rubber Corp. of America (1943) 43 N.Y.S. 2d 444, a New York case, the court held that although a director's right to inspect the corporation's books is ordinarily absolute, where the corporation can show that the director's "entire course of conduct appeared to be prompted by ulterior motives, the basic end sought to be gained in the ruination of the corporation, the court should not interfere to aid the plaintiff in obtaining these objectives."

80. In Dandini v. Superior Court (1940) 38 Cal. App. 2d 32, 100 P.2d 535, the court held that under former Civil Code Section 356 (which, like Corporations Code Section 8334, provided an absolute inspection right, but included no reference to agents or attorneys exercising the right on behalf of the director) a director's right could not be delegated to or exercised by his attorney. The court explained: "There are many sound reasons why the rights conferred by section 356 on a director should not be delegated to an agent or attorney. The first suggesting itself is the customary effort of the minority director to cause trouble and litigation and stir up friction with the majority."

81. Corporations Code Section 7211(a)(7), (8), Findley v. Garrett (1952) 109 Cal. App. 2d 166, Scott v. Los Angeles Mountain Park Co. (1928) 92 Cal. App. 258, 267 P. 914.

82. Corporations Code Section 7211(b) provides that the directors may take action without a meeting in the following manner:

"An action required or permitted to be taken by the board may be taken without a meeting, if all members of the board shall individually or collectively consent in writing to that action. The written consent or consents shall be filed with the minutes of the proceedings of the board. The action by written consent shall have the same force and effect as a unanimous vote of the directors. For the purposes of this section only, 'all members of the board' shall not include an 'interested director' as defined in Section 5233, insofar as it is made applicable pursuant to Section 7238."

83. Civil Code Section 1363.05(b).

84. Title 10 California Code of Regulations Section 2792.20(e) reads as follows:

"(1) The governing body may take actions without a meeting if all of its members consent in writing to the action to be taken.

"(2) If the governing body resolves by unanimous written consent to take action, an explanation of the action taken shall be posted at a prominent place or places within the common area within three days after the written consents of all governing body members has been obtained. If the common area consists only of an easement or is otherwise unsuitable for posting the explanation of the action taken, the governing body shall communicatė said explanation by any means it deems appropriate."

85. Corporations Code Section 7211 reads in full as follows:

"(a) Unless otherwise provided in the articles or in the bylaws, all of the following apply:

"(1) Meetings of the board may be called by the chair of the board or the president or any vice president or the secretary or any two directors.

"(2) Regular meetings of the board may be held without notice if the time and place of the meeting are fixed by the bylaws or the board. Special meetings of the board shall be held upon four dayst notice by first-class mail or 48 hours' notice delivered personally or by telephone, including a voice messaging system or other system or technology designed to record and communicate messages, telegraph, facsimile, electronic nail, or other electronic means. The articles or bylaws may not dispense with notice of a special meeting. A notice, or waiver of notice, need not specify the purpose of any regular or special meeting of the board.

"(3) Notice of a meeting need not be given to a director who signed a waiver of notice or a written consent to holding the meeting or an approval of the minutes thereof, whether before or after the meeting, or who attends the meeting without protesting, prior thereto or at its commencement, the lack of notice to that director. These waivers, consents and approvals shall be filed with the corporate records or made a part of the minutes of the meetings .

"(4) A majority of the directors present, whether or not a quorum is present, may adjourn any meeting to another time and place. If the meeting is adjourned for more than 24 hours, notice of an adjournment to another time or place shall be given prior to the time of the adjourned meeting to the directors who were not present at the time of adjournment.

"(5) Meetings of the board may be held at a place within or without the state that has been designated in the notice of meeting or, if not stated in the notice or if there is no notice, designated in the bylaws or by resolution of the board.

"(6) Members of the board may participate in a meeting through use of conference telephone, electronic video screen communications, or other communications equipment. Participation in a meeting pursuant to this subdivision constitutes presence in person at that meeting if all of the following apply:

"(A) Each member participating in the meeting can communicate with all of the other members concurrently.

"(B) Each member is provided the means of participating in all matters before the board, including the capacity to propose, or to interpose an objection, to a specific action to be taken by the corporation.

"(C) The corporation adopts and implements some means of verifying both of the following:

"(i) A person communicating by telephone, electronic video screen, or other communications equipment is a director entitled to participate in the board meeting.

"(ii) All statements, questions, actions, or votes were made by that director and not by another person not permitted to participate as a director.

"(7) A majority of the number of directors authorized in the articles or bylaws constitutes a quorum of the board for the transaction of business. The articles or bylaws my not provide that a quorum shall be less than one-fifth the number of directors authorized in the articles or bylaws, or less than two, whichever is larger, unless the number of directors authorized in the articles or bylaws is one, in which case one director constitutes a quorum.

"(8) Subject to the provisions of Sections 7212, 7233, 7234, and subdivision (e) of Section 7237 and Section 5233, insofar as it is made applicable pursuant to Section 7238, an act or decision done or made by a majority of the directors present at a meeting duly held at which a quorum is present is the act of the board. The articles or bylaws may not provide that a lesser vote than a majority of the directors present at a meeting is the act of the board. A meeting at which a quorum is initially present may continue to transact business notwithstanding the withdrawal of directors, if any action taken is approved by at least a majority of the required quorum for that fleeting, or a greater number required by this division, the articles or bylaws.

"(b) An action required or permitted to be taken by the board may be taken without a meeting, if all members of the board shall individually or collectively consent in writing to that action. The written consent or consents shall be filed with the minutes of the proceedings of the board. The action by written consent shall have the same force and effect as a unanimous vote of the directors. For the purposes of this section only, 'all members of the board' shall not include an 'interested director' as defined in Section 5233, insofar as it is made applicable pursuant to Section 7238.

"(c) The provisions of this section apply also to incorporators, to committees of the board, and to action by those incorporators or committees mutatis mutandis.

"(d) This section shall remain in effect only until January 1, 1998, and as of that date is repealed, unless a later enacted statute, that is enacted before January 1, 1998, deletes or extends that date."

86. Corporations Code Section 7211(a)(6)

87. Corporations Code Section 7211(c) provides:

"The provisions of this section also apply to incorporators, to committees of the board, and to action by those incorporators or committees mutatis mutandis."

88. There is no statutory provision or judicial decision addressing this issue. The Department of Real Estate Regulations, in Title 10 California Code of Regulations Section 2792.20(d)(1) address the issue as follows:

"(d)(1) Regular and special meetings of the governing body shall be open to all members of the Association provided, however, that Association members who are not on the governing body may not participate in any deliberation or discussion unless expressly so authorized by the vote of a majority of a quorum of the governing body."

89. Corporations Code Section 7211(a)(5) provides as follows:

"(a) Unless otherwise provided in the articles or in the bylaws, all of the following apply:

"(5) Meetings of the board may be held at a place within or without the state that has been designated in the notice of meeting or, if not stated in the notice or if there is no notice, designated in the bylaws or by resolution of the board."

Title 10 California Code of Regulations Section 2792.20(b)(1) reads:

"Regular meetings of the governing body shall be held at a time and at a meeting place fixed by the governing body from tine to time. The meeting place shall ordinarily be within the subdivision itself unless in the judgment of the governing body a larger meeting room is required than exists within the subdivision in which case the meeting room selected shall be as close as possible to the subdivision."

90. In a case addressing the similarly broad definition of "meeting" in the context of the open meeting laws applicable to governmental agencies, Stockton Newspapers, Inc. v. Members of Redev. Agency (1985) 171 Cal. App. 3d 95, 214 Cal. Rptr. 561, the court explained the rationale behind such broad treatment:

> "The collective decision making process consists of both 'actions' and 'deliberations' . . . Thus the 'meeting' concept can not be confined exclusively to either action or deliberation but rather comprehends both or either. Since deliberation connotes not only collective discussion but also the 'collective acquisition and exchange of facts preliminary to the ultimate decision,' the Brown Act is applicable to collective investigation and consideration short of official action."
>
> *******
>
> ". . . 'a statute may push beyond debatable limits in order to block evasive techniques. An informal conference or caucus permits crystallization of secret decisions to a point just short of ceremonial acceptance. There is rarely any purpose to a nonpublic premeeting conference except to conduct some part of the decisional process behind closed doors. Only by embracing the collective inquiry and discussion stages, as well as the ultimate step of official action, can an open meeting regulation frustrate these evasive devices.'"

91. Government Code Sections 11120, et seq.

92. Government Code Sections 54950, et seq.

93. 68 Ops. Cal. Atty. Gen. 34 (1985), 63 Ops. Cal. Atty. Gen. 215 (1980) , 63 Ops. Cal. Atty. Gen. 153 (1980) , 61 Ops. Cal. Atty. Gen. 283 (1978), 61 Ops. Cal. Atty. Gen. 10 (1978).

94. 68 Ops. Cal. Atty. Gen. 34 (1985).

95. Corporations Code Section 7211(a)(6).

96. Corporations Code Section 7211(a)(6)(C).

97. Corporations Code Section 7211 provides in relevant part:

"(7) A majority of the number of directors authorized in the articles or bylaws constitutes a quorum of the board for the transaction of business. The articles or bylaws may not provide that a quorum shall be less than one-fifth the number of directors authorized in the articles or bylaws, or less than two, whichever is larger, unless the number of directors authorized in the articles or bylaws is one, in which case one director constitutes a quorum."

"(8) . . . an act or decision done or made by a majority of the directors present at a meeting duly held at which a quorum is present is the act of the board. The articles or bylaws may not provide that a lesser vote than a majority of the directors present at a meeting is the act of the board. A meeting at which a quorum is initially present may continue to transact business notwithstanding the withdrawal of directors, if any action taken is approved by at least a majority of the required quorum for that meeting, or a greater number required by this division, the articles or bylaws."

98. Corporations Code Section 7211(a)(7).

99. Corporations Code Section 7211(a)(8) states in pertinent part:

". . . A meeting at which a quorum is initially present may continue to transact business notwithstanding the withdrawal of directors, if any action taken is approved by at least a majority of the required quorum for that meeting, or a greater number required by this division, the articles or bylaws."

100. Civil Code Section 1363.05, Corporations Code Section 8320.

101. Civil Code Section 1363(d).

102. Wilson v. Red Bluff Daily News (1965) 237 Cal. App. 2d 87, 46 Cal. Rptr. 591: "The contention [that the officer was entitled to be paid as claimed] rests on a strenuous adhesion to the symbolism of fixed language, eschewing all inquiry into the parties' intent. Seldom does a piece of litigation so resoundingly demonstrate that 'the letter killeth, but the spirit giveth life.' Whether the resolution is clear or ambiguous, it is not to be pursued at the cost of ignoring the unmistakable intention of the parties. . . . Whether a corporate officer is entitled to compensation depends on the intention of the parties. [citations omitted]. The parties may manifest their intention in any of the usual ways, that is, by formal contract, by resolution or simply by their actions. When they do so by resolution, the resolution is not itself a contract but only evidence of it. Consistently with these concepts, California cases hold that the parol evidence rule does not apply to corporate minutes; that the minutes are simply the written records of the events of a meeting; that the record may or may not be true; and, in the absence of estoppel, the corporation or anyone else may show what took place at the meeting."

103. Corporations Code Section 7211(a)(4).

104. Civil Code Section 1365.7(b).

105. Civil Code Section 1365.7(c).

106. Civil Code Section 1365.7 reads in full as follows:

"(a) A volunteer officer or volunteer director of an association, as defined in subdivision (a) of Section 1351, which manages a common interest development that is exclusively residential, shall not be personally liable in excess of the coverage of insurance specified in paragraph (4) to any person who suffers injury, including, but not limited to, bodily injury, emotional distress, wrongful death, or property damage or loss as a result of the tortious act or omission of the volunteer officer or volunteer director if all of the following criteria are met:

"(1) The act or omission was performed within the scope of the officer's or director's association duties.

"(2) The act or omission was performed in good faith.

"(3) The act or omission was not willful, wanton, or grossly negligent

"(4) The association maintained and had in effect at the time the act or omission occurred and at the time a claim is made one or more policies of insurance which shall include coverage for (A) general liability of the association and (B) individual liability of officers and directors of the association for negligent acts or omissions in that capacity; provided, that both types of coverage are in the following minimum amount:

"(A) At least five hundred thousand dollars ($500,000) if the common interest development consists of 100 or fewer separate interests.

"(B) At least one million dollars ($1,000,000) if the common interest development consists of more than 100 separate interests .

"(b) The payment of actual expenses incurred by a director or officer in the execution of the duties of that position does not affect the director's or officer's status as a volunteer within in the meaning of this section.

"(c) An officer or director who at the time of the act or omission was a declarant, as defined in subdivision (g) of Section 1351, or who received either direct or indirect compensation as an employee from the declarant, or from a financial institution that purchased a separate interest, as defined in subdivision (1) of Section 1351, at a judicial or nonjudicial foreclosure of a mortgage or deed of trust on real property, is not a volunteer for the purposes of this section.

"(d) Nothing in this section shall be construed to limit the liability of the association for its negligent act or omission or for any negligent act or omission of an officer or director of the association.

"(e) This section shall only apply to a volunteer officer or director who is a tenant of a separate interest in the common interest development or is an owner of no more than two separate interests in the common interest development."

107. Civil Code Section 1365.7(e).

108. Civil Code Section 1365.7(d).

109. For example, Section 5047.5 of the Corporations Code provides protection for volunteer (noncompensated) directors and officers of nonprofit corporations against lawsuits for money damages when the allegedly negligent act occurred (1) within the scope of the director's or officer's duties, (2) in good faith, (3) in a manner the director or officer believed to be in the best interest of the corporation, and (4) is in the exercise of the director's or officer's

policymaking judgment. Section 5047.5 only applies to nonprofit corporations organized to provide religious, charitable, literary, educational, scientific, social, or other forms of public service and which are exempt from federal income taxation under Section 501(c)(3) or 501(c)(6) of the Internal Revenue Code.

Section 425.15 of the Code of Civil Procedure generally bars the filing of any complaint which includes a claim against a volunteer (noncompensated) director or officer of a nonprofit corporation based on an alleged negligent act or omission, without a prior court order permitting the filing of such a complaint. The statute applies only to corporations which are organized to provide charitable, educational, scientific, social, or other forms of public service and which are exempt from federal income taxation under specified provisions of the Internal Revenue Code.

And, Corporations Code Section 7231(c) protects a director, whether or not the director receives compensation as a director, from personal liability when the director has fulfilled his fiduciary obligations as a director by stating that: "A person who performs the duties of a director in accordance with subdivisions (a) and (b) shall have no liability based upon any alleged failure to discharge the person's obligations as a director, including, without limiting the generality of the foregoing, any actions or omissions which exceed or defeat a public or charitable purpose to which assets held by the corporation are dedicated." To have the beneficial protection of the statute, the director must perform his or her duties "in good faith, in a manner such director believes to be in the best interests of the corporation and with such care, including reasonable inquiry, as an ordinarily prudent person in a like position would use under similar circumstances."

110. Corporations Code Section 7213(a).

111. Corporations Code Sections 7151(c)(5), 7213(a).

112. Corporations Code Section 7213(a).

113. Corporations Code Section 7213(a).

114. Corporations Code Sections 7151(c)(5), 7213(a).

115. Corporations Code Section 7213(b).

116. Title 10 California Code of Regulations Section 2792.21(b)(1). Section 2792.21(b) reads in relevant part as follows:

"(b) The governing body of the Association shall ordinarily be prohibited from taking any of the following actions, except with the assent, by vote at a meeting of the Association or by written ballot without a meeting pursuant to Corporations Code Section 7513, of a simple majority of the members, other than the subdivider, constituting a quorum consisting of more than 50 percent of the voting power of the Association residing in members other than the subdivider:

"(1) Entering into a contract with a third person wherein the third person will furnish goods or services for the common area or the owners' Association for a term longer than one year with the following exceptions:

"(A) A management contract, the terms of which have been approved by the Federal Housing Administration or Veterans Administration .

"(G) A contract for a term not to exceed three years that is terminable by the Association after no longer than one year without cause, penalty, or other obligation upon ninety (90) days written notice of termination to the other party."

117. Title 10 California Code of Regulations Section 2792.21(b)(1)(A).

118. Title 10 California Code of Regulations Section 2792.21(b)(1)(G).

119. Under California Business and Professions Code Sections 10131, however, if property managers engage in certain activities described in the California Business and Professions Code, they are subject to the licensing requirements imposed on real estate brokers and real estate sales persons. Generally speaking, if a person agrees to sell, purchase, lease, or exchange real estate or negotiate any of the foregoing for another person, he or she must be licensed by the State of California as a real estate broker or real estate agent.

120. Civil Code Section 2309 states: "An oral authorization is sufficient for any purpose, except that an authority to enter into a contract required by law to be in writing can only be given by an instrument in writing."

121. Civil Code Section 1624.

122. Civil Code Sections 1624, 2309.

123. Civil Code Sections 1363.1, 1363.2.

124. Civil Code Sections 1363.1(b), 1363.2(f).

125. Under Civil Code Section 1363.1(b) full-time employees of an association and regulated financial institutions operating within the normal course of their regulated business are exempted from the disclosure requirements.

126. Civil Code Section 1363.1. Section 1363.1, which remains in effect only until January 1, 1997 unless the statute is extended by the legislature, reads in full as follows:

"(a) A prospective managing agent of a common interest development shall provide a written statement to the board of directors of the association of a common interest development as soon as practicable, but in no event more than 90 days, before entering into a management agreement which shall contain all of the following information concerning the managing agent:

"(1) The names and business addresses of the owners or general partners of the managing agent. If the managing agent is a corporation, the written statement shall include the names and business addresses of the directors and officers and shareholders holding greater than 10 percent of the shares of the corporation.

"(2) Whether or not any relevant licenses such as architectural design, construction, engineering, real estate, or accounting have been issued by this state and are currently held by the persons specified in paragraph (1). If a license is currently held by any of those persons, the statement shall contain the following information:

"(A) What license is held.

"(B) The status of that license.

"(C) The name of the licensee appearing on that license .

"(3) Whether or not any relevant professional certifications or designations such as architectural design, construction, engineering, real property management, or accounting are currently held by any of the persons specified in paragraph (1), including, but not limited to, certified property manager or professional association manager. If any certification or designation is held, the statement shall include the following information:

"(A) What the certification or designation is and what entity issued it.

"(B) The status of that certification or designation.

"(C) The names in which the certification or designation is held.

"(b) As used in this section, a "managing agent" is a person or entity, who for compensation or, in expectation of compensation, exercises control over the assets of a common interest development. A "managing agent" does not include any of the following:

"(1) A full-time employee of the association.

"(2) Any regulated financial institution operating within the normal course of its regulated business practice.

"(c) This section shall remain in effect only until January 1, 1997, and as of that date is repealed unless a later enacted statute which is chaptered before January 1, 1997, deletes or extends that date."

127. Civil Code Section 1363.1(a)(1).

128. Civil Code Section 1363.1(a)(3).

129. Under Civil Code Section 1363.2(f) full-time employees of an association, regulated financial institutions operating within the normal course of their business, and attorneys acting within the scope of their licenses are exempt from the depository requirements.

130. Civil Code Section 1363.2. Section 1363.2 reads in full as follows:

"(a) A managing agent of a common interest development who accepts or receives funds belonging to the association shall deposit all such funds that are not placed into an escrow account with a bank, savings association, or credit union or into an account under the control of the association, into a trust fund account maintained by the managing agent in a bank, savings association, or credit union in this state. All funds deposited by the managing agent in the trust fund account shall be kept in this state in a financial institution, as defined in Section 31041 of the Financial Code, which is insured by the federal government, and shall be maintained there until disbursed in accordance with written instructions from the association entitled to the funds.

"(b) At the written request of the board of directors of the association, the funds the managing agent accepts or receives on behalf of the association shall be deposited into an interest-bearing account in a bank, savings association, or credit union in this state, provided all of the following requirements are met:

"(1) The account is in the name of the managing agent as trustee for the association or in the name of the association.

"(2) All of the funds in the account are covered by insurance provided by an agency of the federal government.

"(3) The funds in the account are kept separate, distinct, and apart from the funds belonging to the managing agent or to any other person or entity for whom the managing agent holds funds in trust except that the funds of various associations may be commingled as permitted pursuant to subdivision (d) .

"(4) The managing agent discloses to the board of directors of the association the nature of the account, how interest will be calculated and paid, whether service charges will be paid to the depository and by whom, and any notice requirements or penalties for withdrawal of funds from the account.

"(5) No interest earned on funds in the account shall inure directly or indirectly to the benefit of the managing agent or his or her employees.

"(c) The managing agent shall maintain a separate record of receipt and disposition of all funds described in this section, including any interest earned on the funds.

"(d) The managing agent shall not commingle the funds of the association with his or her own money or with the money of others that he or she receives or accepts, unless all of the following requirements are met:

"(1) The managing agent commingled the funds of various associations on or before February 26, 1990, and has obtained a written agreement with the board of directors of each association that he or she will maintain a fidelity and surety bond in an amount that provides adequate protection to the associations as agreed upon by the managing agent and the board of directors of each association.

"(2) The managing agent discloses in the written agreement whether he or she is deriving benefits from the commingled account or the bank, credit union, or savings institution where the moneys will be on deposit.

"(3) The written agreement provided pursuant to this subdivision includes, but is not limited to, the name and address of the bonding companies, the amount of the bonds, and the expiration dates of the bonds.

"(4) If there are any changes in the bond coverage or the companies providing the coverage, the managing agent discloses that fact to the board of directors of each affected association as soon as practical, but in no event more than 10 days after the change

"(5) The bonds assure the protection of the association and provide the association at least 10 days' notice prior to cancellation .

"(6) Completed payments on the behalf of the association are deposited within 24 hours or the next business day and do not remain commingled for more than 10 calendar days.

"(e) The prevailing party in an action to enforce this section shall be entitled to recover reasonable legal fees and court costs.

"(f) As used in this section, a "managing agent" is a person or entity, who for compensation or, in expectation of compensation, exercises control over the assets of the association. However, a "managing agent" does not include a full-time employee of the association or a regulated financial institution operating within the normal course of business, or an attorney at law acting within the scope of his or her license.

"(g) As used in this section, "completed payment" means funds received which clearly identify the account to which the funds are to be credited."

131. Civil Code Section 1363.2(b).

132. Civil Code Section 1363.2(c).

133. Civil Code Section 1363.2(d).

134. Civil Code Section 2295 defines "agent" and "agency" as follows: "An agent is one who represents another, called the principal, in dealings with third persons. Such representation is called agency."

135. Civil Code Section 2309.

136. Civil Code Section 2316, Interinsurance Exchange v. State Board of Equalization (1984) 156 Cal. App. 3d 606, 203 Cal. Rptr. 74.

137. Civil Code Sections 2307, 2310, Rakestraw v. Rodrigues (1972) 8 Cal. 3d 67, 104 Cal. Rptr. 57, 500 P.2d 1401.

138. Royat v. Roberts (1952) 110 Cal. App. 2d 814, 243 P.2d 879.

139. Civil Code Sections 2298, 2300.

140. Hartong v. Partake (1968) 266 Cal. App. 2d 942, 72 Cal. Rptr. 722, McMurry v. Pacific Ready-Cut Homes (1931) 111 Cal. App. 341, 295 P.542.

141. Civil Code Section 2316.

142. Civil Code Section 2019.

143. Civil Code Section 2318.

144. Civil Code Section 2321.

145. Civil Code Section 2322 provides:

"An authority expressed in general terms, however broad, does not authorize an agent to do any of the following:

"(a) Act in the agent's own name, unless it is the usual course of business to do so.

"(b) Define the scope of the agency.

"(c) Violate a duty to which a trustee is subject under Section 16002, 16004, 16005, or 16009 of the Probate Code."

146. Civil Code Section 2304.

147. Civil Code Section 2315.

148. Civil Code Section 2320.

149. Civil Code Section 2322(c), Adams v. Herman (1951) 106 Cal. App. 2d 92, 234 P.2d 695, Sands v. Eagle Oil & Refining Co. (1948) 83 Cal. App. 2d 312, 188 P.2d 782.

150. Rodes v. Shannon (1963) 222 Cal. App. 2d 721, 35 Cal. Rptr. 339, Orfanos v. California Insurance Co. (1938) 29 Cal. App. 2d 75, 24 P.2d 233.

151. Tackett v. Croonquist (1966) 244 Cal. App. 2d 572, 53 Cal. Rptr. 388.

152. Walter H. Leimert Co. v. Woodson (1954) 125 Cal. App. 2d 186, 270 P.2d 95.

153. Restatement. 2d. Agency Section 394.

154. Corporations Code Section 7237.

155. Corporations Code Section 7237(d).

156. Corporations Code Section 7237(g).

157. Corporations Code Section 7237(b).

158. Corporations Code Section 7237(c).

159. Corporations Code Section 7237(b).

160. Corporations Code Section 7237(c).

161. Corporations Code Section 7237(d).

162. Corporations Code Section 7237(e).

163. Corporations Code Section 7237(f).

164. Corporations Code Section 7237(g).

165. Corporations Code Section 7237(i).

CHAPTER IX: FINANCIAL STRUCTURE: ASSESSMENTS, FEES AND RESERVE FUNDS

1. Civil Code Section 1366(a), Title 10 California Code of Regulations Sections 2792.8(a)(4), (5), (6).

2. Title 10 California Code of Regulations Section 2792.8(a) provides the initial authority as follows:

"(a) Governing instruments for the ownership and management of [the] subdivisions . . . including the Covenants, Conditions and Restrictions (CC&Rs), Articles of Incorporation (Articles) and Bylaws shall ordinarily provide for, but need not be limited to, the following:

"(4) Procedures for calculating and collecting regular assessments from owners to defray expenses attributable to the ownership, operation or furnishing of common interests or to the enjoyment of mutual and reciprocal rights of use;

"(5) Procedures for establishing and collecting special assessments for capital improvements or for other purposes;

"(6) Liens upon privately-owned subdivision interests for assessments levied pursuant to the CC&Rs and foreclosure thereof for nonpayment;"

Title 10 California Code of Regulations Section 2792.16(a) then provides that:

"(a) Regular assessments to defray expenses attributable to the ownership, operation and furnishing of common interests by the Association shall ordinarily be levied against each owner according to the ratio of the number of subdivision interests owned by the owner assessed to the total number of interests subject to assessment."

3. Title 10 California Code of Regulations Section 2792.16(b).

4. Title 10 California Code of Regulations Section 2792.16(f).

5. Title 10 California Code of Regulations Section 2792.16(c).

6. Title 10 California Code of Regulations Section 2792.11.

7. Bodily v. Parkmont Village Green Home Owners Association, Inc. (1980) 104 Cal. App. 3d 348, 163 Cal. Rptr. 658.

8. Title 10 California Code of Regulations Section 2792.16(c):

"The subdivider - and his successor in interest, if any - is an owner subject to the payment of regular and special assessments against subdivision interests which he owns provided, however, that the subdivider and any other owner of a subdivision interest which does not include a structural improvement for human occupancy may be exempted by the governing instruments from the payment of that portion of any assessment which is for the purpose of defraying expenses and reserves directly attributable to the existence and the use of the structural improvement. The exemption may include, but shall not necessarily be limited to: Roof replacement; Exterior maintenance; Walkway and carport lighting; Refuse disposal; Cable television; and Domestic water supplied to living units."

9. Title 10 California Code of Regulations Section 2792.16(c)(2).

10. Title 10 California Code of Regulations Section 2792.9.

11. Title 10 California Code of Regulations Section 2792.9(b).

12. Civil Code Section 1366(b).

13. Civil Code Section 1366(a). Section 1366(a) reads in full as follows:

"(a) Except as provided in this section, the association shall levy regular and special assessments sufficient to perform its obligations under the governing documents and this title. However, annual increases in regular assessments for any fiscal year, as authorized by subdivision (b), shall not be imposed unless the board has complied with subdivision (a) of Section 1365 with respect to that fiscal year, or has obtained the approval of owners, constituting a quorum, casting a majority of the votes at a meeting or election of the association conducted in accordance with Chapter 5 (commencing with Section 7510) of Part 3 of Division 2 of Title 1 of the Corporations Code and Section 7613 of the Corporations Code. For the purposes of this section, "quorum" means more than 50 percent of the owners of an association."

14. Civil Code Sections 1365(a), 1366(a).

15. Civil Code Section 1365(c).

16. Civil Code Section 1365(c).

17. Civil Code Section 1365(c).

18. Civil Code Section 1366(b). Section 1366(b) reads in full as follows:

"(b) Notwithstanding more restrictive limitations placed on the board by the governing documents, the board of directors may not impose a regular assessment that is more than 20 percent greater than the regular assessment for the association's preceding fiscal year or impose special assessment which in the aggregate exceed 5 percent of the budgeted gross expenses of the association for that fiscal year without the approval of owners, constituting a quorum, casting a majority of the votes at a meeting or election of the association conducted in accordance with Chapter 5 (commencing with Section 7510) of Part 3 of Division 2 of Title 1 of the Corporations Code and Section 7613 of the Corporations Code. For the purposes of this section, quorum means more than 50 percent of the owners of an association. This section does not limit assessment increases necessary for emergency situations. For purposes of this section, an emergency situation is any one of the following:

"(1) An extraordinary expense required by an order of a court .

"(2) An extraordinary expense necessary to repair or maintain the common interest development or any part of it for which the association is responsible where a threat to personal safety on the property is discovered.

"(3) An extraordinary expense necessary to repair or maintain the common interest development or any part of it for which the association is responsible that could not have been reasonably foreseen by the board in preparing and distributing the pro forma operating budget under Section 1365. However, prior to the imposition or collection of an assessment under this subdivision, the board shall pass an assessment under this subdivision, the board shall pass a resolution containing written findings as to the necessity of the extraordinary expense involved and why the expense was not or could not have been reasonably foreseen in the budgeting process, and the resolution shall be distributed to the members with the notice of assessment.

"(4) An extraordinary expense in making the first payment of the earthquake insurance surcharge pursuant to Section 5003 of the Insurance Code."

19. Civil Code Section 1366(b)(1)-(4).

20. Civil Code Section 1366(c).

21. Civil Code 1367(a).

22. Civil Code Section 1367(b).

23. If it chooses to do so, the association may enforce the assessment against the property owner directly through a variety of mechanisms including: (a) demand letters from the association or its attorney; (b) assignment of the debt to collection a agency; (c) the filing of a Small Claims Court action by the association if the amount of the debt is less than $2,500.00 (or $5,000.00 if the association has not filed more than 2 Small Claims actions anywhere in the State in any calendar year)(Code of Civil Procedure Sections 116.220, 116.231); (d) the filing of an appropriate lawsuit in Municipal Court if the amount of the debt (including prejudgment interest) is $25,000.00 or less (Code of Civil Procedure Section 86); or (e) the filing of an appropriate lawsuit in Superior Court if the amount of the debt (including prejudgment interest, late charges) exceeds $25,000.00.

24. Park Place Estates Homeowners Association, Inc. v. Naber (1994) 29 Cal. App. 4th 427, 35 Cal. Rptr. 2d 51

25. Annandale Golf Club v. Smith (1930) 110 Cal. App. 765 Super., 289 P.806. In this case, a golf club was organized as a nonprofit "cooperative" corporation. The membership of a club member who failed and refused to pay his dues was automatically suspended in accordance with the club's bylaws. More than two years following the date of the suspension, the member tendered to the club a sum of money representing the delinquent dues which had accrued prior to the date of suspension. The member's tender of payment was made on the condition that he not be held liable for the dues accruing between the date of suspension and the date of tender (approximately two years) . The club refused this conditional tender and, instead filed legal action to collect all of the unpaid dues, including those accruing during the period of membership suspension. In holding that the member continued to be liable for payment of his membership dues during the suspension period, the court observed:

> "Under the by-laws defendant was automatically suspended until the payment of his indebtedness for nonpayment of dues. The dues were never paid. Defendant might also have been expelled for nonpayment of dues and payment made by the club for defendant's property interest, but such action was never taken, and defendant still retained his membership, though suspended, subject to all the obligations thereof, including the payment of dues, unless such suspension relieved defendant from all obligation to pay dues. The bylaws do not provide that a member shall cease to pay dues upon suspension for nonpayment."

****

> "Meanwhile [during the period of suspension] the member enjoys all the privileges and possesses all the rights of membership, except social privileges.

Social clubs use dues for operating expenses, for maintaining the club property, and for capital investment, such as payment of the funded debt, making improvements, and acquiring additional property. The property rights which defendant continued to have after suspension were continually being preserved and probably being enhanced with money paid as dues by other members. The defendant could not relieve himself from the obligation to pay dues without surrendering these property rights. . . . There is no reason why a suspended member, who retains all his property rights, should not contribute his share toward maintaining the value of those property rights. Furthermore, by express provision in the by-laws, the member is obliged to pay dues so long as a he remains a member, and the by-laws indicate . . that the suspension did not terminate his membership."

26. Cerro de Alcala Homeowners Association v. Burns (1985) 169 Cal. App. 3d Supp. 1, 216 Cal. Rptr. 84. In this case, the association member ceased to pay assessments levied by the association after he vacated his condominium when he was threatened with foreclosure proceedings by the holder of the first deed of trust. The member argued that because he had vacated his property, he received none of the benefits of the association or its common areas and facilities and should therefore be relieved of the obligation to pay assessments levied after the date he vacated his property. In rejecting the member's claims the court reasoned that:

". . .the key issue is whether a vacating of the premises constitutes either a parting or ceasing of enjoyment of the property . . . We hold that it does not. . . . In order for an owner to abandon a unit in a community association so as to divest himself of the duty to pay assessments, the owner must give the association record notice of the abandonment through the recording of a quitclaim deed, notice of abandonment or other recorded instrument which makes it clear that the owner is relinquishing all of the rights of ownership. Thus, vacating of the premises (mere relinquishment of possession) does not release a homeowner of liability arising from maintenance assessments becoming due. . . . Although [the member] ceased to enjoy the possession of his property, he continued to enjoy other aspects of ownership until the very moment of recordation of the trustee's deed which effected a transfer of the property. As the record owner of the property, [the member] continued to benefit from the homeowners association's ongoing schedule of maintenance and repairs to the common areas. In addition, respondent benefited from the protection of a policy of general liability insurance maintained by the homeowners association. . . . Thus, it is clear that [the member] did not cease to enjoy the benefits of the estate by voluntarily vacating the premises."

Corporations Code Section 7340 also addresses the issue. Section 7340 of the Corporations Code provides the following prohibition on members attempting to escape charges and assessments by simply resigning or abandoning his or her membership:

"(a) A member may resign from membership at any time, although the articles or bylaws may require reasonable notice before the resignation is effective.

"(b) This section shall not relieve the resigning member from any obligation for charges incurred, services or benefits actually rendered, dues, assessments or fees, arising from contract, a condition to ownership of land, an obligation arising out of the ownership of land, or otherwise, and this section shall not diminish any right of the corporation to enforce any such obligation or obtain damages for its breach."

And Section 7351 of the Corporations Code then provides:

> "A corporation may levy dues, assessments, or fees upon its members pursuant to its articles or bylaws, but a member upon learning of them may avoid liability for them by promptly resigning from membership, except where the member is liable for them by contract, as a condition to ownership of an interest in real property, as an obligation arising out of the ownership of an interest in real property, or otherwise. Article or bylaw provisions authorizing such dues, assessments or fees do not, of themselves, create such liability."

27. Civil Code Section 1466, Mountain Home Properties, Inc. v. Pine Mountain Lake Association (1982) 135 Cal. App. 3d 959, 185 Cal. Rptr. 623. Civil Code Section 1466 provides that:

"No one, merely by reason of having acquired an estate subject to a covenant running with the land, is liable for a breach of the covenant before he acquired the estate, or after he has parted with it or ceased to enjoy its benefits."

28. Civil Code Section 1367(b).

29. Civil Code Section 1366(d).

30. Civil Code Section 1367(b).

31. Wilton v. Mountain Wood Homeowners Association. Inc. (1993) 18 Cal. App. 4th 565, 22 Cal. Rptr. 2d 471.

32. Civil Code Section 1367(b).

33. Civil Code Section 1367(c).

34. Cutujian v. Benedict Hills Estates Association (1996) 41 Cal. App. 4th 1379, 48 Cal. Rptr. 2d 166. In this case, the court held that the 4-year statute of limitations begins to run or expire when a demand for performance under the Declaration of CC&Rs is made and the demand is refused.

35. Prior to January 1, 1986, when Section 1367 took effect, under former Civil Code Section 1356, assessment liens expired after one year if no enforcement action was commenced. The former statute provided that: "Unless sooner satisfied and released or the enforcement thereof initiated as hereafter provided such lien shall expire and be of no further force or effect one year from the date of recordation of said notice of assessment; provided, however, that said one-year period may be extended by the management body for not to exceed one additional year by recording a written extension thereof."

36. Civil Code Section 1367(d).

37. Civil Code Section 1367(e).

38. Civil Code Section 1367(d).

39. Civil Code Section 1367(d).

40. Civil Code Sections 1366(d), 1367(b), (d).

41. Civil Code Section 2924c(a), (e).

42. Penryn Fruit Co. v. Sherman-Worrell Fruit Co. (1904) 142 Cal. 643, 645, 76 P.484, Simon v. Superior Court (1992) 4 Cal. App. 4th 63, 5 Cal. Rptr. 2d 428.

43. Civil Code Section 1367(d).

44. Code of Civil Procedure Section 86(a)(6).

45. Code of Civil Procedure Section 729.010(a).

46. Code of Civil Procedure Section 729.020.

47. Code of Civil Procedure Section 729.030(a).

48. Code of Civil Procedure Section 729.030(b).

49. Code of Civil Procedure Section 729.060(b)(l), Lindsey v. Meyer (1981) 125 Cal. App. 3d 536, 178 Cal. Rptr. 1.

50. Code of Civil Procedure Section 729.060(b)(2).

51. Code of Civil Procedure Section 729.060(b)(3).

52. Code of Civil Procedure Section 729.060(b)(4).

53. Code of Civil Procedure Section 729.060(b)(4).

54. Lindsey v. Meyer (1981) 125 Cal. App. 3d 536, 178 Cal. Rptr.1.

55. Code of Civil Procedure Section 726(e).

56. Code of Civil Procedure Section 726(e).

57. Code of Civil Procedure Section 729.040(a).

58. Code of Civil Procedure Section 729.040(b).

59. Code of Civil Procedure Section 729.050.

60. Code of Civil Procedure Section 729.090(a).

61. Code of Civil Procedure Section 729.090(c).

62. Code of Civil Procedure Section 729.080(a).

63. Code of Civil Procedure Section 701.590(a).

64. Code of Civil Procedure Section 701.590(b).

65. Code of Civil Procedure Section 701.590(c).

66. Code of Civil Procedure Section 701.660. The deed must contain: (1) the name of the court where the judgment was entered under which the property was sold; (2) the date of entry of the judgment; (3) the name and address of the judgment creditor; (4) a description of the property sold; and (5) the date of the sale. Code of Civil Procedure Section 701.670.

67. Code of Civil Procedure Section 701.680(a).

68. Code of Civil Procedure Section 701.680(c)(1).

69. Civil Code Section 1367(b).

70. Civil Code Section 1367(c).

71. California Revenue & Taxation Code Section 2192.1.

72. Revenue and Taxation Code Section 2192.1, California Loan & Trust Co. v. Weis (1897) 118 Cal. 489, 50 P.697.

73. Government Code Section 53935.

74. California Civil Code Sections 1213, 1215, 1217, 2897.

75. Internal Revenue Code Sections 6321, 6322, 6323(a),(f). However, even where notice of the lien has been recorded by the IRS, the IRS income tax lien is generally subordinate to state, county and local government tax liens on real property and special assessment liens on real property levied by special assessment districts under taxing authority. Internal Revenue Code Section 6323(b)(6). In addition, the IRS income tax lien, even where notice of the lien has been recorded, is subordinate to certain mechanic's liens on residential real property for certain specified repairs and improvements. Internal Revenue Code Section 6323(b)(7).

76. California Revenue & Taxation Code Sections 2191.3, 2191.4, 2191.5.

77. Code of Civil Procedure Section 701.630.

78. Code of Civil Procedure Section 729.080(e).

79. Title 10 California Code of Regulations Section 2792.16(g) provides that:
"(1) A lien for regular or special assessments against an owner may be made subordinate by the CC&R's to the lien of any first mortgage or first deed of trust (hereafter collectively first encumbrance) against subdivision interests of the owner.

"(2) In the case of a subordination of a lien for assessments to a first encumbrance, the transfer of a subdivision interest as the result of the exercise of a power of sale or a judicial foreclosure involving a default under the first encumbrance shall extinguish the lien of assessments which were due and payable prior to the transfer of the subdivision interest.

"(3) No transfer of the subdivision interest as the result of a foreclosure or exercise of a power of sale shall relieve the new owner, whether it be the former beneficiary of the first encumbrance or another person, from liability for any assessments thereafter becoming due or from the lien thereof."

80. Title 10 California Code of Regulations Section 2792.16(g)(2), (3) provide that:

"(2) In the case of a subordination of a lien for assessments to a first encumbrance, the transfer of a subdivision interest as the result of the exercise of a power of sale or a judicial foreclosure involving a default under the first encumbrance shall extinguish the lien of assessments which were due and payable prior to the transfer of the subdivision interest.

"(3) No transfer of the subdivision interest as the result of a foreclosure or exercise of a power of sale shall relieve the new owner, whether it be the former beneficiary of the first encumbrance or another person, from liability for any assessments thereafter becoming due or from the lien thereof."

81. Code of Civil Procedure Section 701.630.

82. "State tax liens" are defined in Government Code Section 7162 as the following: (1) Oil and gas production tax- Public Resources Code Section 3423; (2) Geothermal resource tax-Public Resources Code Section 3772; (3) Commercial fishing privilege tax- Game & Fish Code Section 8048; (4) Sales and use taxes- Revenue and Taxation Code Section 6757; (5) Vehicle fuel license tax- Revenue and Taxation Code Section 7872; (6) Use fuel tax- Revenue and Taxation Code Section 8996; (7) State gift tax- Revenue and Taxation Code Sections 16063-16064; (8) State personal income tax- Revenue and Taxation Code Section 18881; (9) Bank and corporation income tax- Revenue and Taxation Code Section 26161; (10) Cigarette tax- Revenue and Taxation Code Section 30322; (11) Alcoholic beverage tax- Revenue and Taxation Code Section 32363; and (12) Timber yield tax- Revenue and Taxation Code Section 38532.

83. 11 U.S.C. Section 727(b).

84. 11 U.S.C. Section 362.

85. In the Matter of Rosteck, 899 F.2d 694 (7th Cir. 1990).

86. 11 U.S.C. Section 362.

87. In re Schwartz 954 F.2d 569 (9th Cir. 1992).

88. 11 U.S.C. Section 362(b)(3).

89. Sawyer Nurseries v. Galardi (1986) 181 Cal. App. 3d 663, 670, 226 Cal. Rptr. 502.

90. In re Cohen, 122 B.R. 755 (S.D. Cal. 1991).

91. In re Cohen, 122 B.R. 755 (S.D. Cal. 1991).

92. The Proof of Claim must be filed within the time period prescribed by the Federal Bankruptcy Rules or local court rule of the particular Bankruptcy Court in which the bankruptcy case is pending. Usually, the Notice of First Meeting of Creditors which is supposed to be mailed to all creditors listed by the debtor will state the date of the first meeting of creditors and/or the last date for which Proofs of Claim may be filed.

In Chapter 7 and 13 bankruptcy cases, the last day within which a creditor may file a Proof of Claim is ninety (90) days after the date set for the "first meeting of creditors." Federal Rules of Bankruptcy Procedure, Rule 3002(c).

In Chapter 11 bankruptcy cases, the Proof of Claim filing deadline is ordinarily set by local court rule.

93. Federal Rules of Bankruptcy Procedure, Rule 3002.

94. 11 U.S.C. Section 523(a) (l)-(10).

95. Ordinarily, a bankruptcy debtor obtains a discharge: (a) by liquidation in a Chapter 7 case; (b) by reorganization plan confirmation in a Chapter 11 case; (c) by reorganization plan confirmation and consummation (debtor's completion of the approved plan) in a Chapter 13 case.

96. In re Rosenfeld, 23 F.3d 833 (4th Cir. 1994), cert. denied,_U.S._115 S. Ct. 200, 130 L.Ed. 2d 131 (1994), In re Beeter, 173 Banktcy Rptr. 108 (W.D. Tex. 1994), In re Raymond, 129 Banktcy, Rptr. 354 (S.D.N.Y. 1991).

In In re Rosenfeld, the 4th Circuit Court of Appeals held that: "Thus, the debtor's obligation to pay the assessments arose from his continued post-petition ownership of the property and not from a pre-petition contractual obligation."

97. Matter of Rosteck, 899 F.2d 694 (7th Cir. 1990) , In re Cohen, 122 Banktcy. Rptr. 755 (S.D. Cal. 1991), Matter of Garcia, 168 Banktcy. Rptr. 320 (E.D. Mich. 1993), Matter of Wasp, 137 Banktcy. Rptr. 71 (M.D. Fla. 1992), In re Turner, 101 Banktcy. Rptr. 751 (D. Utah 1989), In re Elias, 98 Banktcy. Rptr. 332 (N.D. Ill. 1989).

98. In re Cohen, 122 Banktcy. Rptr. 755 (S.D. Cal. 1991).

99. Matter of Pratola, 152 Banktcy. Rptr. 874 (D. N.J. 1993).

100. 11 U.S.C. Section 523(a)(16) reads in full as follows:

"(a) A discharge under Section 727, 1141, 1228(a), 1228(b), or 1328(b) of this title does not discharge an individual debtor from any debt -

"(16) for a fee or assessment that becomes due and payable after the order for relief to a membership association with respect to the debtor's interest in a dwelling unit that has condominium ownership or in a share of a cooperative housing corporation, but only if such fee or assessment is payable for a period during which -

"(A) the debtor physically occupied a dwelling unit in the condominium or cooperative project; or

"(B) the debtor rented the dwelling unit to a tenant and received payments from the tenant for such period,

"but nothing in this paragraph shall except from discharge the debt of a debtor for a membership association fee or assessment for a period arising before entry of the order for relief in a pending or subsequent bankruptcy case."

101. In In the Matter of Rosteck, 899 F.2d 694 (7th Cir. 1990), a case decided before the enactment of Section 523(a)(16), the court invalidated a personal money judgment the association obtained in state court following foreclosure of a mortgage senior to the association's assessment lien. After the sheriff's sale, there were insufficient sales proceeds to pay the assessments and the association sought and obtained a deficiency judgment against the property owners personally. In reaching the conclusion that the deficiency judgment was void and obtained in violation of the Bankruptcy Code, the Rosteck Court stated that:

> "Old Willow [the association] contends that allowing the debtors in bankruptcy to escape their obligations for post-petition condominium assessments will allow those debtors to reside in their homes as long as they wish, unencumbered by the obligation to pay assessments that their fellow condominium owners must pay. . . . as a practical matter, Old Willow's fear may be

> largely unfounded. . . . And, as happened in this case, parties holding liens on the condominium (which includes the condominium association ...) can foreclose those liens and end the debtor's possession and ownership."

And, in In re Cohen, 122 Banktcy. Rptr. 755 (S.D. Cal. 1991), the United States Bankruptcy Court for the Southern District of California ruled that the post-petition assessments were a pre-petition debt for which the debtor was entitled to a discharge because the obligation arose pre-petition when the debtor purchased the property. However, the court also indicated that the discharge relief was with respect to the personal obligation of the debtors only and the association could still foreclose its assessment lien:

> "While the result of this opinion is to discharge these debtors from their obligations under [the] CC&Rs, condominium and homeowners' associations are not without adequate remedies in the future. . . . Additionally, the homeowners associations may seek relief from stay in order to attach liens against the property for the amount of the unpaid assessments. If the liens are not paid, the homeowners' associations may foreclose on their liens".

Finally, in In re Affeldt, 164 Banktcy. Rptr. 28 (D. Minn. 1994), the United States Bankruptcy Court for the District of Minnesota ruled that the debtor property owner's personal obligation to pay post-petition assessments was discharged, but that it was not deciding the issue of whether the association's assessment lien arising under state law survived the bankruptcy discharge:

> "Westbrooke [the association] is simply trying to enforce a personal obligation of the Debtor based upon a pre-petition contract [declaration of covenants, conditions and restrictions]. ... I am not deciding, and not being asked to decide, whether Westbrooke's lien arising under state law survives the Debtor's bankruptcy and is still enforceable. . . . All I do decide is that Debtor's personal obligation to pay the post-petition assessments arose pre-petition and was therefore discharged in his bankruptcy."

In re Affeldt, 164 Banktcy. Rptr. 28 (D. Minn. 1994) was affirmed in July, 1995 by the U.S. Court of Appeals for the 8th Circuit, but on entirely different grounds, in In re Affeldt, 60 F.3d 1292 (8th Cir. 1995). In this opinion, the 8th Circuit Court of Appeals referred to new 11 U.S.C. Section 523(a)(16), but held that the new statute benefited neither the bankruptcy debtor property owner or the association because the statute does not apply to bankruptcy cases commenced prior to October 22, 1994. The 8th Circuit Court of Appeals held that the determining factor in choosing which line of cases to follow is whether or not the declaration of covenants, conditions and restrictions, and the obligation to pay assessments, is simply a contract or a real covenant running with the land. The Court expressly declined to adopt any of the three lines of decisions.

102. Civil Code Sections 1365(a), 1366(a).

103. Civil Code Section 1365(c).

104. Civil Code Section 1365(c).

105. Civil Code Section 1365(c).

106. Civil Code Section 1365(b)

107. Civil Code Section 1365(d)

108. Civil Code Section 1365(e)-(i) reads as follows:

"(e) A summary of the association's general liability policy that states all of the following:

"(1) The name of the insurer.

"(2) The policy limits of the insurance.

"(3) If an insurance agent, as defined in Section 1621 of the Insurance Code, an insurance broker, as defined in Section 1623 of the Insurance Code, or an agent of an insurance agent or insurance broker has assisted the association in the development of the general liability policy limits and if the recommendations of the insurance agent or insurance broker were followed.

"(4) The insurance deductibles.

"(5) The person or entity that is responsible for paying the insurance deductible in the event of loss.

"(6) Whether or not the insurance coverage extends to the real property improvements to the separate interests.

"(f) A summary of the association's earthquake and flood insurance policy, if one has been issued, that states all of the following:

"(1) The name of the insurer.

"(2) The policy limits of the insurance.

"(3) The insurance deductibles.

"(4) The person or entity that is responsible for paying the insurance deductible in the event of loss.

"(g) A summary of the liability coverage policy for the director and officers of the association that lists all of the following:

"(1) The name of the insurer.

"(2) The limits of the insurance.

"(h) Notwithstanding subdivisions (e), (f), and (g), the association shall, as soon as reasonably practical, notify its members by first-class mail if any of the policies have been canceled and not immediately replaced. If the association renews any of the policies or a new policy is issued to replace an insurance policy of the association, and where there is no lapse in coverage, the association shall notify its members of that fact in the next available mailing to all members pursuant to Section 5016 of the Corporations Code.

"(i) To the extent that the information to be disclosed pursuant to subdivisions (e), (f), and (g) is specified in the insurance policy declaration page, the association may meet the requirements of those subdivisions by making copies of that page and distributing it to all its members."

109. Civil Code Section 1365(i)

110. Civil Code Section 1365(h).

111. Civil Code Section 1354(i).

112. Civil Code Section 1363.05(e).

113. Civil Code Section 1368(a).

114. Civil Code Section 1368.

115. Civil Code Section 1368(b).

116. Civil Code Section 1365.5(f).

117. Civil Code Section 1365.5(e)(1).

118. Raven's Cove Townhomes, Inc. v. Knuppe Development Company, Inc. (1981) 114 Cal. App. 3d 783, 171 Cal. Rptr. 334.

119. Civil Code Section 1365.5(e), Title 10 California Code of Regulations Section 2792.16(d).

120. Civil Code Section 1365.5(c)(2).

121. Civil Code Section 1365.5(c)(1).

122. Civil Code Section 1365.5(e). Section 1365.5(e)-(h) reads as follows:

"(e) At least once every three years the board of directors shall cause a study of the reserve account requirements of the common interest development to be conducted if the current replacement value of the major components which the association is obligated to repair, replace, restore, or maintain is equal to or greater than one-halt of the gross budget of the association for any fiscal year. The board shall review this study annually and shall consider and implement necessary adjustments to the board's analysis of the reserve account requirements as a result of that review.

"The study required by this subdivision shall at minimum include:

"(1) Identification of the major components which the association is obligated to repair, replace, restore, or maintain which, as of the date of the study, have a remaining useful life of less than 30 years.

"(2) Identification of the probable remaining useful life of the components identified in paragraph (1) as of the date of the study.

"(3) An estimate of the cost of repair, replacement, restoration, or maintenance of the components identified in paragraph (l) during and at the end of their useful life.

"(4) An estimate of the total annual contribution necessary to defray the cost of repair, replace, restore, or maintain the components identified in paragraph (1) during and at the end of their useful life, after subtracting total reserve funds as of the date of the study.

"(f) As used in this section, "reserve accounts" means moneys that the association's board of directors has identified for use to defray the future repair or replacement of, or additions to, those major components which the association is obligated to maintain.

"(g) As used in this section, "reserve account requirements" means the estimated funds which the association's board of directors has determined are required to be available at a specified point in time to repair, replace, or restore those major components which the association is obligated to maintain.

"(h) This section does not apply to an association that does not have a "common area" as defined in Section 1351."

123. Civil Code Section 1365.5(e).

124. Civil Code Section 1365.5(e)(l)-(4).

125. Civil Code Section 1365.5(a)(2).

126. Civil Code Section 1365.5(a)(3).

127. Civil Code Section 1365.5(a)(5).

128. Civil Code Section 1365.5(a)(4).

129. Civil Code Section 1365.5(b).

130. Civil Code Section 1365.5(c)(1).

131. Civil Code Section 1365.5(c)(2). Section 1365.5(c)(1) and (2) read in full as follows:

"(c) (1) The board of directors shall not expend funds designated as reserve funds for any purpose other than the repair, restoration, replacement, or maintenance of, or litigation involving the repair, restoration, replacement, or maintenance of, major components which the association is obligated to repair, restore, replace, or maintain and for which the reserve fund was established.

(2) However, the board may authorize the temporary transfer of money from a reserve fund to the association's general operating fund to meeting short-term cash-flow requirements or other expenses, provided the board has made a written finding, recorded in the board's minutes, explaining the reasons that the transfer is needed, and describing when and how the money will be repaid to the reserve fund. The transferred funds shall be restored to the reserve fund within one year of the date of the initial transfer, except that the board may, upon making a finding supported by documentation that a temporary delay would be in the best interests of the common interest development, temporarily delay the restoration. The board shall exercise prudent fiscal management in delaying restoration of these funds and in restoring the expended funds to the reserve account, and shall, if necessary, levy a special assessment to recover the full amount of the expended funds within the time limits required by this section. This special assessment is subject to the limitation imposed by Section 1366. The board may, at its discretion, extend the date the payment on the special assessment is due. Any extension shall not prevent the board from pursuing any legal remedy to enforce the collection of an unpaid special assessment."

132. Civil Code Section 1365.5(c)(2).

133. Civil Code Section 1365.5(c)(2).

134. Civil Code Section 1365.5(d). Section 1365.5(d) reads as follows:

"(d) When the decision is made to use reserve funds or to temporarily transfer money from the reserve fund to pay for litigation, the association shall notify the members of the association of that decision in the next available mailing to all members pursuant to Section 5016 of the Corporations Code, and of the availability of an accounting of those expenses. Unless the governing documents impose more stringent standards, the association shall make an accounting of expenses related to the litigation on at least a quarterly basis. The accounting shall be made available for inspection by members of the association at the association's office."

135. Civil Code Section 1365.5(d).

136. Civil Code Section 1365.5(a)(1).

137. Civil Code section 1365.5(a)(5).

138. Civil Code Section 1365.5(a)(4).

INDEX

Agency, agents, also see Management
generally, 172, 173
scope of managing agent's authority, 172-174

Age restrictions, 35, 36, 117

Alternative dispute resolution ("ADR"), also see Enforcement of governing documents
completion of process, 61
construction defects, application to, 73
enforcement of governing documents, 59-62
generally, 59, 73
initiation, 60
prerequisite to certain enforcement lawsuits, 59, 62
request for resolution, 60
response to request for resolution, 61

Amenities, community facilities
access to
generally, 63
non-resident owners, 63, 64
persons not property owners, 65
construction defects, see Construction Defects
damage to, 68
maintenance, 4, 11-14, 67, 68
management, 2, 11
repair, 4, 12-14, 67, 68
rules for use of, 44, 45
traffic and parking regulation, 65-67

American flag, restrictions against display, 29

Antennae, see Video and television antennae

Appurtenant
defined, 8
easements, 3, 5, 6, 7, 81
exclusive use common areas, 7

Architectural control committee, see Environmental control committee

Architectural control rules, see Environmental control rules

Articles of incorporation
amending, 100

generally, 89
petition to reduce voting requirements, 102
majority voting requirements, 100
"supermajority" voting requirements, 102
contents, 89
defined, 89

Assessments, also see Assessment liens
abandonment of property, no effect on obligation to pay, 185
attorney's fees, 184
authority for, 9, 179, 180
bankruptcy of property owner, effect of, 196, also see Bankruptcy of property owners
board approval, 182
collection and enforcement methods, 187-194
commencement, 179, 180
defined, nature, 179
delinquent, when, 186
developer's obligation to pay, 181
"emergency situations", assessments for, 183, 184
increases in
general limitation, 94, 182, 183
membership approval of, 94, 182, 183
notice of, 184
specific limitations, 183
interest on delinquent assessments, 184
late charges, 184
limited exemptions from, 181, 182
nonuse of common areas, no effect on obligation to pay, 185
notice of, 184
personal obligation and a lien, 179, 184, 185
regular, 180, 181
special, 180, 183

Assessment liens
authority for, 184
bankruptcy of property owner, effect of, 196-202, also see Bankruptcy of property owners
competing liens and encumbrances, 194, 195
contents and form, 186
creation of, 186
defined, nature of, 184
duration, 187
effect, 184-187
foreclosure
judicial
certificate of sale, 192
"credit bids", 193
deficiency judgment, 191

generally, 189-191
initiation, 190
litigation guarantee, 190
"notice of pending action", "lis pendens", 191
purchaser's deed, 193
redemption, 191-193
nonjudicial
"credit bids", 189
generally, 187, 188
initiation, 188
notice of default, 188
notice of sale, 189
redemption rights, none available, 189
reinstatement, 189
trustee, 188
trustee's sale guarantee, 188
foreclosure of senior liens, effect of, 195, 196
generally, 184-186
"one action" rule, 185, 196
prerequisites to valid lien, 182, 183
priority, 187
recording of, 186
release of lien, 187
required contents of, 186
slander of title, no liability for, 186
subordination, 195

Association
authority and powers generally, 1, 2, 4, 11-14
purposes, 1, 2, 4, 11, 55
responsibilities, 2, 8, 11, 12, 13, 14, 15, 24, 25, 67
votes attributable to association property, 137

Association rules
authority for, 44-46, 55
consistency with declaration, 46, 55
defined, 44, 88

Automatic suspension of membership rights, 52, also see Members

Awnings, 8, 13

Balconies, 8, 13

Ballots
defined, 132
distinguished from proxies, 132
generally, 132
use of, 132

"written ballots", see Written ballots, Members

Bankruptcy of property owners
association's remedies, 199, 200
automatic stay of Bankruptcy Court, effect of, 197, 198
effect on collection of assessments, 196-201
effect on enforcement of liens, 197-201
effect of bankruptcy, generally, 200-201
"post-petition" compared to "pre-petition" debts, 201
recording assessment lien, 198, 199
specific Bankruptcy Code provisions, 201, 202

Bearing walls, 6

Board of directors, also see Directors
action by, 159-161, 164-166
action without a meeting by unanimous written consent, 160
assessment increases, approval by, 114, 115
authority, 143, 144
"business judgment" rule, 25, 148, 149
chairman, 165
collective governing body, 78, 143, 159-161
"Common Interest Development Open Meeting Act", 161-163
deliberations, 164-166
executive session board meetings, 48, 49, 56, 115, 160, 161, 163, 164
inspectors of election, appointment of, 137, 146
meetings, also see "Common Interest Development Open Meeting Act"
adjournment, 166
attendance of directors, methods, 161, 165
calling of, 161
defined, 162-164
emergency, 116, 162
frequency, 91, 156, 162, Ch. VIII note 64
notice of, 156, 162, Ch. VIII note 64
parliamentary procedure, use of, 92, 126, 166
presiding officer, 165
quorum, 160, 165
regular, 91, 156, 161, 162, Ch. VIII note 64
special, 91, 156, 161, 162, Ch. VIII note 64
time of, 91, 156, 161, 162, Ch. VIII note 64
resolutions and policies, 91, 92, 159-161
responsibilities, generally, 149-152

Budgets
contents required, 150, 151, 202, 203
preparation and distribution, 202, 203
pro forma, 150, 151, 202

Business, associations treated as, 84

"Business judgment" rule of association, 25, 148, 149

Bylaws
- amending
  - generally, 87, 101
  - petition to reduce voting requirements, 102
  - majority voting requirements, 101
  - "supermajority" voting requirements, 102
- contents, 90, 91
- defined, 90
- variations from provisions of Corporations Code, 83, 84, 90

CC&Rs, see Covenants, conditions and restrictions, declaration

Ceilings, 6, 8

Chapter notes, 209-291

Committees, also see Directors
- advisory, 154-156
- executive, 154
- generally, 149, 153-156

Common areas
- access to, 63-65
  - property owners and association members, 63, 64
  - non-resident property owners, 63, 64
  - non-property owners, 65
  - tenants, lessees and contract buyers, 64, 139, 140
- damage to, 68, also see Defective construction
- defective construction, see Defective construction
- defined, 3, 7
- delegation of use rights, 139, 140, also see Tenants and lessees, Members
- maintenance responsibilities, 2, 4, 8, 11, 12-14, 67, 68
- "major components", 205, 206
- mutual or reciprocal easements, constituting, 3
- use of, 63-65

"Common Interest Development Open Meeting Act", 115, 116, 160, 161-164, also see Board of directors, meetings, Members

Community apartment
- defined, 7
- exclusive occupancy right, 7
- transfer of ownership, 36, 37, 139, 140

Community facilities
- access to, 63-65
- damage to, 68

defective construction, see Construction defects
generally, 1, 2, 9, 205
maintenance and repair, 2, 4, 8, 11, 12-14, 63, 67, 68
"major components", 205, 206
nonuse by member as excuse for not paying assessments, 185, Ch. IX notes 25-26
reserves for replacement, 9, 14, 182
rules for use of, 44, 55, 63, 64
suspension of member's use rights, 49, 55, also see Discipline of members

Community care facilities, 30

Community living and cooperation, 9, 15, 107, 108, 143

Community services districts
restricting access to public streets and roads, 67
services typically provided by, 67

Conditions, 20

Condominium
boundaries, 6, 7
characteristics, 6, 7
condominium plan, 6
defined, 6
transfer of ownership, 36, 37, 139, 140

Construction defects
association liability, 69
board meeting regarding litigation, 73
certificate of merit required before filing suit, 74, 75
developer liability, 68, 69
disclosure of litigation to property owners, 72, 73
generally, 68
"latent deficiencies", 71, 72
legal recourse, 69, 70, 73, 74
mandatory alternative dispute resolution, 73, 74
"patent deficiencies", 71
prospective purchasers, informing, 75
statutes of limitation, 37, 70
statutes of repose, 71
"substantial completion", 72

Corporations
corporate structure, generally, 77, 78
articles of incorporation, 89, 90, also see Articles of incorporation
bylaws, 90, 91, also see Bylaws
operating rules, 90
parliamentary procedure, 92, 126, 166

Covenant
defined, 18
personal, 18
real, 18
"running", 18

Covenants, conditions and restrictions ("CC&Rs"), also see Declaration
defined, 17
equitable defenses to enforcement
"ambiguity" and "vagueness", 38
"changed circumstances", 39,40
"equitable estoppel", 38,39
"laches", 40
"unclean hands", 40
"waiver", 39
interpretation, generally, 22-26, Ch. III note 18
liberal interpretation required, 25, 26
presumption of validity, 23
reasonableness, 22-24
specific prohibitions or limitations against enforcement
age restrictions, 35, 36, 117
American flag, 29
community care facilities, 30
discrimination prohibited, 25, 34, 35, 117
family day care homes, 30,33
generally, 25, 26
homes for the elderly, 31
mobilehomes, 26
real estate for sale signs, 28,29
selling, renting, leasing, 36, 37
solar energy systems, 27,28
video and television antennae, 29, Ch. III note 23
statutes of limitation, 37, 38
zoning ordinances, relationship with, 40-42

Cumulative voting by members, 109, 110, 112, 113, 129, 130, 133

"**Davis-Stirling** Common Interest Development Act"
application, 80, 81, 83, 87, 97, 108, 120, 151, 180, 205
defined, 80, 81
generally, 2, 80, 81

Declaration of covenants, conditions and restrictions
actual knowledge of, 21
amending
Civil Code requirements, 97-99
deleting developer's provisions, 99
Department of Real Estate regulations, 86
during period of developer control, 86, 95

generally, 95-97
majority voting requirements, 96, 97-99, 101
petition to reduce membership approval requirements, 99, 100
"supermajority" voting requirements, 102
where required level of ownership approval is specified, 97, 98
where required level of ownership approval is not specified, 98, 99
contents, 20, 88
constructive knowledge of, xxvi, 21
defined, 17, 20
enforcement, see Enforcement of declaration of CC&Rs
governing land not controlled by associations, 22
recording, 4, 17, 21, 88

Defective construction of development, see Construction defects

Delegation of membership rights, see Transfer of membership rights

Department of Real Estate
amendment of governing documents, control of, 5, 95, 144
effect on governing documents, 3-5, 86, 96, 129, 150, 169
jurisdiction, 3, 4, 85
regulations, 3, 4, 56, 79, 86, 87, 109, 121, 129, 144, 145, 160, 169, 180, 182

Developer
amendment of governing documents, 5, 86, 95
accurate records of assessments and expenditures, 181
assessments, obligation to pay, 181
bonds, for maintenance and reserves, 182
common area maintenance, obligation of, 182
initial governing documents, preparation of, 4, 86, 87, 95
financial assurances, 9, 182
liability for defective construction, 68, 69
phasing out of, 4, 9, 79, 86, 129, 144
reserves, establishment of, 9
voting power, 129, 144

Development
common characteristics, 3, 22, 80
creation, 80, 81
distinctions between types, 5,6,7
types, 5

Directors
authority, 143, 144
board action, 159-161, 164-166
"business judgment" rule, 25, 148, 149
committees, 153-156
cumulative voting for, 109, 112, 130
developer controlled, 109

elected officials, 4, 109, 143
fiduciaries, 149
indemnification, 175-177
individual directors have no authority, 159
limited liability protections, 166-168
meetings, see Board of directors, also see "Common Interest Development Open Meeting Act"
nomination for election, 145-147
policies, 148
qualifications, 147
removal of, 110, 111, 112-114, 156, 157
responsibilities, 149-152
rights
"absolute" inspection rights, 157-159
filling vacancies on board, 156
generally, 156-159
notice of board meetings, 156
removal, 156, 157
resignation, 156
standards of conduct, 152, 153
term of office, Ch. VIII note 1
vacancies, 156
"volunteers", 167

Discipline of members, also see Enforcement of governing documents
due process requirements, 49-52, 121, 122, 123, 149
executive session requirements, 48, 56, 121
hearing requirements, 56
lawsuits, no discipline for member filing, 124, 125
monetary fines and penalties
authority for, 54, 55
liens for, 56
schedule of fines, adoption and distribution, 54, 56, 57
suspension of membership rights, 49-52, 121-123, 148, 149
automatic suspension, 52, 123
"business judgment" rule does not apply, 123, 148, 149

Discrimination, 34, 35, 58, 64, 84, 117, 140

Doors, door frames, 8, 13

Duration of association, 103

Easements, 3, 5, 6, 7, 81

Elderly, homes for, 31

Emergency board meetings, see Board of directors

Enforcement of governing documents
alternative dispute resolution ("ADR"), generally, 59
completion of resolution process, 61, 62
initiation, 60, 61
prerequisite to certain lawsuits, 62
procedures, 60-62
request for resolution, 60, 61
association enforcement, 4, 48-62
association's good faith, 58
burden of proof, 23, 24
cooperation of owners, 9, 15, 108
defenses to enforcement, see Covenants, conditions and restrictions
expectations of property owners, 15
internal discipline, 48, 49
automatic suspensions, 52, 123
executive session may be required, 48, 56, 121, 161
monetary fines and penalties, 54-57
notice of noncompliance or violation, 53
suspension of membership rights, 49-52, 121-123, 148, 149
due process requirements, 49-52, 121, 122, 123, 149
fair and reasonable, 49-52
hearing opportunity, 50, 51, 122
lawsuits and alternative dispute resolution ("ADR")
injunctive relief, 57, 58
declaratory relief, 57, 58
good faith of association, 58
lawsuits subject to mandatory alternative dispute resolution efforts, 59
owner, enforcement by, 4, 48

Environmental control committee
composition, 43
functions and purposes, 42
generally, 42, 43

Environmental control rules
authority to adopt, 43
consistency with declaration, 43, 88, 93
contents, 42, 43, 88
good faith, 44
reasonable standards, 44
review by courts, 43
subjective judgment permitted, 44

Equitable servitudes
defined, 19
distinguished from covenants, 19
enforcement of, 19, 20, 21, 23
history of, xxv, xxvi, 19, 20

Exclusive use common areas
appurtenant to separate interest, 7, 8, 13
defined, 3, 7, 13
maintenance responsibility, 8, 12, 67

Executive session board meetings, 48, 56, 121, 161, 163

Exterior doors, 8, 13

Family day care homes, 30, 33

Financial resources, association's, 9, 179, 205-209

Financial statement, preparation and review of, 203

Fiduciaries, see Directors
Floors, 6, 8

Foreclosure, see Assessments, Assessment liens

Governing documents
amendment of
articles of incorporation, 100
bylaws, 101
Civil Code requirements governing amendment of declaration, 97-99
declaration to delete developer's provisions, 99
Department of Real Estate regulations requirements, 96
during period of developer control, 5, 86, 95, 96
declaration, generally, 95-99
declarations which specify required level of ownership approval, 97, 98
declarations which do not specify required level of ownership approval, 98, 99
petition to reduce membership approval requirements
declaration, 99, 100
articles of incorporation and bylaws, 102, 103
majority voting requirements, 96, 101
"supermajority" voting requirements, 96, 102
articles of incorporation, 4, 89, 90
association rules, 4, 44-46, 88
bylaws, 4, 90, 91
declaration of covenants, conditions and restrictions, 4, 88
defined, 4, 5, 59, 87
environmental control rules, 4, 42-44, 88
initial
Department of Real Estate Regulations, 85-87
influence of developer, 4, 5, 86, 95
relationship with governing laws, 22, 23, 93-95

Governing laws and regulations
"Davis-Stirling Common Interest Development Act", 2, 80, 81, 83, 87, 97, 108, 120, 151, 180, 205
California Corporations Code, 81-84
Department of Real Estate regulations, 3, 4, 85-87
"common law" or case law, 17, 79
generally, 78-85
other applicable statutes, 84, 85
qualified legal counsel, use of, 87
relationship with governing documents, 22, 23, 93-95
statutes, statutory law, 78, 79

Indemnification of directors and officers, 175-177, also see Directors, Officers

Inspectors of election, 137, 138, 146

Insurance
directors and officers, 167, 177
general liability, 167, 177
statutory liability protections, 166-168
summaries of, 203

Land use control, 14, also see Covenants, conditions and restrictions, Environmental control rules

Maintenance and repair
common areas, 2, 4, 8, 11, 12-14, 67, 68
exclusive use common areas, 8, 1-14
generally, 11-15
separate interests, 3, 8, 12-14

Management
agent's pre-contract disclosure requirements, 170
authority, scope of, 172-174
contract, duration of, 169, Ch. VIII note 116
fiduciaries, 174
indemnification, 175-177
legal relationship with association, 172
licensing requirements, 169
maintenance, accounting and disposition of funds, 171, 172
no commingling of funds without permission, 171-172

Members
action without a meeting
unanimous written consent, 133
"written ballot", 133, 136, 138, 139
association-owned property, votes attributable to, 137
classes of membership, 89, 100, 101, 112, 114, 129, 144
community cooperation, 9, 108

property owners, covenants making all members, 2, Ch. I note 3
defined, 105
discipline, see Discipline of members
list of names and addresses, 119
meetings
eligibility to vote, 138, 139
first meeting of members, 126, 145
frequency, 109, 126
generally, 125-139
inspectors of election, 137, 138, 146
notices of meetings
generally, 127, 128
required contents, 127, 128
parliamentary procedure, 92, 126
quorum
bylaws may vary, 128
defined, 128
inspectors of election, determination by, 137
lack of, 125
reduced, 128
suspended members cannot be counted for purposes of determining, 131
votes withheld for election of directors, proxies and ballots may be counted for quorum, 131, 132
record dates, 138, 139
regular meetings, time and conduct of, 126
special meetings, time and conduct of, 126, 127
voting at members' meetings
cumulative voting, 109, 110, 112, 129, 130, 133
inspectors of election, 137, 138, 146
jointly-owned property, 130, Ch. VII note 113
number of votes, distribution of voting power between developer and other members, 129, 144
proxies and meeting ballots
distinctions between proxy, ballot, "written ballot", 132, 133
form and content, 133-136
generally, 131-133
use, generally, 131, 132
voting power rules, generally, 129, 130
membership certificates, 107
multiple memberships, 106
powers and authority, 108-120
protections
discipline in executive session, 48, 56, 121, 161
limited liability protections, 140, 141
no discipline for filing lawsuits, 124, 125
notice and delivery of information, 120, 116-120, 202-205
suspension of membership rights, 49-52, 121-123, 148, 149
responsibilities, 8, 9, 13, 14, 107, 108

rights
amendment of governing documents, 86, 95-103, 108, 110, 114, 128, 131, 136, 154
approval of assessment increases, 80, 91, 94, 95, 97, 114, 115, 182-184, 208
attendance at board meetings, 115, 116, 146, 157, 160-164, also see "Common Interest Development Open Meeting Act"
calling special meetings, 126, 127
delegation of common area and amenity use rights, 36, 37, 44, 45, 139, 140
election of directors, 4, 109, 110, 143
filling vacancies on board, 128, 156
generally, 108-120
information which must be provided to members
alternative dispute resolution, summary of, 204
assessment lien enforcement policies, 203
construction defects in common areas
notice of litigation regarding, 72-74
survey or questionnaire regarding, 73
financial statements, 87, 91, 94, 116, 117, 118 150, 151, 203-205
governing documents, 117, 118, 120, 204, 205
insurance policies, summary of, 203
minutes of meetings, 116, 117, 118, 162, 204
names and addresses of members, 116, 118-120
pro forma operating budget, 114, 115, 117, 118, 182-184, 202, 203, 204
tax exempt status applications, 117
inspection of association books and records, 116-120, 204
inspectors of election, appointment of, 137, 138, 146
removal of directors
generally, 110, 111
lawsuit for removal, 112-114
voting at members' meeting, 111, 112
responsibilities, 9, 107, 108
suspension of membership rights, 49-52, 121-124, 148, 149, also see Discipline of members

Membership, defined, 106

Meetings, see Board of directors and members, meetings of

Mobilehomes, restrictions against, 26, 27

Monetary fines and penalties, see Discipline of members

Nomination of candidates for election as directors, 145-147

Officers
appointed or elected by board, 78, 90, 91, 168
duties and authority, 90, 91, 98, 99, 102, 127, 145, 146, 148, 149, 150, 151, 153, 155, 168, 169, 173, 186, 207
generally, 90, 91, 148, 149, 150, 151, 153, 155, 168, 169, 173, 186, 207

indemnification, 175-177
limited liability protection, 166-168
president, 98, 168
secretary, 168
treasurer, chief financial officer, 168

Operating funds
maintenance of accounts, 205, 208
nature and purpose, 205
periodic review of, 151, 207, 208
temporary transfer to from reserves, 207

Parliamentary procedure, also see Members, meetings
board meetings, not required, 166
members' meetings, 92, 93, 126, 166
recognized systems of parliamentary procedure, 92, 93, 126
procedures adopted by association, 92, 126

Patios, 8, 13

Pets, animals, regulation of, 21, also see Covenants, conditions and restrictions, Declaration, Environmental control rules, Association rules

Planned development
defined, 5, 6
transfer of ownership, 36, 37, 139, 140

Preservation of development
generally, 2, 4, 9, 11-14, 21, 26, 29, 36, 42, 44, 48, 55, 103, 174, 175
reasonableness of covenants and restrictions, related to, 24

Pro forma budgets, see Budgets

Proxies
defined, 132
distinguished from ballots, 132
duration, 134
form and content, 133
generally, 131
irrevocable, 135
revocable, 135

Public report, 4, 5, 181

Quorum, also see Members, meetings, Board of directors, meetings
directors' meetings, 160, 165
members' meetings, 125, 128, 131, 132
reduced quorums for members' meetings, 128

Real estate for sale signs, 28, 29

Regular assessments, see Assessments, Assessment liens, Reserve funds

Replacement of common areas, community facilities, 9, 12, 14, 63, 151, 181, 182, 202, 205, 206, 207, also see Reserve funds

Reserve funds
- accumulation for replacement, repair, 9, 12, 14, 63, 151, 181, 182, 202, 205, 206, 207
- borrowing from, 151, 152, 207, 208
  - generally, 207, 208
  - litigation, 208
  - temporary transfers, 207
  - written findings by board, necessity of , 207
- developer, establishment by, 9
- estimation, 9, 12, 14, 63, 151, 181, 182, 202, 205, 206, 207
- maintenance of accounts, 205-208
- nature and purpose, 205, 206
- periodic review of, 151, 206, 207
- restoration after borrowing, 207, 208
- signatures for withdrawal, 151, 207
- special assessments to restore, 208
- studies, 206
- use, 8, 9, 151, 206

Reserve studies, see Reserve funds

Restrictions, 20, also see Covenants, conditions and restrictions, Declaration

Separate interest
- defined, 3, 8
- maintenance, 3, 8, 12-14

Servitudes, see Equitable servitudes

Shutters, 8, 13

Solar energy systems, 27, 28

Special assessments, see Assessments and Assessment liens

Statutes of limitation, 37, 70

Statutes of repose, 71

Stock cooperative
- defined, 7
- exclusive occupancy right, 7

transfer of ownership, 7, 36, 37, 139, 140

Subdivider, see Developer

Suspension of membership rights
after hearing, 49-52, 122, 123, 148, 149
automatic, 52, 123
executive session requirement, 48, 56, 121, 161
generally, 49-52, 121-123, 148, 149
hearing requirements, 50, 51, 121, 122
procedural due process, 49-52, 121, 122, 123, 149
when member owns more than one lot or unit, 123

Telephone wiring, 14

Tenants and lessees, 36, 37, 64, 139, 140, also see Transfer of membership rights

Termites, see Wood destroying pests and organisms

Traffic and parking regulation, 65-67

Transfer of membership rights, 64, 139, 140, also see Tenants and lessees

Transfer of ownership of separate interests
generally, 36
restrictions on, 36, 37

Vehicles, see Traffic and parking regulation

Video and television antennae, 29

Volunteers, see Directors

Walls
bearing, of condominium, 6
boundary, of condominium, 6
perimeter, as boundary of separate interest, 8

Windows, 8, 13

Wood destroying pests and organisms
community apartment, repairs, 13
condominium, repairs, 13
planned development, repairs, 13
stock cooperative, 13
generally, 13, 14

Written ballot, 133, 136, 138, 139

Zoning ordinances, relationship with declaration, 40-42

NOTES

NOTES

NOTES

NOTES

NOTES